The
TURNAROUND
SURVIVAL
GUIDE

Strategies
for the
Company in Crisis

■ A. David Silver ■

Dearborn
Financial Publishing, Inc.

While a great deal of care has been taken to provide accurate and current information, the ideas, suggestions, general principles and conclusions presented in this text are subject to local, state and federal laws and regulations, court cases and any revisions of same. The reader is thus urged to consult legal counsel regarding any points of law—this publication should not be used as a substitute for competent legal advice.

Publisher: Kathleen A. Welton
Associate Editor: Karen A. Christensen
Senior Project Editor: Jack L. Kiburz
Interior Design: Lucy Jenkins
Cover Design: Lucy Jenkins

©1992 by A. David Silver

Published by Dearborn Financial Publishing, Inc.

Printed in the United States of America

92 93 94 10 9 8 7 6 5 4 3 2 1

Library of Congress Cataloging-in-Publication Data

Silver, A. David (Aaron David), 1941–
     The turnaround survival guide : Strategies for the company in
crisis / A. David Silver.
         p. cm.
     Includes index.
     ISBN 0-79310-307-X
     1. Corporate turnarounds — Management. 2. Business enterprises —
Finance. 3. Corporations — Finance. I. Title.
HD58.8.S55 1992   91–44496
658.1'6 — dc20   CIP

Dedication

JOSEPH E. "PATSY" LANDOLFI

Other Books by
A. David Silver

- Corporate Venture Capital Investing
- The Radical New Road to Wealth
- Upfront Financing, Revised Edition
- The Entrepreneurial Life
- Who's Who in Venture Capital, 3rd Edition
- Entrepreneurial Megabucks
- The Silver Prescription
- Successful Entrepreneurship
- Venture Capital
- When the Bottom Drops
- The Business Bible of Survival
- Your First Book of Wealth
- The Inside Raider
- The Middle Market Leveraged Financing Directory
- The Middle Market Business Acquisition Directory
- The Bankruptcy, Workout and Turnaround Market
- Close Any Deal

Acknowledgments

Although I am responsible for the lyrics of this book and its two companion directories, the music was supplied by several hardworking and competent technicians. Kathy Welton, my editor at Dearborn Financial Publishing, Inc., provided the orchestration. Special thanks to Kate M. Mitchell for gathering directory information. Dorothy E. Moore provided the keyboard solo in her usual perfect fashion.

My wife, Jeri, graciously volunteered her advice and professional library for the crisis-management chapters. Michael Koblitz, Gruntal Financial Corporation's workout specialist, cheerfully answered technical questions in the emerging area of workouts and reorganizations. To all these allies, a hearty "thank you."

A. David Silver
Santa Fe, New Mexico
August 1991

Table of Contents

Introduction

Your company's creditors are literally or figuratively breaking up furniture in the waiting room. Your key sales manager has resigned. The company's credit cards have been canceled. You can't pay for advertisements placed months ago. The process server brings three lawsuits a day demanding payment. Your accounts payable clerks cannot stand the stress of taking dozens of calls each day and not having a new story to tell the creditors. The production department lacks raw material to produce saleable merchandise. Dun & Bradstreet is calling you persistently for an updated financial report. A reporter for one of the industry's trade journals is calling to confirm a rumor that your company is in deep trouble. The stress is building and your head is pounding.

Your lawyer encourages you to meet with a bankruptcy attorney. The attorney recommends that your company file for protection under Chapter 11 of the Bankruptcy Act, explaining that "this will give you time to reorganize, perhaps six months, during which time no creditor can put you out of business." The bankruptcy lawyer's argument is persuasive. You pay an exorbitant amount of money to prepare the filing, and in a few days, you sign the papers and your company is in Chapter 11.

True to the bankruptcy lawyer's word, all creditors are backed off. The creditor telephone calls stop. Cash builds up because only the essential bills are paid. And for the first time in months, you begin to find some peaceful moments in your office to think about the business.

You tell yourself to think fast and think smart. Very few companies emerge from Chapter 11. The number is one in five. Here are some things many owners and managers think about when in Chapter 11:

- How did I get into this mess? (Regret)
- Maybe I'm not cut out for this business. (Doubt)
- If that blankety-blank customer had paid its bills. (Blame)
- If that ignoramus banker of ours had come through with the loan renewal that he promised. (More blame)
- I want out. I want someone to buy this company and let me walk away from it. (Escape)
- What if we can't come out of this? (Fear)
- I'm a failure. (Shame)
- I have failed my people, my family, everybody. (Thoughts of death)

These are not productive thoughts. These are not the thoughts of someone thinking about saving his or her business. These are thoughts of someone in a high state of distress and agitation.

You don't have to file for protection under Chapter 11 to work yourself into a state of extreme distress and anxiety. You can do that outside of Chapter 11 and it is less expensive. In fact, you can do lots of things outside of Chapter 11, including back off your creditors, generate cash, negotiate stretchout plans with your creditors and rehabilitate your company. Oh, yes. You can manage your crisis also. Chapter 11 should be regarded as a last gasp, not a first step. Anyone can put his or her company into Chapter 11 when it is insolvent, but it is certainly not the first step to take.

THE CRISIS AND THE INSOLVENCY

I am not going to tell you that saving your troubled company is a simple thing. There is no simple solution. But there is a process for saving the troubled company, just as there is a process for starting a company or expanding a company, for buying a company or selling a company. And the process for saving the troubled company begins with drawing a line between the crisis and the company's illiquidity. One problem is emotional and the other is structural. Crisis is the *result* of stress that builds on itself until it becomes distress and explodes into uncontrolled chaos.

Illiquidity is the *symptom*, but not the cause, of the company's crisis. There are structural problems within the company that have depleted its cash, with its liabilities exceeding its assets. The causes of insolvency vary from company to company, but most workout and turnaround specialists will agree that the primary reasons are as follows:

1. Managers are unprepared for trouble.
2. Managers tiptoe around stressors until they become crises.
3. Managers do not know where and how to slash expenses and raise cash.
4. Many of today's managers never have lived through seriously troubled times.
5. Managers think sales growth can disguise problems within their organizations.
6. Companies are undercapitalized.
7. Managers fail to respond to the market by continually reviewing products or services.
8. Managers fail to stay in contact with customers and to continually ask what they want.
9. There are not enough talented people in middle management.
10. Owners and managers become emotionally involved with their companies.

This analysis is empirically interesting, but not when creditors are outside your office threatening to break up the furniture. Or when a big customer goes out of business owing you $150,000. Or when your major vendors refuse to ship products unless you pay them COD. Or when payroll can't be met. Or when your bank calls your loan, and the company's key salespeople are resigning in droves.

Years ago, these would be signals for an owner to put a company into liquidation. (Back then, it was called Chapter 10.) But with our society becoming increasingly credit-driven, the modern way of dealing with crisis is to save and rehabilitate the company so that creditors will receive more than they would get in liquidation.

Today, the owner or manager of a troubled company has choices: (1) informal reorganization, (2) formal reorganization under Chapter 11 of the Bankruptcy Act, (3) liquidation, known as Chapter 7, which means that the company is shut down and its assets sold off to pay creditors or (4) the prepackaged bankruptcy, or "prepack." The fourth option has the attenuation of time that favors informal reorganization coupled with the cleansing feature of Chapter 11 delivered by a bankruptcy judge who crams the plan down the throats of dissenting creditors. The Chapter 7 option is not really a choice. It is the result of procrastination when three creditors get together to throw the company into bankruptcy, or as was the case with Eastern Airlines, when the company filed for protection under Chapter 11 with sufficient assets to cover all debts but with an extremely angry group of creditors. But the choice between an informal and a formal reorganization can be taken away from a distressed owner or manager who makes the wrong telephone call.

A CALL TO THE LAWYER

Every company has a lawyer, and because the lawyer is in the distress business, he or she usually is the first to be called. But that call could take away the informal reorganization option because most bankruptcy lawyers are specialists in bankruptcy and not in the business of rehabilitating companies outside of bankruptcy. A medical comparison would be when you feel severe chest pains, is your first call to a heart surgeon to saw through your ribs and begin open-heart surgery, or do you go in for a checkup instead? Many lawyers do not know the process of saving troubled companies outside of bankruptcy. Thus, they ask for a big retainer up front — because all payments by a company in Chapter 11 must be approved by the court — and put the company into a long and expensive bankruptcy proceeding.

THE RISE IN BUSINESS FAILURES

There were approximately 19,600 corporate bankruptcy filings in America in 1990, according to the American Bankruptcy Institute, or nearly three times the number in 1980. The rate was 30 percent higher in the first half of 1991 compared with the first half of 1990. Recent academic analyses lay the cause at the feet of strained debt-to-worth margins spurred by the junk bond craze and the financing of growth with debt instruments. But aside from the handful of junk-bond-financed leveraged buyout (LBO) failures that have made front-page news, such as Southland, Campeau, Revco, Carter Hawley Hale, Interco and Tracor, most managers know how much debt their companies can tolerate and they operate within their comfort zones.

Businesses fail simply because *their owners or managers are unprepared for crises.* They either cannot see the stressors that precede the crises, or they detour around the stressors, or they see the stressors but work on solutions in the wrong areas. Managers of troubled companies frequently got there by expanding too fast, taking on unprofitable customers and acquiring peripheral businesses. They have too many things to worry about because their businesses are too complex. Many of them no longer can locate the *core*, the business that they need to get back to.

American industry has two primary species of managers: *traditional* and *entrepreneurial.* The former are trained to produce year-to-year growth of profits, and the latter aspire to produce innovative products each year. Both managerial strategies frequently consume capital, create energy-diverting peripheral divisions and bloat overhead expenses in the race to outperform the prior year's results. Many traditional and entrepreneurial owners and managers respond to trouble by borrowing money to build sales and cash flow, relying on their peripheral divisions for additional cash flow, surrounding themselves with managers who believe that growth will be the salvation and telling stories to their creditors. When this happens, the company's accounts payable stretch from 90 to 120 to 180 days, some vendors refuse to ship, litigation bursts out, credit is canceled and a full-fledged crisis erupts. That is the moment at which most owners and managers realize that the situation is beyond their control.

Managers who understand the fundamentals of managing troubled companies — we will call them *crisis managers* — know how to "right size" their companies: to get rid of peripheral business, to operate with minimum overheads, to maximize cash and to develop multiple cash flow channels for the core product or service. They know how to slash expenses and raise cash quickly, spin off peripheral assets, select a gritty battalion of teammates to design a battle plan and speak candidly with creditors to win their support while the company works itself out of its crisis. By the time you finish reading this book, you will understand the fundamentals of crisis management.

THE EMERGENCE OF THE INFORMAL REORGANIZATION

It was the restructuring of the federal Bankruptcy Act of 1978 that gave rise to the crisis manager who knows how to forestall bankruptcy and liquidation. The 1978 act recognized that we live in a credit-intensive society and that people and companies will get into trouble by borrowing too much money. Creditors no longer want to break the trading bench of debtors — the word *bankruptcy* comes from the Italian *banca rotta*, "to break the bench" — but to recover some of their money through the reorganization and rehabilitation of troubled companies.

But filing for protection under Chapter 11 stretches the reorganization process from nine months to four years, on average, and is at least ten times more expensive than an informal reorganization. This means that *creditors of a troubled company almost always will receive more money in an informal reorganization than via bankruptcy proceedings*. The crisis manager can shorten the reorganization process, *outside of bankruptcy court*, from three months to nine months. If he or she cannot ferret out "free cash" — that is, cash not designated for specific creditors — or if he or she cannot negotiate an informal plan of reorganization with creditors, the debtor company still can file for protection. The option always is there.

Success or failure in a workout usually is determined by how effective the crisis manager is in convincing the company's creditors that no matter how many stories they have heard, no matter how many checks were being put into the mail and no matter how grossly unfair their treatment, the crisis manager will get them paid if they cooperate. If the creditors do not trust the company's chief executive officer (CEO), then the company's crisis manager should be another executive within the company whom they do trust. Failing that, a workout consultant can be hired. Workout consultants are less expensive than bankruptcy lawyers and typically operate more rapidly. The crisis manager must buy time and trust. Why should creditors trust him or her? Because in bankruptcy, the creditors will receive less money and will have to wait longer to get paid. Legal fees will eat into payments to creditors. Crisis managers are skilled at carrot-and-stick negotiating. "This is the best plan we can offer you and if you don't accept it, we are prepared to file for protection where you will receive less and it will take much longer to get you paid."

THE WORKOUT AND TURNAROUND PROCESS

There are six steps in the workout and turnaround process. They follow each other in sequence and although the crisis manager may double-back on step number five to reexamine the information and conclusion he or she filed away in step number one, the sequence must be followed in a systematic manner for the company to be rehabilitated outside of a Chapter 11 filing or liquidated in Chapter 7.

Step One: Diagnosing the Crisis

The crisis manager first learns as much as possible about the nature and extent of the company's crisis by listing all the accounts payable by amount and degree of seriousness. Concomitant with the analysis of the nature of the crisis, a *viability assessment* is done to see if the business can be saved in its present form, if it should be liquidated or if it should be "right sized" into something smaller and more valid. The payables are arranged in terms of their degree of severity. None of the liabilities can be trivialized, but some are more life-threatening than others.

Step Two: Mitigating the Crisis

This step is the one in which you buy time to effect a workout plan. A crisis management team of five loyal and courageous managers is put together, and they immediately meet with the nervous people who are the gatekeepers at the flash points, calm their fears and win their support. These probably will include employee groups (or union leaders), the company's principal lender, key suppliers and important customers. The operative phrases are "negotiate standstill agreements" with the creditors to buy time and "damage control" to see that the gatekeepers are properly communicated with, which is central to the success or failure of negotiating the standstill agreement.

Step Three: Generating Cash

The crisis management team next will turn its attention and experience to generating a pool of cash. This will be done by slashing expenses, selling off unused assets, sale leasebacks of fixed assets, spin-offs of divisions, production changes, adding new channels of distribution, changing the terms by which customers pay and possibly raising bridge capital. It is impossible to rehabilitate a company without locating free cash or raising cash through a financing. Fortunately, there are many lenders to and investors in companies that are in a formal or information rehabilitation process. They are listed in the directories in the appendixes at the back of this book.

Step Four: Preparing a Turnaround Plan

Before the ink is dry on step three, the crisis management team begins to develop a rehabilitation plan that will return the company to normalized operations, albeit possibly as a different size or type of business. The plan will include restructuring debt, negotiating new terms with suppliers, redeploying assets and personnel and raising capital (if the cash on hand is inadequate). Creditors usually are offered a stretchout plan, or an installment note of several years, plus equity, if needed. They often are offered an upside kicker in the event of a merger or refinancing or the raising of capital. Among the more tried-and-true rehabilitation plans is to buy a cash-flow-positive company using LBO financing techniques, then to apply its excess cash flow to pay installment notes given to creditors. This is known as the "when you're broke, buy something" plan.

Step Five: Negotiating the Plan

The crisis manager will present the plan to the largest and most important creditors first. They may request modifications or they may refuse to accept it. If they refuse, return to step four, or call in the bankruptcy lawyer to prepare a filing as a threat, but also be ready to file in case the threat backfires. The plan must be negotiated quickly, clearly and in a manner that leaves the company enough back doors and circuit breakers to make alterations or to find cash if the plan cannot be lived up to. The prepack is increasingly being used to obtain the consent of holdout creditors via the Chapter 11 "cram-down" provision. Chapter 11 provides that if only one impaired creditor (not secured) votes for a plan, the judge can cram it down all creditors.

Step Six: Implementing the Plan

Once the plan is accepted by all creditors, it is implemented and carefully monitored for two to three months to make sure that it is working smoothly. This is a critical period that tests the crisis manager's ability to do what he or she said could be done. A downtick in revenues or cash receipts could seriously upset the company's plan and cause the creditors to grow restless. The crisis manager may have to backpedal to step four to see if he or she made some incorrect assumptions about monthly cash flows, then renegotiate a new plan in step five and implement the revised plan, all of which will test the patience of creditors.

WORKOUTS CANNOT BE RUSHED

A troubled company is not very popular. Friends that you have networked with in the past, people you thought you could count on for financial or moral support, may give you the cold shoulder. If your company employs many people in the community and some of them are laid off, you and your family may be the object of scorn in the community.

Keep a low profile. Keep your head under the hood and fix the motor. Don't look up to tell the community of critics that you have just about got it fixed. You haven't. Workouts are unsteady processes, and you will do quite a bit of backsliding before you have tunneled through the dark. If the light at the end of the tunnel appears to be 90 days away, it isn't. It is more like 180 days away. If you think it is 90 days away and you promise your creditors that they will receive a scheduled payment in 120 days, you probably will be apologizing to them for another delay in 120 days and pleading for an extension. They may resist.

A QUICK STUDY

When a company has its shoulders on the mat, there is not much time for extracurricular activities. Even reading this book is an investment in time that you may feel you can ill afford. So let me give you some quick time and worry savers: Ted Turner put a cot in his office and slept there when Turner Broadcasting System was in crisis. H. Ross Perot visited the spouses of his salespeople and gave them shares of EDS stock to win their allegiance when he needed his sales force to remain at customer sites for months on end. Unpaid withholding taxes are the most serious account payable, but the government will accept a stretchout up to six years if you present your story to them openly and honestly. Collection agencies are a step between the creditor and litigation, and they usually will accept negotiated settlements. If you are in trouble because your bank called its loan before it was due and without interest or principal in arrears, you usually can bring the bank back into normalized relations with the threat of a lender liability lawsuit. Aggressive creditor lawyers who breach the fine line between bold advocacy and improper actions can be stopped by asking a judge to sanction them for vexatious litigation and contemptuous behavior. Keep a damage-trail notebook to record any damages that overzealous creditor lawyers might cause you. Open a company bank account outside of the county where you are located to prevent a surprise attachment of your bank accounts by a creditor who persuades a local judge that you are about to flee with the assets. Gather your family and closest friends around you; tell them openly and honestly about the troubles you are facing and ask them for their support. You will need lots of it.

■ CHAPTER ONE ■

Crises Are Turn-Ons

CRISIS AS A SPRINGBOARD

It is not only possible, but it should be your goal, to use a crisis to pole-vault to a higher level of success than the company achieved before the trouble hit. Crises are meant to be springboards for success, but many managers are not trained to manage their businesses through crises. The conventional wisdom is that crises will plow us under, and if we still have a company at the end of the turmoil, it will be smaller, uncomfortably debt-ridden and without many prospects for returning profits to its stockholders. The conventional wisdom also says that our reputations will be dogged by continual reminders of our previous failure. Nothing could be further from the truth. Most fortunes are made in hard times. Most successful entrepreneurs springboard out of crises. Here are some examples.

Sam Walton, the founder of Wal-Mart Stores, Inc., might have been the owner of a small five-and-ten but for his crisis. Walton built a successful Ben Franklin general merchandise store in Newport, Arkansas, while in his mid-30s. He had signed a five-year lease that terminated in 1950, but he had failed to negotiate a renewal clause. Actually, Walton's lease contained a renewal option, but "at terms to be negotiated." The landlord wanted the store for his son, so he would not give Walton a renewal.

Walton's lawyer, Fred Pickens, Jr., said to him: "I hope to God the next time you take over a lease from somebody, you check to make certain it contains a proper renewal clause. They're not going to let you keep the store. The plain truth is, they want Douglas Holmes to run a Ben Franklin in that building! You've shown the whole town what a money-maker it can be."[1]

Walton was driven out of Newport, went to Bentonville, Arkansas, and opened what became the retailing miracle known as Wal-Mart Stores.

Fred Smith, the founder and chief executive officer of Federal Express Corporation, pulled the company through deep financial crises, political crises brought on by aggressive competitors and numerous operating problems, but none greater than when the Ayatollah Khomeini raised the cost of fuel 400 percent in 1975. But not one of these crises was as severe as the time he was charged with a federal crime.

> On Friday, January 31, 1975, Smith was formally indicted for obtaining funds from the Union Bank by use of false documents. And on Monday, February 3, a warrant was issued for his arrest. But, this was only part of his trouble: Late that same night he had been indicted, when he hit and killed a pedestrian who was jaywalking. When apprehended, he claimed he did not realize he had hit anybody, and this was the reason he failed to stop. Smith was charged with leaving the scene of the accident as well as driving with an expired license.[2]

The board of directors immediately sought Smith's resignation, but the senior managers threatened to leave if he was ousted. The board retained Smith but stripped him of much power until his litigation was resolved. Shortly thereafter, Smith was exonerated on all charges and returned to build Federal Express into the leading overnight small-package courier in the world.

Barbara Proctor Gardner, founder and owner of Proctor & Gardner Advertising, Inc., in Chicago, one of the fastest-growing advertising agencies in the country, was fired from her job in 1970. A single mother in a white male-dominated business, Proctor had the courage to defend her convictions. Her agency wanted her to write a shaving cream TV commercial to parody the civil rights sit-ins of the time by calling it a "foam-in." Proctor refused because it demeaned the civil rights movement.

With no alternative but to put her own ideas to work, Proctor formed her own advertising agency. She latched onto the idea that large advertisers wished to appeal directly to the black consumer and needed guidance to do so. She also wanted to protect the black community from questionable advertising pitches. An $80,000 Small Business Administration (SBA) loan was Proctor's launching fuel, and today Proctor & Gardner Advertising dominates its niche.

Personal Experience

My perspective on turning around the troubled company does not come merely from observing Walton, Smith, Gardner and other resilient entrepreneurs. I was in serious business trouble when an investor in my company sued me and my auditors for a serious breach of fiduciary responsibility and then gave a damaging story to the press. The other investors and my company's banks abandoned me as well. I was violated and left to rebuild my reputation in the financial community and to generate cash flow by whatever means I could muster. The cash flow had to be sufficiently large to finance my legal defense and counterclaim as well as provide for my family.

Owners and managers of troubled companies who hire my services value my firsthand knowledge. When I consult with them about the importance of fearlessness, tenacity and standing up to rich, chicken-hearted creditors, they know that the words are coming from someone who has walked in their shoes. I feel for them as a battle-scarred veteran feels for a clean-shaven recruit.

THE CLONING OF FAMILY THERAPY

I have the good fortune of being married to a family therapist and having access to an extensive body of knowledge in this relatively new field. Family therapy grew out of a response to the narrow didactic of Freudian psychology, which treats the individual for emotional pathologies. Family therapists treat the family rather than the individual. They do not treat a crisis within the family, such as the father's alcoholism or the teenager's substance abuse, as an isolated instance of emotional illness. Rather, they treat it as a family problem.

Some family therapists regard businesses as having many of the characteristics of families, and they have begun treating companies in their practices. If someone in your community is skilled in treating the crises of companies and moderating the distress felt by key decision makers and valued employees, it would be a good idea to interview that person to determine if he or she can be helpful. Charles Bahr, president of Bahr International, Inc., a Dallas work-out consulting firm, recently added a psychologist to his staff. Bahr says, "If the top management is well, we can make the company well. But if not, then no amount of work will work."[3]

When interviewing family therapists for your company, here is a checklist of points to consider:

1. You will want a therapist who shares the mission and gut values of the company. A therapist who disdains your company's product or service will not respect your values and is not likely to give you quality time.

2. You will want someone who can help you speculate on what the issues in your company's crisis are likely to be. Find out if the therapist is good at forecasting. You will detect this if he or she begins asking you "if-then" questions. A therapist does not have to know your business; in fact, that might not be a benefit. But he or she should ask you to focus on the effects of crisis and to list its variables.

3. You can't make an omelet without breaking eggs. Will the therapist be tough and talk straight to the key personnel? Clarity is an important attribute when you must identify a crisis and its solutions.

4. The therapist's main objective should be the strengthening of traditional values — a group benefit — without losing sight of individual strengths. He or she must be good at identifying individual strengths and weaknesses that can be stitched together for the collective good.

5. The therapist should outline his or her theory of problem solving as it relates to crisis management. Look for the following concepts:

- objectives: desired results or solutions
- endogenous variables: factors within your control
- exogenous variables: factors beyond your control

As a business manager and a leader, you undoubtedly are good at stating your objectives and handling variables within your control. It is the exogenous variables, those that appear to be outside of your control, that can desiccate your company. The therapist you hire must have the ability to help you identify the variables that appear to be outside your control before they strike.

Shared gut values, ability to forecast, clarity, toughness and an organized approach to problem solving — these are the qualities you are seeking in a therapist.

There is little written material in the field of crisis management for business, but there are many books and audiotapes available on family crises. Read them and listen to them. The parallels are there. The alcoholic parent whom family members tiptoe around is much like the executive who denies his incompetencies while his subordinates tiptoe around them. You can learn how to deal with a serious Pirandellian problem inside your company by picking up a good book or tape on family therapy and learning as much as you can on crisis-meeting resources.

THINK OF YOUR COMPANY AS A FAMILY

The family presents "a common front of solidarity to the world, handling internal differences in private, protecting the reputation of members by keeping family secrets, and standing together under attack," observes sociologist Reuben Hill.[4] The family lives in a greater state of tension today than it did 50 years ago because it carries the burden of the social order. In a society of rapid social change, there are more problems striking the family than there are solutions, and all of the uncertainties and frustrations of modern life are played out within the family. With few exceptions, people return from work or school to rehearse their daily frustrations within the family, where they hope to gain the necessary understanding and resilience to return to the fray.

Most families have had a long history of troubles and have worked out procedures and a division of responsibility for meeting crises as they arise. Notwithstanding that the family is badly organized for problem solving, it has been doing a better job of it than practically any other organization you can name. Families are heavily weighted with dependents; they cannot freely reject weak members and recruit stronger teammates. Its members receive unearned acceptance; they pay no price for belonging. In short, the family is an awkward decision-making group, poorly structured to withstand stress, yet society has assigned to it the heaviest responsibilities for meeting the emotional needs of all citizens, young and old.

A crisis-provoking event is a *stressor*: a situation for which the family has had no preparation. The stressor often creates complications that demand competencies from the family that the event itself may have temporarily paralyzed. Companies are better organized to deal with crises. They can replace incompetent players with competent ones; they can exact a price for membership; and they do not have to shoulder the weight of dependents. Furthermore, companies are geared for problem solving (although usually not crisis solving). To them, a problem is merely an opportunity in work clothes. Its leaders are irrepressible fighters in most business situations but poorly trained in crisis management.

CASE STUDY OF A FAMILY-OWNED BUSINESS

In a family-owned business, the crisis that attacks the company often has repercussions within the family. Carol Mann comanages the workout consulting company of Triage, Inc., which specializes in family-owned and family-operated businesses. Before becoming a business turnaround specialist, she and her husband owned a family business, Family Electronics.

Family Electronics was a 23-year-old firm involved in the U.S. distribution of specialized electronic assembly equipment manufactured in Japan, Germany and Switzerland. Founded by Carol Mann's husband, the business had grown to annual sales of $8 million when the falling value of the dollar suddenly turned what should have been hundreds of thousands of dollars in profitable sales into massive losses.

Meanwhile, her husband had, in Mann's view, developed an extravagant life-style. Despite the mounting debts, when he wanted a new sports car, he took money from the business to buy it. "He had reached a point," remarked one associate, "where his life-style was no longer a by-product of the business. Rather, the business existed solely to maintain that life-style, regardless of the consequences to the business."

Family Electronics had assets of $1.5 million, but it had built up a debt of $2.1 million and the debt was still mounting. Its accounts payable were running 120 to 150 days late.

Mann and her husband went to the bank to seek an additional $250,000 line of credit for working capital, to pay down vendors and to put a new business plan into effect. The bank's reply stunned them.

Not only did the bank refuse them the additional line of credit, but it announced that effective immediately it was calling in its previous loans. "Starting today," the bank told the Manns, "we are taking 80 cents of every dollar you deposit for repayment. And if you try to deposit your money anywhere else, other than this bank, you will go to jail." The bank also demanded Carol Mann's personal guarantee. Because she was only 21 and had very few assets, she refused. "If you need *my* personal guarantee," Mann said, "you should not be loaning money to this company."

Mann, who had no previous business experience but a lot of common sense, concluded that their only hope for survival was to reorganize the company under Chapter 11 protection. Her husband was an emotional wreck and could not deal with the crisis or participate in business decisions. She told him to take a backseat while she handled the workout.

With Family Electronics' assets and receivables effectively frozen out of reach by the bank, the law firm the Manns contacted demanded an up-front payment of $50,000 in cash. The Manns had no choice but to use their personal assets. "I remember sitting on the floor counting up our IRA certificates," said Mann. The lawyer was paid.

With the Chapter 11 filing, Carol Mann swung into action.

First, she slimmed down the company's work force. She discontinued a research-and-development project on which the company already had expended $350,000 and sold it to another company for $40,000.

She totally revamped the sales organization and its compensation system. Sales representatives, who previously received a combination of salary and commission, were put on straight commission. They were given quotas, and those who did not meet the quotas after four months were dismissed.

She tightened credit requirements for customers, insisting on complete credit checks for all accounts before shipping merchandise. She brought in a telemarketing expert to collect receivables by telephone. In short order, receivables collections were reduced from an average of 80 days to 32 days.

Mann instituted a quality-control program. In the past, Family Electronics never returned or charged back faulty products to vendors; instead, its own people would repair a faulty piece of equipment that a vendor shipped. Mann put a stop to that. She pressed vendors for improved quality standards and began returning and charging back faulty merchandise. She also began buying forward contracts to lock in current prices for future purchases.

She slashed all expenditures that did not directly produce a profit. The advertising budget, which had been $1.2 million annually, was reduced by more than half and redirected from magazines to targeted direct mail to improve its effectiveness.

Mann personally went into the shop to work with managers and employees. She improved shop management techniques and taught the people there how to figure company costs of jobs so they could be priced profitably.

She instituted a tracking program for the company's products. Slow-moving and unprofitable lines were dropped. She inaugurated a prospect-qualification program. Previously, Family Electronics shipped to anyone that requested demonstration units, whether or not they were prospective customers. Now the company would not ship expensive demonstration units to any firm unless it met a new qualification test.

The reorganization resulted in a sales volume that was half what it had been — $4 million versus $8 million at the company's peak. But, whereas the company lost money on $8 million in sales, it was showing a positive cash flow on $4 million. With costs cut, profits up and cash flow improved, Mann then arranged a new bank loan to provide the company with working capital.

In just seven months, a remarkably short time, she had reorganized the company to the point where it was again a profitable entity and no longer in need of Chapter 11 protection. She also found that the administrative, manufacturing and marketing management skills she developed during the workout and turnaround could be used to rescue other businesses in trouble. She left her husband, who continues to operate Family Electronics, and set her cap to become a company physician to family-owned businesses.

STURDY IMMIGRANT FAMILIES

Immigrant families generally are good at crisis management because they have experienced the sudden removal of the father or the oldest son by conscription or false imprisonment. A vertical study of thousands of war-torn American families by Reuben Hill found six significant hardships:

1. Sharp changes in income
2. Housing inadequacies
3. Enforced living with relatives
4. Illness of wife or children
5. Wife's having to work and act as mother and father
6. Child discipline problems stemming from father's absence

Some of the nation's most successful entrepreneurs emigrated to America in fear of their lives and survived at the most meager level while preparing themselves for great business achievements. Nothing in the business world seems to frighten them because they have escaped the ultimate crisis. Alex Manoogian, the founder of MASCO Corporation, the nation's largest manufacturer of plumbing supplies, escaped persecution in Turkey as a young man. Juan Benitez, the head of production at Micron Technology, Inc., fled Cuba. One of the founders of Intel Corporation, Andrew Grove, fled Hungary in 1951 and landed in New York unable to read a newspaper. Three years later, he graduated as valedictorian of his class at City College of New York.

K. Philip Hwang, founder of TeleVideo Systems, Inc., was born in Hungnam, North Korea, and escaped to South Korea at the age of 14. He sold pencils and pads and studied rigorously to qualify for overseas study. Eleven years later, he enrolled at Utah State University with a scholarship and $50 to his name. He would have starved in his first year except for a Christmas basket of damaged cans of pumpkin pie filling given him by a friendly Presbyterian minister.

Rose Blumkin, 97, who recently launched a new furniture store to compete with Nebraska Furniture Mart, which she sold in 1983 to Warren Buffett for $60 million, came to America from Russia in 1917 without a penny to her name. She began in business in the basement of a pawnshop when she was 43 with a borrowed $500. She helped her husband run the pawnshop until 1950. When her husband died, Blumkin had to make her own way in the world. In 1917, she bribed her way past a Russian border guard and came to America in a peanut boat via China and Japan. Her drive to succeed was an offshoot of her drive to be free. When asked the secret of her success, the illiterate daughter of a poor Russian rabbi responded, "Sell cheap, tell the truth, don't cheat nobody and don't take kickbacks."

Warren Buffett, frequently referred to as America's shrewdest investor, trusts Blumkin so much that he bought her business without conducting an audit. He told *The Wall Street Journal*: "Put her up against the top graduates of the top business schools or chief executives of the *Fortune* 500 and, assuming an even start with the same resources, she'd run rings around them."[5]

GUILT, DEPRIVATION AND MOTHER
STROKING—PROFILE OF AN ENTREPRENEUR

Several years ago, I became curious about the factors that caused entrepreneurs such as Rose Blumkin, H. Ross Perot, Fred Smith, Ray Kroc and K. Philip Hwang to succeed against overwhelming odds. I sent questionnaires to several hundred male and female entrepreneurs who had made more than $20 million in personal wealth, and I received an unusually high response rate, considering how many requests these individuals receive each day. I categorized the responses and, with the assistance of two psychiatrists, came up with a profile of the successful entrepreneur.

The entrepreneur is driven by guilt, was deprived in childhood, because of a physical, economic or geographic impairment, and was raised in a home where the father was absent or, in the case of females, in a home where the father emboldened his daughter to do anything the boys could do. "Who is the successful entrepreneur?" I asked. Here is what I found.

The entrepreneur is someone dissatisfied with his or her career path (though not with his or her chosen field) who decides to make a mark on the world by developing and selling a product or service that will make life easier for a large number of people.

The entrepreneur is energetic and single-minded and has a mission and clear vision; he or she intends to create out of this vision a product or service in a field many have determined is important, to improve the lives of millions. Consider the number of successful entrepreneurial ventures undertaken over the past 15 years in the computer, biomedical and communications industries. Yes, the entrepreneur probably will make a lot of money and knows it; when, who knows and who cares.[6]

The typical entrepreneur is a male between 27 and 34 years old. This is not a reflection on the entrepreneurial capabilities of women. In fact, an increasing number of dynamic young women are becoming dissatisfied with their corporate roles and are leaving them to start more personally rewarding businesses. There is no difference from my point of view between men and women entrepreneurs. But because mostly men responded to my questionnaires, and because almost all the entrepreneurs I've worked with over the past 20 years have been male, for the remainder of this chapter I will refer to the typical entrepreneur as "he."

To some, this archetypical individual represents a contradiction. Until the time he conceived of his entrepreneurial (ad)venture, he worked fully within the scope of traditional societal values, for a corporation, perhaps, or for a laboratory, a medical school or a research center. He was hired, he believed, for his creative potential and was rewarded, he believed, for his creative contributions. He was well satisfied.

Lurking in the wings, however, was a foil. For although initially he trusted that the organization valued him and rewarded him principally for his creative potential and output, as he became more energetic and needed more latitude and funding for invention, the organization's commitment to creative output and its willingness to invest in his personal research and development efforts emerged as less than he expected. At first surprised, he became increasingly dissatisfied, though for a time he did nothing.

As trust in the workplace faded, strong commitment to his own capabilities unfolded. More and more, he felt a sense of direction; an inner voice was asking him questions about his personal values—not philosophical stock-taking questions that often are raised by people in their mid-30s and 40s, questions such as What have I accomplished in my life? What tracks have I left in the sand? What will I do with the rest of my life? Those questions are as likely to come to the entrepreneur as to anyone else. But at this point in his life, the big question for the entrepreneur was: What will I do with my creativity?

He is intense, deadly serious about homesteading somewhere and being able to exercise his confidence in himself. So, before he even knew it had started, the entrepreneurial race was on. For a time, as he continued to do his job for his employer, dissatisfaction increased and the idea for the one product or service would take the marketplace by storm was putting down roots in his mind. The first growth might be a primary shoot that withers, but the root system was secure, come sunny weather or violent storm. He will be protected by enormous potential to replenish psychic energy, by intense pleasure at his activity and, if he is to be successful, by excellent communication skills and exquisite judgment: the ability to do the right thing rather than the capability to do a thing right.

At this point, he comes to me.

I have the enormous pleasure, then, of meeting complex, intense, determined, imaginative people who have faith in themselves and whose energy isn't sapped by pervasive anger or disappointment. The workplace has not been satisfying and hasn't rewarded what they most respect in themselves, but they go on to create their own reality. Thus, the true entrepreneur does not feel victimized. He accepts that the organization will not provide a place to do what he wants to do and he decides to create such an organization on his own.

The creative intelligence the entrepreneur brought to the employer's business now is directed toward designing a product or service and positioning it for the marketplace. He examines opportunities, perhaps for licensing, sees none he likes, may work for a short time as an independent consultant or for a consulting firm, continues to see the need he identified and finally decides to create his own opportunity.

He is getting ready to carve out his niche and build a place in the sun. He is not interested in empire building. Rather, he is planning for self-reliance, a quality-controlled provision for creative output. He talks about building an organization where people will not get lost; where creativity will be rewarded; where salaries and benefits will be just; where participative management (though he doesn't call it by that name) will be the rule, not the exception.

The undercurrent of optimism and trust in his professional power, the certainty that his expertise in his field is unequaled, govern a clear decision to be on his own and succeed. He has no fear of failure, though he makes careful, detailed plans to avoid it. Statistics of new business and small business failure offered to him by well-meaning friends and family are dismissed as irrelevant. Then he goes on with his presentations and telephone calls to bankers, brokers, friends of friends. Failure is simply not a possibility. He has spotted an opportunity and is leaping forward to take advantage of it as rapidly as possible.

POSITIVE STRESS

Positive stress drives the successful businessperson. It enables the manager of a troubled company to get through periods of distress that would overwhelm the inheritor of a business or a divisional manager in a corporate hierarchy. Positive stressors include an absent father (or in the case of a female, a supportive father), the need to drop out of school and work to supplement the family's income, serious childhood illness, bankruptcy in the first venture, with a moral obligation to repay all creditors, and escape from a dictatorial regime coupled with months of hand-to-mouth survival.

In a 1960 research paper for the Small Business Administration, David Moore of Cornell University interviewed 110 entrepreneurs and found "a high incidence of parental death or divorce which creates massive insecurity and makes the person more self-reliant." Raised by a strong-willed mother who pushed for achievements, competence and public recognition, the successful entrepreneur seeks to work in a well-regarded establishment organization. Then he leaves in a burst of motivation to succeed at all costs in an effort to erase forever the hurt that the crisis once caused his family.

The lore of entrepreneurship contains countless examples of individuals who were motivated by positive stressors, but perhaps the best example is C. Kemmons Wilson, founder of Holiday Corporation (nee Holiday Inns of America, Inc.). Wilson's father died when he was nine months old, and he was raised as an only child by his mother, Ruby, called "Doll" because she was less than five feet tall. Doll supported the family with a variety of low-paying jobs, but when she got sick, Wilson dropped out of high school and began an early career in the vending-equipment business: pinball machines, jukeboxes and cigarette machines. Wilson once bought 250 cigarette machines with six postdated checks of $10,000 each and pulled the quarters out of each machine three or four times a day to cover the checks.

From 1943 to 1945, he served as flight officer in the Air Transport Command. He returned to civilian life in 1946 and expanded his home-building business while operating theaters in Memphis, Tennessee; St. Louis, Missouri; and Louisville, Kentucky.

In 1951, Wilson took his family on what he refers to as "the most miserable vacation trip of my life" because of the cramped, costly lodging available. The motels charged $2 per child even though they bunked in the same room as their parents. Little did Mrs. Wilson realize that her husband's ranting about building a chain of motels that never would charge extra for children would turn into a reality. In 1952, the first Holiday Inn was built on Summer Avenue, one of the main arteries into Memphis. Since that time, the chain has grown into 1,750 establishments in 50 states and on every continent except Antarctica. The company now has branched into casinos, bus transportation and steamship services.

Wilson retired from Holiday Inns in 1979 because of a heart attack but has since branched into other entrepreneurial activities. The word *retirement* doesn't exist in the vocabulary of developer and entrepreneur extraordinaire C. Kemmons Wilson.

Giving Meaning to the Stressor

The ability to ride out the stressor event without paralysis or disorganization depends on what meaning the family or company gives to it. The stressor becomes a crisis only if the family or company defines it as such. Figure 1.1 shows Hill's conceptual framework of the stressor-to-crisis event.

The second and third determinants — family or company resources and definitions of the event — lie within the family or company itself and must be seen in terms of their structures and values. The hardships of the event, which make up the first determinant, lie outside the family or company and are an attribute of the event itself.

Workout consultants cite time and again that procrastinating and denying the early warning signals of stress will turn a one-alarm fire into a destructive blaze. The people in your organization who say, "No problem, boss. I can handle it," probably have their heads in the sand. They will have to be let go, along with other poor teammates described in chapter three.

FIGURE 1.1   From Stressor to Crisis

A (the event) → interacts with **B** (the family's or the company's crisis-meeting resources) → interacts with **C** (the definition that the family or the company gives to the event) → produces **X** (the crisis).

SOURCE: Reuben Hill, "Generic Features of Families Under Stress," in *Crisis Intervention: Selected Readings*, ed. Howard Parad (New York: Family Service Association of America, 1965), 40.

The Willy Loman Trap

Biff and Hap, the sons of Willy Loman in Arthur Miller's *Death of a Salesman*, could not see Willy's stress as an impending crisis because Willy raised them to chase the dream. The Loman family, unable to give meaning to the stressor event, suffered the terrible consequences. Emotions explode in a cathartic scene in which Biff breaks down, sobbing, telling his father to "take that phony dream and burn it before something happens."[7]

How many times have we watched managers in crisis hold onto "that phony dream"? Robert Campeau, who purchased Bloomingdale's and five other retail chains, was literally rearranging the deck chairs on the *Titanic* by choosing products for his flagship stores while the stores' managers were barraged with calls from screaming creditors. Bobby R. Inman, who acquired Tracor, Inc., a large defense contractor for whom he incurred mountains of debt in a leveraged buyout, blamed the outbreak of peace and Tracor's slump in sales for the company's demise. He missed the simple fact that you don't buy capital equipment manufacturers with debt because their inevitable cyclicality will pull the companies under while leaving their managers screaming like Ahab at the whale of ineluctable truth: "How can this happen to my dream?"

The B factor in Hill's equation — crisis-meeting resources — determines the family's or company's capacity to meet obstacles and shift courses away from its vulnerable points. Crisis-meeting resources include agreement by all members as to role structure, subordination of personal ambitions to the organization's goals and compatibility of the emotional needs of its members and the goals toward which the family or company is moving collectively. "When companies hit rough waters, employees in general become less communicative," says Canton, Ohio, workout consultant Kenneth Glass. Incompatible crisis-meeting resources must be discussed seriously and openly among department heads. If one department head is unwilling to accept the organization's definition of the stressor event and the organization's plans for meeting the crisis, then he or she must be replaced so that the company can move collectively to meet its goals.

A combination of deficiencies within the family's or the company's organization coupled with a tendency to define stressor events as terminal can make an organization crisis-prone. Large corporations frequently are crisis-prone because they are poorly organized, because their members are personally ambitious and because the lines of communication are so poor that facts become rumors, and rumors become crises. Crisis-prone corporations are easy prey for corporate raiders who dismember them with the ease of taking candy from a baby.

LITIGATION-INDUCED CRISIS

Litigation is a business, the intent of which is to place the opponent in crisis. Lawyers in America, where plaintiffs are not penalized for bringing lawsuits, however unrealistic, have developed a skill in unbalancing defendants and pitching them headfirst into crisis. As there are very few business managers equipped to deal with litigious crises, the business of litigation has grown to $300 billion per year. Here is how Peter Huber, author of *Liability*, adds up the cost of litigation:

> It adds more to the price of a helmet than the cost of making it. The tax falls especially hard on prescription drugs, doctors, surgeons, and all things medical. . . . Because of the tax, you cannot use a sled in Denver city parks or a diving board in New York City schools. You cannot buy an American Motors 'CJ' Jeep. . . . You can no longer buy many American-made brands of sporting goods . . . . The tax has curtailed Little League and fireworks displays,

tax has curtailed Little League and fireworks displays, evening concerts, sailboat races, and the use of public beaches and ice skating rinks.[8]

These are examples of tort liability that are brought against manufacturers of consumer products and providers of consumer services in an attempt to win outrageous settlements. The United States Supreme Court permits juries to award punitive damages — awards to the plaintiff in excess of the alleged damages — so settlements can be very high. Thus, Wal-Mart once had to pay $11.5 million in damages to a customer who suffered minor injuries in a slip-and-fall accident. And a school board once had to pay $350,000 to a burglar who fell through the school's faulty skylight.

In addition to the punitive-damage missile, lawyers also attempt to bury opponents with Racketeer Influenced and Corrupt Organizations Act, or RICO, charges to obtain coerced settlements. RICO seeks treble damage awards and makes lawsuits more intense and ferocious than they otherwise would be. To charge an opponent with RICO, the plaintiff must show merely that the defendant allegedly committed two or more acts of fraud, hence, a pattern. As Walter Olson observes: "With the twin weaponry of RICO and punitive damages, [lawyers] can charge opponents with shocking-sounding wrongdoing under vague, shifting retroactive legal standards."[9]

The bottom line is no downside risk for the party that brings a tort or RICO lawsuit. Under the legal systems in most other Western countries, a plaintiff who loses a lawsuit pays the winner's legal fees. But in America, if you are sued and win, you still have to pay legal fees. How does one survive the attack of a vicious and unwarranted lawsuit?

Business as a Battlefield

To win a sudden and severe lawsuit, one first must regard it for what it is: a military battle. The enemy is the plaintiff, and everything we have learned about running our businesses will not work in a litigation. Conventional business tools do not apply. Military tactics must be quickly learned and implemented.

Victory does not lie in crushing your opponent, but in outthinking him or her and in blanketing yourself with greater moral and intellectual strength. You must frustrate your opponent's plans. As Sun Tzu wrote 2,500 years ago: "To subdue the enemy without fighting is the acme of skill."[10] Battles are won without loss of life, Sun Tzu wrote, only by realizing that the primary battlefield is in the mind of the opposing commander.

If you are a manager who never has been tested in the litigation battlefield, let me give you some advice, because I survived the crisis of having been wrongfully sued.

1. *The damage trail.* Immediately begin to maintain an accurate record of the damages that the litigation causes your business to suffer. You will need the damage trail when you bring your counterclaim.

2. *Chancellorsville strategy.* In the Civil War battle of Chancellorsville, Stonewall Jackson implemented the pincers strategy, by which he split his battalion into two groups that silently surrounded the opponent and opened fire at their backs. Assign some intelligent employees to research the opponent company in depth, looking for facts that will weaken its case and fire your salvos at these unprotected positions.

3. *Adversarial communications training.* There are consulting firms that specialize in training business managers faced for the first time with having to communicate in adversarial situations. They listen to the charges made against you, then ask you to make a speech in your defense. The speech typically is full of self-pity and recrimination. Then they rebuild your personal image and reshape your speech. Oliver North's performance during the Iran-Contra investigation was the result of learning adversarial communications skills.

4. *Holding down legal fees.* The conventional wisdom is that the side with the most money will win a lawsuit because it will hire the best lawyer. That may be true, but if you don't have so much money as your opponent, then you will have to either hire a smart, experienced affordable lawyer or defend yourself. I have done both, and I can assure you that defending yourself is an interesting experience and much less expensive, although you will need to buy a library of books published by Nolo Press and

others on the subject of acting *pro se*. You also will need professional advice on the mechanics of lawyering.

5. *Communicating with your teammates.* Some employees, managers and members of the community in which your company operates will assume that because you have been sued you are guilty — guilty of racketeering or making a dangerous product or whatever the lawsuit states. But the company that brought the suit is big, rich and chickenhearted. It will be disgraced and will have to abandon the litigation once you have a chance to present your case. If any of your teammates do not join your cause, it will be a good time to excuse them from your inner circle.

The wrongful and ferocious lawsuit is a serious crisis that must be addressed vigorously, yet strategically. It is different from other crises because there is very little that prepares one for it. Nonetheless, adjusting to it follows the prescription for adjusting to crises in general.

ADJUSTING TO CRISIS

A company in crisis takes an outburst of shots into its operating system that imbalances it in three key areas that must be reexamined and reconstituted to find a pathway out of the crisis. These areas are the company's *values*, the *roles* of its key people and its *communications* system.

Values refer to the system of ideas, attitudes and beliefs that consciously or unconsciously bind together members of the company "family" in a common culture.

The second factor that characterizes a company is the patterning of *roles*. This patterning defines who does what, when and under what circumstances (obviously influenced by the system of values). In crises, the carrying out of tasks must be reexamined and realigned.

The third dimension, *communication*, is a network for carrying messages and transmitting information and ideas among managers and employees of the nuclear company as well as between the company and the outside community. "It includes definitions as to which messages are perceived as worth transmitting (again very much influenced by the value system) and provision for channels for transmission."[11] Who says what to whom is a critical decision in the workout and turnaround process — so critical that a new breed of consultant recently has emerged to handle it.

> So along with the growth in bankruptcy has emerged a new breed of expert: the Chapter 11 communications consultant. "In the first twenty-four hours of a bankruptcy, there's a window of opportunity when you can win or lose your employees' support," said Harris Diamond, a partner with the Sawyer/Miller Group in New York, which has handled Chapter 11 announcements for Ames Department Stores, Resorts International and Southland.[12]

The company will succeed in adjusting to a new value system and new role delineations if it also implements a revised communications system. One major effect of crisis is to cause changes in these role patterns, particularly as they relate to the need-to-know issue. With shifting expectations, members of the organization have to work out different patterns of communication.

Employees first must adjust to their relationships with the marketplace and with creditors. Who should be told? How much should they be told? Who should not be told? There is a need-to-know principle that requires *role playing* by members of the organization. Those who need to know should be told, "Yes, we are having some difficulties in certain areas. What company isn't? And we're having some successes in other areas. I don't want to burden you with all the details; but you should know that we have our arms around the problem. We think we understand it, and we are dealing with it. We will come out of it very well. Just watch us."

The customers' and creditors' responses will help you gauge the degree of assistance they will provide. Some will say, "You have been an important customer [or supplier] to us for many years, and we value your relationship. If we can help you, you can be sure that we will." But others will turn their backs on you until you trampoline out of trouble. Then they will be the first to say, "See, I knew that trouble would blow over."

Some additional advice on what to say to whom comes from one of the most successful poker players of our day, Anthony Holden. His advice applies to what to say to opponents at the beginning of a poker game to cause them to bet into you when they think you are bluffing, but in fact you have a pat full house. Note the similarities with the instructions of Sun Tzu.

> Whether he likes it or not, a person's character is stripped bare at the poker table. If the other players perceive him as better than he really is, he has only himself to blame for subsequent losses. Unless he is both able and prepared to see himself as others do, flaws and all, he will be a loser in cards as in life.[13]

Holden explains the art of bluffing: "Misplaying hands deliberately can at times be a higher art form than playing to win."

Holden recommends appearing unsophisticated up front to get the other players to bet into you wildly when you have a full house later on. This is a good strategy in poker playing. How does it transfer to business?

- Appear in need of assistance from your prospective lender. Ask for his or her involvement and participation. This appeals to the new banking strategy: relationship banking. It makes a banker feel useful and involves him or her in the workout strategy.
- Always understate your projected cash flow. Always understate the liquidation value of your assets. You will need the cushion later on as the full amount of your liabilities becomes known. That's good poker playing and good deal making.

When writing about how a family adjusts to the crisis created by an alcoholic spouse and parent, Joan Jackson identifies seven stages of adjustment:

1. Attempts to deny the problem;
2. Attempts to eliminate the problem;
3. Disorganization;
4. Attempts to reorganize in spite of the problem;

5. Efforts to escape the problem; the decision to separate from the alcoholic spouse;
6. Reorganization of the family without the spouse; and
7. Reorganization of the entire family.[14]

One of the great misconceptions held by owners and managers of businesses that are facing crises for the first time is that their ruin will come suddenly and swiftly. A major New York real estate developer, whose properties were in jeopardy when his banks became unable to fund him during the recession of 1990–1991, told me that his first thoughts were of humiliation, ruin and suicide. He was ill-prepared for crisis and could not adjust to it. I had to explain to him that a workout and turnaround period is a *process*, that it has certain learnable steps that, when taken properly, begin to sound out a rhythm of rehabilitation. Do it right, and you can hear your own turnaround. You can hear it in the voices of your vendors, lenders, key customers and teammates.

CRISIS FORMULATION

When oil prices fell sharply in 1985, John Madden, president of Houston's Rex Machinery, Inc. ($30 million sales), realized that oil drillers would have very little need for drilling equipment, Rex's primary product. Madden assumed that the crisis would be deep and prolonged. What would the industry need? A means of getting rid of equipment, less-expensive used equipment and a mechanism for carting away and storing equipment. Madden then formed three new businesses: moving, warehousing and used-equipment sales, and he moved mid-level managers from new-equipment sales to head the three new divisions. Rather than stand by and watch his company slide into bankruptcy, Madden boosted its overall sales and earnings in the midst of the crisis with three new divisions to respond to the needs of the marketplace.

Madden's crisis was brought about by an industry recession that was particularized to the Southwest. He correctly perceived that the need for new equipment would dry up suddenly, but the need for services would be strong. The shift from Rex's former operating systems to its recession business, however, would be painful and upsetting. To stanch the flow of blood, Madden began cutting costs immediately: across-the-board pay cuts, layoffs, elimination of advertising, less use of professional services, even down to using incoming paper clips.

By formulating the nature of the crisis and then adjusting to it, Madden saved his company. Crisis formulation paid off for Rex Machinery while other oil and gas companies went down the tubes. Take a tip from Madden: When doing layoffs, do them all at once. If you do them over time, the remaining employees will become demoralized and unproductive.

As you formulate the potential crisis, create a notebook of facts. Separate symptoms from problems. Write your own questions in the notebook: Is the crisis mentality forming among all of your customers and suppliers? Is it geographic, demographic or psychographic? Conduct your own telemarketing campaign to see how certain customers and suppliers are reacting to your crisis.

THE NATURE OF A STATE OF CRISIS

While stress is a negative condition, crisis has growth-promoting potential. Stress is a burden or load under which a person survives or cracks. Crisis, on the other hand, is a catalyst that disturbs old habits, generates new responses and creates new developments. A crisis is a call to action. The challenge it provokes may bring new coping mechanisms that strengthen the individual's adaptive capacity.[15]

Gerald Caplan defined crisis as an "upset in a steady state." The company strives to maintain a state of equilibrium — homeostasis — through a series of adaptive maneuvers and problem-solving activities. Over time, situations arise that disturb the homeostatic state and result in disequilibrium. These discontinuities are dealt with through conventional adaptive mechanisms such as replacing personnel, rolling over a loan, intensifying customer service.

In a state of crisis, the usual adaptive responses are inadequate to achieve balance. The response to crisis is threefold: to take the impact head-on, to recoil from it and to begin energizing solutions.

If solutions do not materialize, the family or company will disorganize and disintegrate.

I advise clients who are mired in self-pity to think about diving boards and trampolines; to think about the recovery process; to try a number of solutions to see which one works. Money comes into companies through several spigots, the conventional ones being sales, borrowings and the sale of equity. But there are other solutions to finding cash such as renting the customer list, licensing the brand name, lease financing and selling components rather than the entire product.

The Birth of the Moped

Crises were a way of life for Soichira Honda, the most brilliant mechanical engineering entrepreneur since Henry Ford, who was pierced by one unique, fixating idea that was to drive him through periods of hunger, pain and falling bombs. In 1938, Honda was in a desperate, around-the-clock pursuit of a perfectly cast piston ring. He slept at his machine shop, covered in grease, without savings or friends, and having pawned his wife's jewelry. The first batch of piston rings was rejected by Toyota Corporation, so he went back to the drawing board. At his industrial-engineering classes, Honda's designs brought laughter from his professor.

Two years later, Toyota found the piston rings satisfactory and placed an order, but the Japanese government was tooling for war and denied Honda the cement to build a plant. Undaunted, Honda and his men learned how to make their own cement. When the war came, Toyota advanced the badly needed working capital of $260,000 while Honda began training women to replace the men who went to war. His factories were bombed out twice, but after each attack, Honda rushed out to pick up the extra gasoline tanks that U.S. fighters threw away as they flew by. Honda called these cans "Truman's gifts" because they provided raw materials for his manufacturing process. When an earthquake finally leveled his factory, Honda sold his piston-ring operation to Toyota for $125,000.

After Japan's surrender, Honda created a fast rotary weaving machine, but he ran out of funds in 1947 before the manufacturing stage. Because of the gasoline shortage, he was unable to use his car to get food for his family. In desperation, Honda attached a small motor to his bicycle. A neighbor asked for one and then another neighbor, and another, until his supply of motors ran out. Then he decided to build motors.

Because there was no gasoline in war-ravaged Japan, Honda made a motor that ran on pine resin mixed with gasoline bought on the black market.[16]

With the income from motorbikes, Honda set out to fulfill his dream of speed and build real motorcycles. He brought in Takeo Fujisawa as a full partner and gave him complete authority in finance and strategic marketing. By 1951, Honda's machine was ready for the market, notwithstanding a lack of working capital. Fujisawa relied on customer financing. He wrote letters to Japan's 18,000 bicycle shop owners and told them about Honda's dream, the history of the bicycle and its evolution to the motor-driven bicycle, and finally, he sold the dream of a new Japan and their role in it. Five thousand dealers signed up, but only the hard-core motorcycle riders wanted Honda's dream. He needed to downsize the motorcycle to a small, inexpensive, quiet, step-through, motor-driven bicycle to expand the market from "class" to "mass." The small motorbike, called the Cub, became an overnight winner, and Honda was awarded the emperor's medal.

It was Honda's good judgment to bring Fujisawa in to handle finance and marketing. Because Fujisawa had been raised in the home of a frequently failing small businessperson, he knew how to design stretchouts for bankers and creditors and how to stretch the stretchouts. As the company prepared to expand into Europe and the United States in 1953, it overextended itself with the purchase of $1 million of machine tools, and if the loan from the Mitsubishi bank had been called, Honda Motor Company would have been gobbled up by the atavistic Mitsubishi Heavy Industries. Fujisawa persuaded the bank to extend the loan and the company remained independent. By 1955, the Honda motorbike was on its way to capturing the hearts and minds of the postwar baby boomers in Europe and America. Honda and Fujisawa built a dealership network in the United States from bicycle dealers who were looking for a new product with a high profit margin. When Honda Motor

Company introduced its automobile to the United States in the 1970s, its dealership organization was in place.

Each crisis in Soichiro Honda's business life was met head-on with creative solutions: "Truman's gifts," operating his factory with women workers and resin from pine root.

CRISES HAVE TIME LIMITS

Does facing desperation and riding through it safely prepare the manager for future crises? I believe that it is of greater benefit than hiring a therapist because it instructs the person in the most important fact about crises: They have time limits. Crises do not go on forever. The better prepared and more adaptable the company is before the crisis hits, the shorter the period of reorganization will be.

Crisis managers do not grieve or deny. They have an action-oriented code of behavior that instructs them to keep firing in all directions. And like the Marines hitting the beach at Iwo Jima, if something falls down from their shots, they hightail it in that direction.

Department heads and key personnel within the company, however, may not know that crises have time limits. They may not know that their leader has need-response electrons in his or her brain that trigger "if–go to" and "if not–go to" instructions that lead instinctively to appropriate responses and near-perfect resolutions of problems. Hence, the need for communication and clarity. The crisis manager must continually explain the objectives of the company and how he or she expects key personnel to deal with crises.

The leader should clearly define the difference between stressor events and crises and outline appropriate responses to each. Key personnel will perceive stressor events as crises unless they are told otherwise, especially if they recently worked for large corporations whose reactions to problems is typically to make them worse through active denial, massive litigation or a public-relations blast that obfuscates reality. "Spinning" a story to anxious creditors diminishes the company's integrity and makes employees worry about management ethics. It fuels the fire of concern and should not be in the workout playbook.

Caplan is very clear about the need for good internal communications when a family is in crisis:

> *Communication* is a network for carrying messages and transmitting information, feelings, ideas, among the various family members of the nuclear family (internal communication) as well as between the family and the outside community (external communication). It includes definitions as to which messages are perceived as worth transmitting (again very much influenced by the value system) and provision of channels for transmission (word symbols, body behavior, gestures).[17]

PAYING ATTENTION TO DETAILS

In business, as opposed to the sciences, we strive for satisfaction rather than perfection. But the company in crisis must strive for exactitude. People get sloppy when things are going well, but when the company is in crisis, all details must be attended to.

Prevent any proposal, bid, legal action, offering circular, funding memorandum or important letter from leaving the company unless it is accurate and neat. When sending documents by courier, record the airbill number. When asking that a check be sent via overnight courier, give the check sender your credit card or courier account number or better yet, send him or her a courier envelope and your self-addressed airbill. If you have convinced the customer to wire transfer funds, be sure to add the receiving bank's ABA routing number. Then alert your bank that a wire transfer is coming and to call you when it arrives. Have secretaries repeat messages back to you to be certain they are accurate. Even your damage-trail notebooks must be completely accurate. Every document must be dated.

In the midst of a crisis, the office may become chaotic. Papers can get lost. The cleaning service may throw away some papers that are inadvertently placed on the floor. Strive for neatness. Otherwise, a worried supplier or banker may drop in unexpectedly and have his or her worst fears confirmed. Make sure that everyone is paying attention to details.

FEARLESSNESS

As we move through the six steps of the workout and turn-around process, remember that you are the leader. People will be looking to you as their Moses. You may not be a fearless leader by nature, but there is no time like the present to begin.

Fearlessness is a learned behavior. I wasn't raised to be fearless, nor did I face death in Vietnam as did Pepi Piedre, replacement chief executive officer of Seattle Silicon, a brilliant turnaround manager. I became fearless in business by surviving as a money finder for entrepreneurial and turnaround companies in periods when there seemed to be no money. Then, having rescued them, I had to collect my fee to feed and clothe my family. My own business has gone through a crisis with the concomitant symptoms of illiquidity, loss of clients and ferocious litigation. Therefore, when I describe the workout and turnaround process, I do so as one who has been financially devastated, maligned by litigation and scarred on the battlefield of crisis. Yet I am still smiling, still winning, and nothing in business frightens me.

Endnotes

1. Vance Trimble, *Sam Walton: The Inside Story of America's Richest Man* (New York: Penguin Group, 1990), pp. 56-57.

2. Robert Sigafoos, *Absolutely Positively Overnight* (New York: New American Library, 1983), pp. 115-16.

3. James Drummond, "Taking a Burn for the Better," *Nation's Business*, May 1991, pp. 44-48.

4. Reuben Hill, "Generic Features of Families Under Stress," *Social Casework* 39, nos. 2-3 (1958).

5. Frank James, "Furniture Czarina, Still a Live Wire at 90; a Retail Phenomenon Oversees Her Empire," *The Wall Street Journal*, May 23, 1984, p. 1.

6. A. David Silver, *The Entrepreneurial Life* (New York: John Wiley & Sons, Inc., 1983).

7. Arthur Miller, *Death of a Salesman* (New York: Viking, 1949), pp. 132–33.

8. Peter Huber, *Liability: The Legal Revolution and Its Consequences* (New York: Basic Books, 1988), p. 3.

9. Walter Olson, *The Litigation Explosion: What Happened When America Unleashed the Lawsuit* (New York: Truman Tolley Books, 1991), p. 10.

10. Sun Tzu, *The Art of War* (circa 500 B.C.), trans. by Samuel Griffith (New York: Oxford University Press, 1963), p. 41.

11. Howard Parad and Gerald Caplan, "A Framework for Studying Families in Crisis," in *Crisis Intervention: Selected Readings* (New York: Family Service Association of America, 1965), p. 58.

12. Nancy Marx Bette, "Putting the Best Face in Bankruptcy," *New York Times*, April 7, 1991, p. F23.

13. Anthony Holden, *Big Deal* (New York: Penguin Group, 1990).

14. Joan Jackson, "The Adjustment of the Family to Alcoholism," *Marriage and Family Living* 18, no. 4 (1956), pp. 361-69.

15. Lydia Rapoport, "The State of Crisis: Some Theoretical Considerations," *The Social Service Review* 16, no. 2 (1962).

16. George Gilder, *The Spirit of Enterprise* (New York: Simon & Schuster, 1984), p. 179.

17. Gerald Caplan, "Patterns of Parental Response to the Crisis of Premature Birth," *Psychiatry* 23 (1960), pp. 365–74.

■ CHAPTER TWO ■

Let's Review Your Options

Now that you have decided to treat the workout and turnaround as an intellectual process, just as you would any other significant stage in the life of the company, let's review the options that are available to you. These will depend on how much debt the company has, the nature of the debt, how much free cash flow the company can ferret out of its assets and the ability of the company to attract outside capital, based on your viability assessment.

SIZING UP THE COMPANY'S PROBLEMS

The optimum troubled condition is as follows:

GRADE A: The Best Troubled Condition

One (or a few) secured creditor that has a lien on all of the company's assets and many unsecured creditors that are individually owed small amounts of money; cash that can be freed up by slashing overhead expenses and selling off peripheral assets; a positive viability assessment.

If your troubled condition is Grade A, then Chapter 11 is not for you, unless it is a prepack, and that will depend on your ability to attract outside capital. Donald J. Trump's trouble is Grade A, but with some minor complications stemming from his very high level of personal guarantees. You can bet that he will not file corporate bankruptcy, but, because of his personal guarantees, the question of his personal bankruptcy still is an issue.

The second best troubled condition is the following:

GRADE B: *The Second-Best Troubled Condition*

Many secured creditors, all with liens on different assets; a few unsecured creditors, several of whom are owed a lot of money; possibly loyal customers, but requiring continual reassurance with advertising; a positive viability assessment in a market with strong competitors.

The Grade B condition describes a company that must act decisively because it can be flipped into a Chapter 7 by an angry band of creditors. Grade B is a high-wire act. If several unsecured creditors, even two disgruntled former employees with back pay or back commissions due, each of whom is owed more than $5,000, decide to liquidate the company and take their chances at auction, the Grade B company will be history.

The critical conditions of the Grade B situation are the number of creditors and the amount owed to the unsecured creditors. If they are not kept happy, they could be troublesome; and with that in mind, some companies are doing prepackaged Chapter 11s to thwart the troublesome unsecureds. It is a Sun Tzurian strategy of pinching off riotous creditors before they are fully armed.

Try to avoid the Grade C condition at all costs because all your equity could be wiped out, stockholders could lose their investments and the company could be dissolved. This could happen if your company meets the following conditions:

GRADE C: *The Worst Troubled Condition*

There are no secured creditors, or perhaps a few, but most of the company's assets are not collateralized; many unsecured creditors, large enough to afford experienced creditor-advocate lawyers and workout consultants; nervous customers who question the company's product and service quality; a negative or dubious viability assessment.

In this situation, the company has serious enemies poised on all sides. The secureds want more collateral. The unsecureds want to be collateralized. Sales are shrinking and customers must be persuaded to stay in the fold. Effecting a workout outside of Chapter 11 will require a masterful negotiating feat with the objective of giving something to each adversary while preserving some equity for the stockholders. Angry and powerful unsecureds can force concessions from secureds and stockholders. Perhaps if the unsecureds can be negotiated with from the onset, the company can be turned around without a Chapter 11 filing. The company's viability, however, is negative to begin with. Thus, raising capital to finance a turnaround is out of the question and a new business plan will have to be implemented. Some solutions to the Grade C condition are suggested in chapters nine and ten of this book.

MISPLACED BLAME

Pay no attention to those who cast aspersions on the managers of companies in trouble. It is in the nature of a competitive marketplace that some companies will fall on hard times and attempt to recover. In Japan, where there are fewer bankruptcies than in the United States, companies cooperate more, and banks often own large blocks of stock in corporations and keep them propped up.

Businesses fail because they have structural problems. They do not fail because they exhaust their cash resources or because their banks call their loans or because they amass too much debt. These are *symptoms* of troubled companies, not causes. You can point to the excessive leverage that was accumulated to effect junk-bond-leveraged buyouts as a causative factor in well-known business failures such as Campeau, L. J. Hooker, Revco, Southland, Tracor and Ames Department Stores. But these were actually *transaction-caused failures* created by the confluence of ego-driven corporate raiders and fee-driven investment bankers who, to the delight of their owners, overpaid for companies with high-interest loans that were lapped up by institutional lenders.

The finger of blame on the graves of defeated companies is pointing at junk-bond-based leveraged buyouts of the 1980s and their creator, Michael E. Milken. This is unfair. Milken, for all his moral flaws, was a financial genius who roused corporate directors to a more cost-conscious way of conducting business. He is mentioned here for his contributions to the art of the workout.

THE INSTRUCTIONS OF MICHAEL MILKEN

Milken was employed by a third-rate investment bank that had no important corporate clients. Status on Wall Street is correlative with fee income because the more prestigious the investment banker's client list, the more it can charge for its services. The top-drawer investment banks derive enormous fees from raising capital and advising on mergers and acquisitions for their *Fortune* 500 clients. Milken's employer, Drexel Burnham Lambert, had marginal clients going into the 1980s. Its clout and profitability were destined to remain small for years to come because it was sacrosanct among the captains of American industry that their financial transactions carry the imprimatur of Wall Street's finest, which did not include Drexel.

Milken changed the financial markets and industrial management for years to come. He did this with a product, the junk bond, in a service industry.[1] The junk bond is a high-interest-rate (more than 16 percent), usually unsecured, bond, the interest and principal repayments of which are uncertain at best, and impossible to meet at worst. Milken introduced junk bonds as the means of overpaying for takeover targets in corporate raids. Typically, companies are taken over by entrepreneurs via leveraged buyouts that involve borrowing on the assets of the takeover target and repaying the borrowings out of the company's cash flow. The excess by which the price exceeds the amount that could be borrowed on the company's assets is typically 5 percent to 10 percent of the purchase price and is funded by the entrepreneurial team. If the cash flow of the takeover is insufficient to service debt, pay back the risk equity and provide the entrepreneurs a reasonable return, a lower price is offered or the buyers walk away. Money rarely chased deals pre-Milken.

"Though Drexel had not pioneered the LBO," writes Connie Bruck, "it was a match made in heaven. It was a philosophical fit: The leveraged buyout (LBO) represented a shift of control from a bureaucratic organization into entrepreneurial hands. And it was an extension of what Milken had been doing since 1977, when he started to help his clients to leverage their balance sheets with high levels of debt, through the issuance of junk bonds."[2]

By dramatically overpaying for deals — more than twice the amount that could be borrowed on the target company's assets — Milken created a win-win-win situation for all the participants in the takeover market:

1. *Secured lenders.* The usual lenders in the leveraged buyout market were pleased with all of the takeover activity because their loans were fully secured and they were making lots more of them.

2. *Junk bond buyers.* Mutual funds, pension funds, insurance companies and savings and loan institutions were thrilled to be loaning money at more than 16 percent interest. They were told that when an interest or principal payment came due but could not be paid out of cash flow, Milken's firm would find a source of payment.

3. *Managers of takeover companies.* Although some managers put up a semblance of a fight for public consumption, most had golden parachute deals that would make them multimillionaires after the takeover. Furthermore, the takeovers were frequently at stock prices that they could not hope to generate in five years of the most adroit management.

4. *Stockholders of takeover targets.* Stockholders of takeover targets were happy to be offered a dollar for something that the most efficient auction market in economic history said was worth not a penny more than 50 cents. Stockholders of nontargets in the same industry benefitted as well when their holdings rose in sympathy to their breakup value: the projected aggregate price at which their company's parts could be broken up and sold off.

5. *Investment bankers.* The best deal of all fell to the investment bankers, of which Milken's firm, Drexel Burnham Lambert, became the most proficient, the most highly regarded and the

most profitable. Whereas investment banks traditionally earned one or two fees for arranging acquisitions for their corporate clients, Milken multiplied the number of fees to at least six per transaction and increased their size. The potpourri of his fees included:

- Finder's fee for introducing the target;
- Valuation fee charged to the buyer for stating that the price was fair;
- Financing fee for raising the money to buy the company;
- Equity fee, or part ownership in the takeover target, for being its initiator;
- Spin-off fees (several, depending on the number of spin-offs earned by selling off divisions to raise cash); and
- Refinancing fees to refinance the junk bonds when it was clear to all that the debt could not be serviced.

Other investment banks jumped into Milken's enormously profitable arena, while his personal income exceeded $500 million per year on occasion. The competition to do Drexel-type deals to generate fees pushed the takeover game to such extremes that spin-offs and refinancings could not be handled fast enough to stanch the flow of blood. Commercial banks did not collateralize themselves properly. Raiders did not manage companies to maximize cash flow, so some of their trophies ended up in bankruptcy. "Junk bonds are by definition junk," said H. Ross Perot. "I didn't name them. The guys who created them named them. They are going to be worn like animals around the necks of the companies that sold them. They have nothing to do with anything except making fees."[3]

The premise of the junk-bond-backed LBO binge of the 1980s was quite simple: Let's overprice takeovers and see who buys the program. Nearly everyone whose name was called signed up for Milken's deals, notwithstanding that the entrepreneurs the junk bonds were financing had no proven management ability. Names like Ronald Perelman, who acquired Revlon; Nelson Peltz, who acquired Triangle Industries; Carl Icahn, who acquired TWA; T. Boone Pickens, who attempted to acquire Phillips Petroleum; and Bobby R. Inman, who acquired Tracor.

There have been some junk-bond-backed LBO bankruptcies, but for the most part the jury is on the side of the raiders. Putting aside the economic validity of the Milken-inspired age of takeovers and the felonies he committed during this period, the *deal* that he conceived, developed, implemented and sold to some of the most astute lenders and investors in the country is awesome.

In a rational world, money managers entrusted with billions of dollars of savings and pension funds simply do not buy junk bonds that yield 16 to 18 percent per year if the financial statements presented to them clearly indicate that there is inadequate cash flow to service the debt. Institutional investors are fiduciaries. Justice Louis Brandeis defined a fiduciary as someone to whom money is entrusted and who is supposed to exert greater care in its management than in the management of his or her own money. Why did these gatekeepers of the nation's savings take such incredible risks?

The "Godfather" Proposition

Milken (and the competitive investment bankers who tried to play catch-up to Drexel from 1985 to 1989) made institutional investors a series of offers that they could not refuse. First, they received a *commitment fee* upon subscribing to buy junk bonds. Thus, if the deal was lost to a competitive bidder, if the takeover broke down or if the full amount of the financing could not be raised, the subscribing financial institution received payment for reading the offering circular and documents. The commitment fees ranged from 3/8 of 1 percent to 7/8 of 1 percent. Thus, a $10 million commitment resulted in a payment to the institution of approximately $50,000 for reading the deal and voting yes.

Milken's junk-bond-offering circulars were shipped to institutional money managers in tightly bound manila envelopes that literally screamed, "Open me, ye who seek undreamed of riches!" The investor had to respond to a Drexel deal within 24 to 48 hours. Institutional investors were not used to being ordered about by investment bankers, but they took orders from Drexel. They could either subscribe to the deal in two days, and see more junk bond deals in the future, or they could pass, and they probably would not see any more Drexel deals.

Milken changed the buyer-seller dynamics. He positioned junk bonds as solutions to the problems faced by institutional investors; that is, their need to earn sufficiently high yields to cover operating expenses and payouts to policyholders, pensioners and passbook holders to whom they were offering higher yields to capture their loyalty. Before Milken, if an institution could lock in average yields of 12 per annum, it made ends meet. Junk bond yields of 16 to 18 percent permitted operating expenses (read: management salaries and bonuses) to rise without jeopardizing statutory payouts. An investment officer in a large institution frequently receives a bonus if his or her portfolio yields more than a predetermined target rate of return, such as 10 percent per year. A salaried investment officer earning $100,000 a year pre-Milken could bump his or her take-home pay by an additional $100,000 by investing in junk bonds. That is a very strong inducement.

The final leg of the stool was Milken's tacit promise to junk bond buyers that if the borrower is unable to pay interest or principal on the debentures when due, Milken and his team would either refinance the initial junk bond with a new one that offered superior features or sell a peripheral division of the borrower to raise cash to meet the payment deadlines. Drexel had a highly skilled investment banking crew that was capable of rolling over the debt when it came due with debt restructurings or cashouts.

Drexel's promise to refinance junk bond principal when it came due was tantamount to a *guarantee* that the buyer would make and not lose money. As long as Milken was around to honor that guarantee, the institutions did not lose money. He replaced their old debt with new. But when he was removed from the industry he created in 1989, the spool of thread began to unravel.

THE DEMISE OF JUNK BONDS

Drexel dominated its competitors for five years. Figure 2.1 lists the dollar amount of junk bond financings effected between 1984 and 1988, grouped by underwriter. Although Drexel's share of junk bond financings declined from 69 percent in 1984 to 41 percent in 1988, it remained the dominant junk bond house.

FIGURE 2.1   Competition in Junk Bond Underwritings, 1984 to 1988

	$ Amount	Percentage
Drexel Burnham	$ 57.4 billion	40.1%
Morgan Stanley	13.5 billion	9.4
First Boston	10.9 billion	7.6
Merrill Lynch	10.6 billion	7.4
Other	50.8 billion	35.5
Total	$143.2 billion	100.0%

SOURCE: *Investment Dealers Digest* and Morris & Co., Inc.

To play catch-up ball, Drexel's competitors offered higher prices to takeover targets and embellished the junk bonds with equity kickers, higher interest rates and improved terms. We can get a sense of the competition among America's most prestigious investment banks to underwrite junk-bond-based takeovers in a book about the largest junk bond takeover of them all, RJR/Nabisco.

> Of particular interest to Johnson [CEO] were the many uses the bidders had found for the strain of junk bonds known as pay-in-kind securities, or PIK. The management group's decision to "pile on the PIK" in place of cash still boggled his mind. . . .
>
> . . . we have found something that's better than the U.S. printing press. And they've got it down here on Wall Street. And nobody knows it's going on. . . . It's a brand new currency. . . .[4]

The party that we came to know as the Great Takeover Bash of the late 1980s became a drunken brawl. All the participants were making more money than they ever dreamed possible. Stockholders were selling out at double their investment. Managers were jumping out of target companies and floating to the lush fairways of Scottsdale and Tarpon Springs on golden parachutes. Institutional investors were showing more profits than at any time in their history, and their money managers' billfolds were crammed with the rewards of their financial acumen. The raiders built empires and sewed up net worths as large as their Social Security numbers. The investment bankers generated six to seven times the traditional fees of the business, and Milken alone made more money than the gross national products (GNPs) of half of the countries in the United Nations.

Very little thought was given to the ability to repay more than $260 billion in junk bonds. Some of the takeover targets defaulted. Some fraudulent inside trading by high-profile arbitrageurs — investors who bet on takeovers — sent jitters through the institutional investor crowd. Legislators who caused the savings and loan industry debacle by voting in 1982 to deregulate it without proper speed bumps needed a scapegoat, so they blamed the Milken crowd and the junk bonds they "forced" on institutional investors. As quickly as the party began, it ended. American industry is in recession, some 75,000 employees in the investment banking industry lost their jobs in 1989 and 1990, and New York area real estate prices sank to record lows and pulled down other markets as well.

DEFENSIVE MANAGEMENT

Although it is the strongest in the world, the U.S. economy is not always a calm and safe harbor. It continually attracts flight money from people who accumulate wealth in less stable countries and consumer and investor capital from relatively safe markets such as Japan. Yet the U.S. economy is not recession-proof. It is capable of temporary slumps that can pull down entire industries. "In the aftermath of the worst Christmas selling season in nearly a decade," reported *The Wall Street Journal* on April 9, 1991, "it is estimated that more than 300 retailers have filed for protection under Chapter 11 of the Bankruptcy Code so far this year."

The ripple effect when retailers cannot pay their bills is dramatic. One sufferer is Bullfrog Knits, a maker of moderately priced children's clothes. During the past year, 150 of its retail accounts filed for Chapter 11 protection. "It was the first time we lost money since we started in business in 1972," says Daniel Schiff, president. "The loss was due entirely to the bankruptcies of our accounts. It's tough to survive, because you don't know who to ship to."[5]

There were no structural deficiencies among the 300 retailers that sought protection from creditors in the 1990–1991 recession. Consumers simply kept their billfolds locked up during Christmas of 1990. They were cautious as the real estate and banking failures on the East Coast began to spread throughout the country. Then the Persian Gulf war preoccupied many consumers, turning January and February of 1991 into disastrous retailing months. The companies that were not prepared for the swift and prolonged downdraft in sales were wiped out. Because of the problems besetting the commercial banking industry, when retailers turned to their banks for help, the banks slammed the loan windows shut on their fingers.

Gerald Paul, CEO of Paul Harris Stores, a 377-store women's apparel chain based in Indianapolis, could not persuade the company's banks to loan it money following a substantial 1990 loss. To obtain financing, Paul placed the company in Chapter 11, where creditors are blocked from suing to collect on accounts payable. The banks came through with a $19 million debtor-in-possession, fully secured financing to enable the company to ride out the storm. The banks charged a 2 percent or $380,000 commitment fee to provide the new financing, whereas prior to filing for protection, Paul Harris Stores customarily paid its banks a 1 percent commitment fee when its loan came up for renewal.

Although it may be too late to warn you that the terrible swift sword that devastated the retail apparel industry in 1990 and 1991 could fall on your industry, I will offer some cautionary words. We all learn defensive management at some time in our business lives, usually after we have suffered a loss or a very difficult year. But some of the great business and sports heroes always practice downside, or defensive, management as a way of cushioning themselves for a fall.

PREPACKAGED CHAPTER 11s

At this point, you are familiar with two options within your control at the onset of a crisis: Chapter 11 or informal reorganization. There is a third option that is very well suited to a Grade B condition: the prepackaged Chapter 11, or "prepack." The opportunity to do prepacks has been around since Congress changed the Bankruptcy Act in 1978, but nobody began using them in earnest until Southland Corporation proposed one in 1991.

Southland, owner of the 7-11 chain of convenience stores, was stumbling under a massive amount of junk debt bearing interest at 18 percent per annum. It tried an informal reorganization by offering each holder of $1,000 of junk to exchange the bond for a $257 bond bearing interest at 4 percent per annum. The bondholders refused.

Southland then lined up a Japanese investor willing to pump in $430 million of new capital for 70 percent of the company. But the new investor wanted a "protective" shield from claims of creditors who were not thrilled with Southland management's offer to cut their hair with a hedge clipper. On the other hand, Southland could not drag the Japanese investor through a two- to four-year Chapter 11 proceeding without its interest waning.

The solution: Sweeten the haircut offered the bondholders with a small amount of stock, then obtain their preapproval on a plan of reorganization before filing for Chapter 11. The judge approved the prepack and Southland emerged from Chapter 11 in four months with new equity and its debt shrunk by three-fourths.

INVOLUNTARY BANKRUPTCY

If the unsecured creditors are sufficiently angry, they may force the company into *involuntary bankruptcy* (Chapter 7) whether or not they anticipate receiving any value for their claims. Because most people act rationally, an involuntary bankruptcy is more likely to occur when there are some unsecured assets to be auctioned to raise cash to pay unsecured creditors. A procrastinating debtor who has stretched his or her credibility with creditors to the breaking point or the existence of (or the creditors' belief in) unsecured assets that can be liquidated to pay creditors 50 percent or more of the amount of their note or account payable usually is enough to force an involuntary bankruptcy on the debtor.

Some degree of cooperation among creditors is required to effect an involuntary bankruptcy. If the debtor corporation has 12 or more creditors, then any three of them who are owed $5,000 or more in the aggregate can petition the bankruptcy court to force a company into Chapter 7. If the debtor has fewer than 12 creditors, then one creditor who is owed at least $5,000 can force a company into Chapter 7.

In Chapter 7, the court appoints a trustee whose job is to sell the assets and apply the cash thus received to pay creditors. The trustee is insensitive to the debtor's pleas to seek higher prices by holding onto the assets for a while longer. The trustee has an incentive to convert assets into cash quickly: He or she receives a fee for services equal to a percentage of the cash realized through auction or otherwise. The fee is the same among the 286 bankruptcy court jurisdictions throughout the country: approximately 3 percent of the amounts raised through foreclosure and sale. Thus, a liquidation that realizes $2 million in cash for the benefit of creditors will result in a fee of $60,000 for the trustee. You can see that an attempt to persuade the trustee to wait six months to realize perhaps another $200,000 probably will not be successful.

The key to surviving a troubled situation, however, is to remain in control of the workout and turnaround process. Because Chapter 11 and Chapter 7 proceedings remove much of your control and cede it to lawyers and the presiding judge, it is important to try to effect the workout on an informal basis. Just how much control passes from you to others in a bankruptcy proceeding is explained in chapter six of this book.

THE ARGUMENT FOR INFORMAL REORGANIZATION

Why try to avoid Chapter 11? Quite simply, *to preserve stockholder value*. After all, the purpose of business is to create wealth, or at least a return on stockholders' equity. This is virtually impossible in Chapter 11, where bankruptcy judges normally favor creditors over stockholders.

In workouts, senior creditors give up more than they would receive in Chapter 11. They give other creditors and stockholders a portion of what they are legally entitled to in order to avoid the legal hassles and delays of Chapter 11. The definitive study of realized values in Chapter 11 versus workouts was done by Julian Franks and Walter Torons at the London Business School in May of 1991 and reported in *The Economist*:

> [T]he study (which looked at 88 big, troubled firms, 41 in Chapter 11 and 47 in workouts, between 1983 and 1990), [shows] that creditors give up some of their seniority rights as a carrot to get management to agree to a deal.
>
> The 41 Chapter 11 deals gave some $878m to claimants that was not . . . due to them.
>
> [S]enior creditors give up even more in workouts than in Chapter 11 deals, although the write-downs of their claims tend to be a lot less. Of the $1.7 billion shifted from losers to gainers in workouts, senior creditors gave up $1.3 billion.[6]

Obviously, there is going to be a shifting of values in a turnaround, whether it is a Chapter 11 or an informal reorganization. Your position in the company often determines which course you take. If you are the hired gun without any equity to speak of, perhaps your allegiance is to your management team and to keeping your job. But if you own a reasonable amount of stock, your personal goal will likely be to preserve a large slice of value for the stockholders. Different motivations are behind each workout. As the best plumber in Putnam County, New York, Patsy Landolfi would say when faced with difficult water-related questions: "It's all accordin'."

FIGURE 2.2 Payments to Unsecured Creditors in 12 Recent
Chapter 11s

	Percentage of Outstanding Debt Paid to Unsecured Creditors
Allis-Chalmers	16.0%
AM International	61.1
Beker Industries	1.1
Care Enterprises	50.0
Coleco	5.2
Crystal Oil	55.8
Evans Products	79.4
Global Marine	39.3
McLean Industries	11.6
Towle	56.3
Wickes	83.5
Zenith Labs	95.0
Average	46.2%

The Benefits to Creditors of an Informal Reorganization

To survive your crisis, you must get inside the minds of your opponents. They want their money back. In a Chapter 11, they may not get it, or they may receive less. In 12 of the most recent large Chapter 11s, the average payment to unsecured creditors was approximately 46 cents on the dollar (see Figure 2.2).

Even more compelling than telling creditors they will get more money if they work things out with you is telling them they will receive nothing if they push too hard. This condition is best explained by an analogy from the world of music.

The Bobby McGee Condition

In the Kris Kristofferson song "Me and Bobby McGee," the singer describes the condition of a perfect candidate to remain out of bankruptcy: "Freedom's just another name for nothing left to lose." If all of a company's assets are pledged to secured creditors, then should the unsecured creditors try to force the company into Chapter 7 — a liquidation for the benefit of creditors — they will receive nothing. Thus, the debtor company has freedom to avoid its liquidation and to choose a reorganization plan, either informally or formally in Chapter 11.

Let me give you an example. A wholesale produce distributor that I recently assisted with a workout had pledged all its assets to a lender but remained in business, selling $850,000 per month with one of the most upside-down balance sheets imaginable (see Figure 2.3).

The company's gross profit margin was 15 percent, and it was paying a factor and interest rate of 21/2 percent per month, or 30 percent per annum. Thus, it was losing 15 percent on every sale. Losses kept mounting, but the suppliers kept shipping because the company supplied some of the best restaurants in the city, and they paid their bills within seven days. The company paid its current bills in 30 days but could not make a dent in more than $2 million of old accounts payable. By turning its receivables fast and furiously, the company was able to pay its operating expenses, interest, payroll and current accounts payable while staying current on withholding taxes.

But its suppliers never threatened it with liquidation, never sued, didn't withhold shipments and, except for a few instances, did not demand that their old invoices be paid. Why not? Because of the Bobby McGee condition. The secured lender — the factor — had a lien on all assets. In liquidation, the creditors would receive nothing. Moreover, the inventory was perishable. So even if the factor is paid dollar for dollar from the accounts receivable, the inventory could not be sold to pay the trade suppliers a few cents on the dollar.

The Bobby McGee condition creates a predicament for the trade creditors. A trade creditor is stuck like a linebacker whose feet are in six inches of mud when the fleet-footed running back hurdles the line and cuts deftly in front of him.

The crisis manager can be most effective when the company is in the Bobby McGee condition because the unsecured creditors are boxed out from forcing the debtor company into liquidation. This is not to say that they will believe the owner or manager who says

FIGURE 2.3   Balance Sheet of Produce Distributor

Assets		Liabilities and Stockholders Equity	
Cash	$ (70,000)	Notes payable	$ 500,000
Accounts receivable	600,000	Accounts payable	2,600,000
Inventory	450,000	Accrued expenses	250,000
Current assets	980,000	Current liabilities	3,350,000
Equipment — net	300,000	Stockholders' equity accumulated (Def.)	(2,070,000)
Total assets	$1,280,000	Total liabilities and stockholders' equity	$1,280,000

to them, "If you force us into Chapter 7, there will be no money to pay you. But if you give us time to work ourselves out of our trouble and come up with a plan, we will be able to pay you some of what we owe you."

The Bobby McGee condition is no bluff. Knowing its power, some troubled companies pledge all of their assets to a secured creditor to stonewall them ahead of the oncoming vigilante. But if the company files for protection under Chapter 11 within six months of having fully secured a loan, new or old, the bankruptcy judge can reverse the decision. Therefore, it is not a good idea to preemptively pledge all of a company's assets unless you are certain of avoiding Chapter 11 for at least the better part of a year.

Donald J. Trump's Condition

There are no heroics in how Donald Trump is managing to forestall bankruptcy notwithstanding that some of his companies cannot pay interest on their loans, much less principal. Now that you know about the Bobby McGee condition, it is obvious that all of Trump's assets are pledged to banks. He is parting with ownership in his companies, but not losing them. Trump's assets are not perishable; they are not bananas and lettuce. But his casinos and hotels rely on food, linens, liquor and a host of services provided by small vendors, and these suppliers will not cater to a company in bankruptcy. Thus, what appears to be a fascinating high-wire act by the imperious Mr. Trump is actually just plain business.

More than any single factor, the raiders of the 1980s whose businesses are being mopped up by bankruptcy lawyers in the 1990s were tripped by their needs to sign personal guarantees. Dr. Sonja Rhodes, author of *Cold Feet*, says about Trump: "Donald was the son who took on the responsibility to succeed on behalf of the family when his older brother died of alcoholism. He was trying to achieve power, wealth and fame to win his father's respect and in so doing he attempted to please bankers, the public, investors and customers. The task was awesome. It was doomed from the start."[7]

Trump personally guaranteed $500 million of $2.1 billion in borrowings to build his empire. In New York City, where the appropriate aphorisms roll easily off the tongue, a personal guarantor is called "a schmuck with a fountain pen." To guarantee $500 million personally is a "grandiose responsibility," to use John Bradshaw's words.

Trump's empire before he began missing loan interest payments appeared as in Figure 2.4, as reported in *Forbes*. At its peak, the Trump assets totaled $3.7 billion (market value) and the Trump liabilities aggregated $3.2 billion, according to *Forbes*. But as American Trump watchers have come to learn through endless reports, "the Donald's" fortunes have withered and he has had to yield partial ownership in one casino and complete ownership in the Trump Shuttle, the Grand Hyatt Hotel in New York City and Trump Plaza. The Trump Organization is being "right sized" in an informal reorganization. Chapter 11 (or liquidation, for that matter) has been and will be avoided. The Bobby McGee condition is the explanation.

Eastern Airlines

Whereas Trump has a positive consumer following and a supportive, loyal customer base, some companies' revenues sag demonstrably when news of their travail hits the front pages. One such

FIGURE 2.4   Trump's Empire

Property	Estimated Value
Taj Mahal	$ 834,700,000
Westside Yards	200,000,000
Trump Plaza Casino	616,000,000
Trump Castle Casino	416,000,000
Plaza Hotel	400,000,000
Trump Shuttle	400,000,000
Trump Tower	100,000,000
Condos, coops, hotels	356,000,000
Personal assets	345,800,000
Total assets	$3,668,500,000
Less: debt	3,169,300,000
Net worth	$ 499,200,000

SOURCE: Excerpted by permission of *Forbes* magazine, May 14, 1990, pp. 92–96. © Forbes Inc., 1990.

company is Eastern Airlines, which as I write is being liquidated in Chapter 7.

Eastern's Chapter 11 case was adjudicated in the New York Federal Bankruptcy Court of Judge Burton Lifland, arguably the most pro-debtor bankruptcy judge in the country and certainly the busiest. He is handling many of the nation's biggest bankruptcy cases: Pan Am ($2 billion in assets), Best Products ($1.5 billion), Hills Department Stores ($1.3 billion) and G. Heileman Brewing Company ($1.2 billion) in addition to Eastern. LTV Corporation has been in Judge Lifland's court since 1986, perhaps a record length of time for a company to remain in Chapter 11.

After Eastern landed in Judge Lifland's court in 1989, the judge released approximately $600 million in cash for management to use for operations, thus depriving the creditors of cash to pay down indebtedness. The creditors were angry, and angrier still when in a March 1989 filing, Eastern listed the liquidation value of its assets as greater than its liabilities yet ignored creditor demands to sell off its airplanes, landing rights and other assets immediately to pay all debts.

Instead, Eastern management attempted to operate the company. Stronger competitors, however, entered its profitable Miami hub and advertised aggressively. Travelers backed off from flying Eastern. The airline business relies to a great degree on consumer confidence and Eastern management did next to nothing to reassure its customers.

Whenever Eastern's creditors went to court to demand that Eastern shut down, or at least be prevented from spending more money, ticket sales slumped. "You could tell which days the stories ran in the newspaper from looking at the sales charts,"said Martin Shugrue, Jr., Eastern's trustee in bankruptcy.

In liquidation, Eastern's creditors are receiving less than 50 cents on the dollar. The Bobby McGee condition did not work for Eastern Airlines because it failed to hold its customers.

SUMMARY

Everybody gives up something in an informal reorganization and in a Chapter 11, but everyone also receives something. Informal reorganizations leave more equity in the hands of stockholders, leave management in place (if new investors regard them as credible) and provide creditors more money, at least the amount that would have been spent on legal fees. The least desirable alternative is involuntary bankruptcy, largely because the debtor company has no control over the disposition of its assets.

This chapter outlined the options available to a troubled company and the consequences of each. Before you can determine which is best for your situation, you must analyze the causes of your company's problems. The diagnostic process is covered in chapter three.

Endnotes

1.   Service spin-offs of product companies succeed more often than do product spin-offs of service companies.

2. Connie Bruck, *The Predator's Ball* (New York: Simon & Schuster, 1988), p. 99.

3. Todd Mason, *Perot: An Unauthorized Biography* (Homewood, Ill.: Dow Jones, 1990), p. 10.

4. Bryand Burrough and John Hilyar, *Barbarians at the Gate* (New York: Harper & Row, 1989), p. 489.

5. Jeffrey Trachtenberg, "Close-out: The Credit Crunch Is Latest Harsh Blow for Smaller Retailers," *The Wall Street Journal*, April 9, 1991, p. A-1.

6. "The Kindness of Chapter 11," *The Economist*, May 25, 1991, p. 83.

7. Sonja Rhodes, *Cold Feet* (New York: G.P. Putnam, 1989).

■ CHAPTER THREE ■

Diagnosis

Following is a menu of nine factors to consider when determining the nature and depth of the trouble, the likelihood that your company is salvageable and the cost of recovery. Each factor will be explained in this chapter.

1. Time and creditor anger
2. The personal exposure of the owner or manager
3. The existence of free cash flow
4. The crisis-readiness of the management team
5. The capitalization of the company
6. The prospects for raising capital
7. The prospects for selling the company
8. The courage of the owner or manager
9. The economic validity of the business

TIME AND CREDITOR ANGER

The longer a company waits to address its crisis, the more desperate the situation becomes and the angrier the unsecured creditors become. Workout consultants agree that procrastination is the principal reason behind the need for their services. As workout consultant Chris Niermann of The Competere Group says, "When a company gets into trouble, its management either ignores the signals, tries to fight its way out by getting creditor cooperation over and over again, or uses ineffective workout strategies such as trying to increase sales, all of which consume time and usually make a bad situation worse."

If a management team responds immediately at the first sign of trouble, it can diagnose the problems and develop remedial strategies within four to six weeks. But if management ignores the problems until lawsuits have been filed and creditors have been stiff-armed for 120 days, it will require a Homeric effort to save the company.

The Value of the Diagnosis

Last summer, I was called by the CEO of a Kansas horse-feed and dog-food producer with a superb 40-year reputation among the breeders and farmers in four midwestern states. The founder of the company, the CEO's father, now in a nursing home, was stricken with Alzheimer's disease two years ago but had continued running the company. Some of his judgments, including borrowing heavily to buy land, had created an illiquidity crisis. A senior secured lender was threatening to force the company into a Chapter 7. The CEO, a college professor, had been called in to manage the company, although he had practically no business experience. Sales had declined from $8 million to $4 million annualized, and the CEO was grasping for solutions.

I asked the CEO to send me a couple year's worth of year-end financial statements and the most recent interim financial statements, plus copies of the loan agreements, promissory notes and all correspondence between the hostile lender and the company. I would study them on the airplane and hit the ground running when I arrived at the Kansas airport.

You have to be a bit of a Perry Mason to make it in the workout business. For instance, a few things stood out from the conversation with the CEO. Why did the bank loan money to an older man who was exhibiting obvious signs of Alzheimer's? There must have been an inducement to the bank. What was it: personal guarantees? Side collateral?

Did sales begin to decline when the founder still was the day-to-day chief operating officer or only when the professor-son came in to run the company? The financial statements showed that declines began under the father's management. Surely the bank saw this; yet it loaned more money to the company.

Forty-year-old companies are tough to kill. They usually have loyal customers, faithful employees and a broad supplier network. Agricultural companies usually can whistle past the graveyard because they have weathered many tough economic periods. The difference in this instance could be the new CEO. A professor by training, he probably knew little about the nuances of business, to say nothing of crisis management.

The plane ride also gave me a chance to find a solution to the problem of the company's imminent demise. The bank had gotten itself into a *lender liability* problem and probably could be persuaded to cooperate in an informal reorganization.

Sure enough, when the founder borrowed money and the business began sputtering, the banker demanded the septuagenarian wife's signature. She had cosigned notes in the past, but the circumstances were different. Her husband then was young and healthy. The bank knew that the wife had assets in her name, and it was looking to them as primary collateral, but without informing the wife. In fact, I learned the bank had the husband obtain her signature rather than ask for it directly.

Winning by Intimidation

When faced with losing your company because of a hostile, heavy-handed lender, the first place to look for a solution is the manner in which the bank obtained its loan in the first place. If it coerced the signer without properly informing him or her of the dire circumstances that the business was falling into, the signer can intimidate the lender with the threat of lender liability litigation. These kinds of lawsuits have become fairly popular recently as banks look for wiggle room in their loan agreements and attempt either to oversecure their loans, as in this case, or to call in their loans in a precipitous fashion to generate much-needed cash. The crisis manager, or his or her attorney or workout consultant, can set an appointment with the bank and bring along two folders, one under each arm.

Picture yourself as Perry Mason in a trial setting, but instead of a judge or a jury, you are presenting your case to the senior credit officer of a bank that thinks it has nothing to lose in a foreclosure because it has a lien on all the company's assets, plus side collateral.

"Mr. Banker, in this folder is our workout plan, and our cash flow statement projections. You can see how your bank will be repaid, which is not immediately by any means, and it requires your cooperation."

You place the folder in front of the banker and pause for a moment. Then you reach for the other folder and say:

"Mr. Banker, in this second folder is a lender liability lawsuit my attorney has prepared. We think we have a pretty good case against your bank for overreaching and playing hardball."

Then you place the second folder alongside the first and say:

"The choice is yours. Work with us on the repayment plan, or we will take you into court where a jury made up of men and women who live and work in this community will decide your fate."

Bankers, like all managers in large corporations, have a great fear of bringing bad publicity to their corporations. And a lender liability lawsuit can damage years of laying pipe with the community. Most banks would rather work with a debtor than face a lender liability lawsuit in their community.

Commercial bankers fear that they will not get repaid. They face loan committees; internal audits; and external audits by their CPA firms, by the Comptroller of the Currency (if they are national banks) and possibly by the Federal Deposit Insurance Corporation (FDIC). It is no wonder that they become nervous when their loan to your company is overdue or when you miss an interest payment.

If your loan is fully collateralized, your banker will be less nervous about the possibility of your filing for protection under the Bankruptcy Act. A fully secured creditor cannot lose its collateral in a bankruptcy. Fungible assets such as Treasury bills or accounts receivable provide the greatest comfort to the banker. Even so, there is always the risk that the banker failed to file a Uniform Commercial Code evidence of collateral (UCC-1) properly or that someone else filed ahead the bank. Your banker also fears that if your company goes into Chapter 11, the collateral may diminish in value and put the bank in the position of an unsecured creditor.

As a result, your banker probably will work with you to keep you solvent and out of bankruptcy. If you have a meeting to clear the air, he or she might advance you a new loan tying up all of your assets; stretch the repayment on the new loan for six months, with interest due at the end; or take other steps to see you through tough times. The banker probably will agree to give you immediate credit on your customer deposits as well. If the sheriff comes with a court order to attach your accounts, however, there is nothing your banker can do to prevent the attachment. That is a good reason to open new depository relationships while working with your current lender.

Coming in Late

Many companies in crisis react to overreaching banks or creditors after they have attached the companies' bank accounts and raised havoc with cash flow and bounced checks. This usually comes after a warning, which in the case of a bank is a *demand letter*, and in the case of the Internal Revenue Service (IRS) is a *warning* that assets will be liened. Surprisingly, many managers do not take these warnings seriously. Bankers get upset when they think they won't be repaid. They tend to strike fast and hard so that there is no mistaking their intent.

Companies that maintain small depository relations suffer the most when banks overreact in economic hard times. Suddenly, lines of credit are capped, overdrafts are not permitted, payroll checks are not cashed. In some cases, the company's banker leaves, and the new loan officer does not understand the company. When the manager and the chief financial officer sit down with the new banker to explain their company, they are met with a stifled yawn.

As part of your survival plan, change banks. Begin a larger depository relationship at the new bank. Pick an independent bank — if possible, a newly formed one. Take $200,000 of the cash you recently found (see chapter seven) and buy a certificate of deposit for 90 days. Then tell the bank president that you want to borrow $100,000 for 90 days secured by the CD. When you repay it, you will have established an excellent credit rating with your new bank.

Moreover, if it is a newly formed bank, you will have made the president a hero by opening a new account.

Read your local newspapers, looking for new bank formations and for the names of the new presidents. They need to bring in new business accounts. Open a payroll account and a business account at the new bank while keeping a small balance and some activity at the old bank. Maintain an excellent relationship at the new bank, and if you must take risks, do that at the old bank, where you are subject to less favorable treatment because you were a borrower or a client of a banker who may have been transferred or let go because of troubled loans.

If you travel out of town, you might open a safety valve account there as well. This will be a place to keep cash away from the sheriff if a lender or creditor gets a prejudgment attachment on your local bank accounts.

Surprise Attachments

A prejudgment attachment can occur when a company owes a bank or supplier a sum of money. The lender or supplier merely posts a bond for 100 percent of the amount owed in the county where the borrower has offices; then the lender makes an appointment with the United States District Court judge and persuades him or her that the obligor is likely to flee the state with the assets or the money that belongs to the creditor. The creditor's lawyer visits the judge *ex parte* — that is, without your lawyer present. Thus, you are a sitting duck for an attachment if you have been unable to pay an obligation for a period of time.

Once the judge signs a writ of attachment, the creditor's lawyer is supposed to inform your lawyer that he or she has notified the sheriff or the U.S. marshal to remove your assets from your business and, if you are a general partner or a guarantor of the obligor, from your home. It is my experience that some lawyers treat this convention with disdain.

Be ready for a prejudgment attachment, and keep the bulk of your cash out of the county. But do nothing unusual that would create the suspicion that your company is transferring assets out of state to avoid the repayment obligation. If flight is suspected, the attachment will be sustained when you and the lender go head to head in court later on. Do not commit fraud by conveying assets to third parties. You will lose your reputation with creditors at a time when you most need it. And do not flee with any assets.

Thoughts from Buddha

One of the more businesslike quotes from Buddha is the following:

There is no fire like passion,
There is no shark like hatred,
There is no shame like folly,
There is no torrent like greed.

To this I would add, at the risk of immodesty: *There is no balm like cash.*

In the diagnostic stage of the workout, some managers delude themselves into believing that the turnaround will come through increased sales, more advertising, greater sales incentives or more emphatic and direct sales promotions. Other managers believe that the problem is illiquidity, when in fact that is the symptom; they seek to raise more capital from investors, lenders and suppliers (by stretching them out further). But the turnaround will not occur without a focus on *cash*.

Get the Cash before You Crash

In chapter seven of this book, we will discuss cash-raising strategies that have immediate effects. But at this juncture, the crisis manager must take stock of the causes of the company's illiquidity and make some difficult, self-effacing, hard business calls. Causes differ from one company to the next, and between manufacturers and distributors. The most typical, however, are the following:

- Product obsolescence
- Regional recession

- Key customers go out of business
- Aggressive price competition
- Industrywide recession
- Key suppliers go out of business
- Aggressive foreign competition
- Faulty production leading to cost overruns and shipping delays
- High overheads
- Ineffectual middle management

These causal factors can be pinpointed by observing three years' worth of the company's financial statements. A declining gross profit margin coupled with slower inventory turnover often bespeaks product obsolescence or aggressive price competition. A high product-return ratio could mean faulty production. Slower receivables turnover is a management problem or a tip-off that key customers are suffering the cash shorts. Rising overheads, particularly in health insurance, professional fees, rent and communications expenses, are easier to deal with if the rest of the company is fairly sound. A decline in operating ratios such as sales/employee, sales/product, sales/working capital suggests that management is not attentive to the fundamentals of business.

The diagnosis should reveal whether or not the company has a fifty-fifty chance of surviving in its present business or whether it must forsake its present business, generate *free cash* and emerge as something entirely different. Face the truth, but remember that without cash these decisions will become moot.

PERSONAL EXPOSURE OF THE
OWNER OR MANAGER

Nothing complicates a company's troubles more than the personal guarantees of the owners and managers. It is one thing for a company's existence to be at risk, but quite another for its owners or managers to place their assets — homes, cars, furnishings, securities — in jeopardy. In this situation, the crisis manager needs a greater depth of understanding to protect the owners' or managers' assets and to save the company.

Personal guarantees are issued when a company is unable to obtain sufficient credit without additional collateral, or a backstop for the company's collateral. The optimistic owner or manager believes that the company's cash flow will improve and thus his or her personal guarantee never will be called on. Moreover, creditors generally have a time- and experience-tested guarantee form that many owners and managers sign without the benefit of a legal review. This is frequently an inflexible document that permits the creditor to demand payment from the guarantor if it is not paid by the primary obligor.

The crisis manager usually can find a loophole in the language of the personal guarantee, a condition in the state's laws pertaining to when a guarantee can be called or, as a last resort, financial logic to persuade the guaranteed creditors to think twice before forcing the company and the guarantor into involuntary bankruptcy. And because the crisis manager is not frightened by creditor drum-beating, he or she can work methodically and carefully on this thorny area.

My method of assisting managers of troubled companies who have personal guarantees outstanding involves the following steps:

1. Read the signed personal guarantee carefully to look for steps that the creditor must take before demanding payment from the guarantor. This may include selling off the assets that secure the debt in a "commercially reasonable" manner. Permitting the creditor to take back its goods, sell them at auction and then determine if there is a balance owing from the guarantor may obviate a bankruptcy proceeding because it favors one creditor over the others.

2. Review the state's laws, particularly recent case law, with the company's counsel to see how the judges have been reacting to creditors who hastily pursue a personal guarantor. The laws may set up several hurdles for the creditor to jump before it can take the guarantor into court and demand payment. These may include establishing the exact amount owing, for example.

3. Review the invoices submitted by the creditor to the company and the correspondence with the intent of finding a *service* feature to the relationship or a series of goods returned for defects. If I am fortunate enough to find inconsistencies in the vendor's service record, shipping history or product quality,

then perhaps I can persuade the creditor that it will not prevail if it sues the guarantor.

4. With the results of my diagnosis carefully assembled, I telephone the creditor and ask for a visit. At the meeting, I present my case for patience while an informal reorganization plan is set in place. I promise to communicate regularly and honestly, and I attempt to convert an enemy into an ally.

These steps do not always fend off the creditor posse, but there are many steps between organizing the posse and the eventual hanging.

Guarantor Protections

Most personal guarantee forms favor the lender or creditor. They do not provide that the creditor first must attach the company's fungible assets that secure the loan, sell them in the marketplace in a *commercially reasonable manner* and then go after the guarantor. Should you ever decide, against my better judgment, to sign a personal guarantee, remember to establish these speed bumps:

1. The lender first must attach the primary assets that secure its note.
2. The lender then must sell these assets in a commercially reasonable manner.
3. The lender then must give the personal guarantor 90 days to come up with the difference in amount owing.
4. The lender then may demand payment from the personal guarantor.

Some state laws strongly favor the personal guarantor and prescribe following these four steps for collecting on a personal guarantee, even when the personal guarantee is not written that way. It certainly blunts the lender's grab for personal assets to sue if it does not follow these steps. A 60-day delay while the matter is heard by a judge can give a besieged debtor a little time to sell the assets and pay off the debt.

In one of my less spectacular business ventures, I personally guaranteed the shipment of computers to a computer chain in which my venture capital fund had an investment. I did not guarantee the shipment personally, but the venture capital fund was a partnership, its general partner was a partnership and I was the general partner of the general partner, which meant I was the one who actually guaranteed the repayment of the loan secured by personal computers.

The lender demanded the return of approximately $450,000. When it was not forthcoming, the lender backed up a couple of trucks to the computer chain's warehouse and stores and hauled off its collateral. It ran an advertisement in the classified section of a regional newspaper, received some bids and sold the computers for less than $200,000.

When the lender knocked on my door for the balance, I responded with a lawsuit that charged it with failing to sell the computers in a commercially reasonable manner. I charged the lender with dumping the assets. I said it did not advertise broadly enough and that it did not allow enough time to circulate the news that it had 500 brand-new personal computers to sell at auction prices. My lawsuit got its attention. We settled on the courthouse steps for less than 30 cents on the dollar for the amount still owing.

The Double Garnishment

Some managers of companies in crisis have more than one exposure to personal guarantees. The second (or third) exposure is typically for unpaid withholding taxes. Approximately 25 percent of an employee's wages must be deposited each quarter with the IRS, but this obligation occasionally is overlooked intentionally by managers who believe they can put the toothpaste back into the tube at a later date while using the government's money today for marketing or advertising. This borrow now, pay later scheme rarely works, and the IRS goes after everyone who is directly responsible for the payment of withholding taxes. This includes the chief financial officer, the chief executive officer and members of the board of directors.

The unpaid withholding taxes debt never can be compromised. The IRS will accept only dollar for dollar. It will, however, negotiate an installment payment, and it is legally empowered to go out as far as six years. It will open the negotiations with possibly one year, but know that it has far greater flexibility.

Once you have begun the repayment, however, if the company misses one or two months, the IRS may attach the debtor company's bank accounts, then come after the aforementioned principals and attempt to garnish their wages. But the law allows only one garnishment at a time. Thus, if another creditor has been granted a garnishment — the right to receive direct payment of wages — the IRS cannot be granted one. One per debtor is all that is allowed.

Moving Assets

Endangered personal guarantors who put most of their assets in their spouses' names at the onset of the crisis may have to reverse themselves a few months down the road if they file for protection under the Bankruptcy Act. The act calls this tactic fraudulent conveyance, and the bankruptcy judge is empowered to reverse the transfer if it was made within six months of the date of filing. Once it is reversed, all the creditors have an equal chance of being repaid from the sale of the assets that now are back in the pot.

To counter the preemptive shifting of assets, many creditors seek the spouse's guarantee. In community-property states, the spouse's guarantee is automatically on the paper. Thus, if the owner of a business personally guarantees a loan in one of these states, the spouse has pledged his or her assets as well.

Limiting Your Exposure

The workout and turnaround plan that you craft with the company's creditors may require that you provide a personal guarantee to one or two lenders whose faith in your promises has worn thin. You know how the language of the personal guarantee should read — that is, the speed bumps to put into the document. But there is more in the way of protection, particularly if you are not the sole owner of the business.

The goal of any lender is to have three ways to get repaid: cash flow, liquidation of the collateral and personal guarantees. You cannot fault lenders for asking, but do not be so quick to give it to them. In the first place, there are different kinds of guarantees, some more severe than others. The *joint and several guarantee,* if signed by you and the other founding stockholders, permits the lender to sue each of you for the full amount of its loan. The *limited guarantee,* which limits your obligation to an exact dollar amount, is the only type of guarantee you should consider signing. You also should make the argument to your lender that if you have a sizable amount of personal money committed to the deal, a personal guarantee is not warranted. You may not win the negotiation, but you may win a limited guarantee.

THE EXISTENCE OF FREE CASH FLOW

The owner or manager of the seriously troubled company is frequently too paralyzed with fear or shame to look for sources of cash to meet its obligations. Experienced crisis managers, when they seize control of a troubled company, divide the liabilities into three major categories: bullets, criticals and occasionals. The terminology varies from one workout team to the next, but the categories are the same:

- *Bullets.* Those obligations that if not paid probably will put the company out of business suddenly and unequivocally
- *Criticals.* Those obligations that are critical to the company's operations but for which timely payment is not critical
- *Occasionals.* Those obligations that should receive at least partial payment some of the time to let them know they haven't been forgotten

There may be variations within these categories, and there may be additional categories depending on the depth of the crisis. For example, if the workout strategy begins after the owner or manager has been sued by a handful of creditors and they have been awarded judgments by the court and the sheriff is seizing assets, then there is very little to do except file for protection under Chapter 11 and develop a plan of reorganization to help the company springboard out of it.

But if the workout strategy is adopted early on, then there usually is ample time to categorize the liabilities, contact the creditors, diagnose their degree of bloodthirstiness and set up payment schedules for bullets and criticals. To do this successfully requires creating weekly cash flow statement projections and modifying them as frequently as needed. The cash flow statement projection is the troubled company's road map out of the swamp.

After examining the categories of liabilities, the crisis team will determine the need for a specific amount of cash every week, another amount every other week, another every month and yet another every two months. What the team is seeking is *free cash flow*. Not cash flow required for payroll, raw materials and operating expenses, but over and above that, to pay the bullets and the criticals. If the company's senior management doesn't know where this cash flow will come from, or if it's not there, a workout consultant will be needed to probe more deeply for sources of overhead that can be slashed. The cash is hidden in assets and overhead, and it does not require a metal detector to find it.

The situation could be so desperate that the workout team cannot find all the cash it needs to help the company dodge the bullets, in which case a Chapter 11 filing is prepared. But with an open mind to slash expenses and sell unneeded assets quickly, any troubled company can generate free cash flow. Here are some of the places I look first:

- *Facilities costs*: Buildings, warehouses, equipment, airplanes, trucks, vans, cars and other fixed assets
- *Communications costs*: Postage, couriers, telephone, facsimile and electronic mail
- *Travel costs*: Airplanes, rental cars, hotels, restaurants and customer entertainment expenses
- *Employee health insurance expenses*: Generally considered the largest and the fastest-rising overhead expense
- *Legal expenses*: The cost of services rendered by the company's outside law firms
- *Audit and accounting expenses*: An analysis of these services to determine which of them may be brought in-house

- *Advertising expenses*: A review of their importance to product sales and the effectivity of lower-cost alternative forms of creating product awareness such as direct-response marketing and public relations
- *Borrowing costs*: An examination of all loan agreements, trade credit, letters of credit, employee credit cards and bank charges
- *Employee costs*: Can the company be run with fewer employees?
- *Peripheral division expenses*: The workout consultant's task is to save the company's core, which may require selling off peripheral divisions.

Crisis-hardened workout consultants attempt to find cash in overhead and to do so quickly. In this respect, they are like corporate raiders who take over companies with mountains of borrowed money and immediately ferret out cash to repay the debt. I wrote about the expense-slashing strategies of raiders in my book *The Inside Raider*.[1]

Many owners and managers in crisis are so frozen with fear that they will lose their company as it now exists if they cannot react objectively to what must be done. The workout consultant focuses on cash first and tries to free it up in the most logical place: corporate overhead.

THE CRISIS-READINESS OF THE MANAGEMENT TEAM

Many management teams are not battle-scarred. They are unfamiliar with the early warning signals of crises, or they choose to disregard them. Many management teams are expansion-oriented, trying to make their company or division grow above the previous year's level.

When a crisis develops, there is a downward slump in the organization. Work is done with less enthusiasm. Conflicts within the organization are expressed or converted into tensions. Relations become strained. Eventually, the company begins to disintegrate. When the workout team intercedes and begins to create order, things improve. New routines are put into effect, and members of the company reach new agreements about how the goals are to be reached. Middle managers begin to rally around the crisis managers when they see how the crisis managers systematically use the dynamics of the company to generate new sources of cash and calm the troubled creditor waters.

The stages in adjusting to a crisis in a company were set forth in chapter one of this book. The overall adjustment process can be viewed as a roller coaster ride. Naturally, a company cannot go through a bumpy roller coaster ride without some personal shocks. Weaker companies lose members at the earlier stages through either shock, disbelief, numbness or mourning. Well-integrated and adaptable companies, particularly those that identify the crisis at an early stage, take the roller coaster ride in stride. They rise to a higher level of homeostasis after the crisis is past.

The Reputations of the Creditors with Debtor Companies

Today, credit managers have experience with a multitude of debtors. The lap-top personal computer (pc) goes to creditor meetings these days, and it can quickly compute the creditor categories, the amounts owing each and the cash flow ability to service debt. Moreover, the creditors know each other well in many instances. They hire workout consultants to represent them in the larger situations. They know the bankruptcy lawyers very well, and they frequently hire the best in the business to keep the debtor from hiring them.

Try to know the mind-sets of your creditors. Find out through personal investigations if they bludgeon their debtors to the point of submission or if they are malleable. How will they react to different proposals? How patient will they be before a plan of reorganization is proposed? How likely are they to react to various plans submitted to them? What may be going on inside their minds?

Naive debtors will not be considered charming and innocent by creditor committees today. They will be tossed into Chapter 7 and their companies liquidated unless they approach their workout problems in a businesslike and professional manner. A debtor who tries to face down a roomful of angry creditors without an experienced crisis manager riding shotgun is going to be in for a big surprise. The creditors want someone in the crisis-riven company who understands them and, if possible, who has worked with them before.

THE CAPITALIZATION OF THE COMPANY

The typical financially troubled company is one with too much debt in relation to its equity. We know that many companies such as Tracor, Campeau and Hooker are in bankruptcy proceedings because they were aggressive junk-bond borrowers and buyers of companies at premium prices. The corporate raiders who took over these companies with massive amounts of 16- to 18-percent-interest-rate junk bonds could not generate cash quickly enough via spin-offs and asset sales.

But it is not always excessive debt that leads to business failures. After all, financial service companies, leasing companies, commercial banks and trading companies operate successfully with debt/equity ratios of ten to one and more. When they stay with their core businesses, they succeed handsomely. When they reach for risky loans or leases or when they go on an acquisition tear as did Bank of New England in the late 1980s, however, they are courting disaster.

Leverage cuts both ways. When a business is growing and generating new channels of cash flow, leverage is a fulcrum that raises the company to new heights. But when adverse circumstances strike, debt cannot be serviced and leverage is blamed for the company's failure. A company can get into trouble by not borrowing to finance growth and having competitors take bites out of its market share. On the other hand, a company can get into serious trouble faster by borrowing.

Because interest payments on borrowed money are deductible from income taxes and dividends on preferred and common stock are not, many owners and managers prefer to finance their companies' growth with borrowed money rather than with the sale of stock. If they do so too aggressively and circumstances clobber their carefully sculpted cash flow projections, it is practically inevitable that in their plans of reorganization they will issue common or preferred stock to creditors as a means of confirming a plan of reorganization. What goes around comes around, as the saying goes. Businesses are pendulums. If they swing too far out on the debt curve, they are likely to be forced to swing back in the other direction and sell equity in their companies at a later date at distress prices.

Workout consultants have a broad grasp of the optimum capitalization structures in a variety of industries. They can apply certain quick tests to determine if a company is overleveraged for its industry. The most frequently used ratios are shown in Figure 3.1.

"I can go in and do a quick and dirty on a troubled company's capitalization," says Diane M. Freaney, a Delaware Valley workout consultant. "That analysis will usually tell me how much time I have to try and turn the company around." For example, if a company's ratio of cash to current liabilities is less than .1 and if its ability to service debt ratio is less than 1.0, the company is not only severely overleveraged, but it is on the edge of the diving board overhanging an unfilled swimming pool.

On the other hand, if a company's total debt/net worth ratio is in excess of 5:1 but its ability to service debt ratio is slightly more than 1.0, it is certainly overleveraged, but it is not sitting on a time bomb. This company may need *recapitalization* — that is, the replacement of some of its short-term debt with longer-term debt or preferred stock.

An overly leveraged capitalization is generally a predictor of bankruptcy in one class of industries, while other financial ratios we will discuss are indicators of significant bankruptcy potential in certain other industries.

Short-term illiquidity and excessive total debt/total assets and total debt/net worth ratios can be deadly in the mining, paper processing, chemical processing, retail, wholesale distribution, construction and service industries. These industries are subject to outside forces, such as sudden changes in demand or supply factors, that can make excessive leverage particularly punitive.

Notwithstanding the selectivity of leverage in killing certain companies faster than others, the workout consultant realizes at some point that he or she probably will have to recapitalize the company, and this means raising capital.

FIGURE 3.1   Ratios That Measure Leverage

Overall leverage	Total debt/total assets
Short-term liquidity	Short-term debt/total debt
Cash position	Cash/current liabilities
Banker's view of leverage	Total debt/net worth
Ability to service debt	Annual interest plus principal payment/cash flow

THE PROSPECTS FOR RAISING CAPITAL

Details on the process of raising capital for troubled companies are provided in chapter eight of this book. The directories in the appendixes at the back of the book list many financial institutions that provide capital to troubled companies.

THE PROSPECTS FOR SELLING THE COMPANY

Experienced crisis managers say that the asset they seek to maximize above all others is *options*. The fewer the options to save the company, the smaller their probability of success. And like a physician whose death rate is higher than the norm, a workout consultant with a high rate of failure will receive fewer referrals because there are no survivors to give positive references to potential clients.

"There are two overriding goals that workout specialists strive for," says C. William Gano, a Memphis, Tennessee, problem solver: "To achieve a financing and to accomplish an informal plan of reorganization."

A financing and an acquisition are similar, but in most situations, a company loses its identity when it is acquired at a distress price. If a company is sold out at the bottom of the roller coaster ride and then recovers and rebounds to a higher level of success, the acquirors receive the benefits. On the other hand, if it accomplishes a financing at a boneyard price and then rockets back to life, the stockholders, although seriously diluted, have the opportunity to recapture their investment and perhaps make a small gain.

During the high-technology investments craze of the 1970s, many venture capital funds formed to invest in start-up and rapidly emerging companies became vulture capital funds in the early 1990s. These are investment companies that prey on wounded companies that have proprietary markets, definable niches and demonstrable economic validity, but that have exhausted their capital and their credibility with investors.

In many instances, the technoids who started these companies are ill-equipped to manage them in a crisis and must be replaced. It is difficult to change existing management without a change in ownership; thus when the vulture capitalists offer to invest $2 million, for example, to rescue the company, they usually seek control. It is a foregone conclusion that they will bring in a workout manager to run the company. A change in control coupled with a change in management is a *de facto* acquisition.

There are many shrewd acquirors who realize that they can acquire a troubled company for less if the acquisition is made through the bankruptcy courts than they could if they acquire it before it files for protection. This is not the most desirable result for the stockholders, who will receive nothing in that circumstance, or for the workout specialist, who will not have a positive client reference if the company slides into bankruptcy. Beware the anxious suitor who proposes an acquisition pre-Chapter 11 and then continually pushes back the wedding date.

To enhance the prospects for selling a crisis-torn company, the workout consultant must be hired as early as possible. If the crisis overwhelms a management team that is unprepared for battle, the prospects for selling the company will evaporate along with its price.

Selling the troubled company is a backdoor option: not a first choice, not a second choice, but an option for preserving the company nonetheless. Those managers who rage against their fate rather than formulate a survival plan virtually shut the back door and eliminate their option of selling the company.

In my workout and turnaround assignments, I make it very clear up front that acquirors and sources of financing will be pursued simultaneously and with equal energy. I want the client to have as many options to choose from as possible. I telephone my staff from the client's office and ask them to run searches through my "golden Rolodexes": public and private companies in industries that have acquired companies similar to the client, and acquisition funds that list the client's industry, size and region among their criteria. By the time I return to the office, stacks of annual reports, 10-Ks, Standard & Poor's tear sheets and photostated directory pages are on my desk waiting for me to qualify a dozen potential investors and a like number of acquirors.

THE COURAGE OF THE OWNER OR MANAGER

The owner or manager in crisis needs great courage to get through difficult times. If you have never been there, you cannot imagine the din of threats, process servers in the outer office, collection calls, lawyers screaming, creditors telling you what part of your anatomy they're going to "sue off," key personnel resigning, managers begging for product and deathly silence in the wee small hours of the night except for nightmares of liquidating auctions in the company's parking lot. One way to get through this period is to hire the services of a workout specialist who fears nothing that a creditor, collector or lawyer can do to the company because he or she has stared them down before.

THE ECONOMIC VALIDITY OF THE BUSINESS

The business your company has been in no longer may be valid. It may not be worth saving. But before you decide to enter a new business, first determine if you should fetch the old horse and try to ride it again. This means assessing the company's likelihood of success once you put it back together again.

Before setting out to save the existing business, the workout specialist performs the DEJ (demonstrable economic justification) factor test (see Figure 3.2). If the business meets all eight requirements of the DEJ factor test, *the workout specialist or the owner/ manager can be almost assured of success. And the cost of saving the company will be less than $500,000.*

FIGURE 3.2   DEJ Factor Test

DEJ Factor	Ask Yourself These Questions	Cost
1. Existence of qualified buyers	Are the consumers to whom the product or service is marketed *aware* that they have a need for it?	Advertising
2. Large number of buyers	Are there lots of consumers who need this product or service?	Competitive pressure on *price*
3. Homogeneity of buyers	Will the market accept a standardized product or service or must it be customized?	Manufacturing, tooling, die costs
4. Existence of competent sellers	Is the product or service so complex to explain that customers will need 90 days or more to test it?	Salespersons' salaries and expenses
5. Lack of institutional barriers to entry	Is governmental or industry association approval needed before the product or service can be marketed?	Working capital that burns while approval is awaited
6. Easy promotability by word of mouth	Can the merits of the product or service be described by word of mouth?	Advertising

FIGURE 3.2   DEJ Factor Test (Continued)

	DEJ Factor	Ask Yourself These Questions	Cost
7.	Invisibility of the inside of the company	Is there a need to reveal profit margins to the public?	Competitive pressure on price
8.	Optimum price/ cost relationship	Is the selling price at least five times the cost of goods sold?	Restricts the number of marketing channels

Managers who fail to ask these eight questions may refinance the troubled company only to have it fail again. The DEJ factor test is a predictor of success and a measure of the cost of seizing the opportunity. Here's the rule:

- *Super DEJ.* If the business possesses all eight DEJ factors, refinancing it will cost less than $500,000, and the probability of success will be about 90 percent.
- *Majority DEJ.* If the business possesses seven out of eight DEJ factors, saving it will cost up to $2 million, and the probability of success will be about 80 percent.
- *Marginal DEJ.* If the business possesses six out of eight DEJ factors, saving it will cost up to $20 million, and the probability of success will be about 60 percent.
- *Below six DEJ factors.* The business is a reject and the manager should think in terms of creating a new vehicle (see chapter nine).

As you review the eight DEJ factors, think of the marketing failures within your company. Which factors nailed its coffin shut? If you can't come up with an example inside your company, remember DeLorean Motor Company, a $165-million fatal plunge.

Imagine trying to save a defense contractor (Lockheed) or an automobile manufacturer (Chrysler). The former has institutional barriers to entry and needs to wait years to be paid for contracts. The latter needs mountains of advertising and a large dealership network to sell its products to consumers. Is it any wonder that these companies required government bailouts? Both have six out of eight DEJ factors and required nine-figure refinancings. Where would the capital have come from if not from the government? Existing stockholders would have been sorely diluted.

Questions about a company's economic viability are valid but are not always asked by managers or owners in crisis. The crisis manager is an objective observer, like the field surgeon in the Civil War movies who grits his teeth, holds back his fear and tells the wounded soldier, "Son, I have to take off your leg to save your life. Take a swig of this and hold on."

SUMMARY

The diagnostic process provides a quick assessment of the level of crisis in your company and the causal nexus of the problem. It is the first step in the workout and turnaround process. The nine factors discussed in this chapter are guideposts to follow when diagnosing your company's problems and its outlook for recovery.

Well-integrated and adaptable companies, those that identify the crisis at an early stage, take the roller coaster ride in stride. Some even rise to a new level of homeostasis after the crisis. As the owner or manager of a troubled company, you may not have the skills or courage to lead the workout team, but you must take the lead in facing the truth. If you can admit that your company is in trouble and look for honest answers to explain why, you already are well on the road to recovery.

Endnote

1.   A. David Silver, *The Inside Raider* (New York: Harper & Row, 1990).

■ CHAPTER FOUR ■

Managing the Workout

When the diagnostic period begins, you will see exactly how much money the company actually owes and how little cash there is to pay all the bills. Like most people of strong moral fiber, you will take the impact personally. When the knowledge of your illiquidity crisis sets in, you also begin to realize that you might have some control over the events you are involved in. You may feel terribly sad, but at the same time very alert to the signals that have been unclear but disturbing for quite some time, much like James Agee described in *A Death in the Family*[1]:

> His rage and despair and the shock of the blow had so quieted and sobered him that now he was beyond even self-hatred. He felt gentle and dear. The sadness grew and became all but insupportable, and for the first time that evening, one of the few times in his life, he began to see things more or less as they were.

But the time for blame and rage has gone. You are a manager, and your company is out of cash. You can take four steps without the help of outsiders to turn your company around. Each step will be discussed in detail in this chapter. They are as follows:

- Select a crisis-management team.
- Sell assets to raise cash.

- Slash expenses.
- Improve employee morale.

SELECT A CRISIS MANAGEMENT TEAM

If you are accustomed to year-to-year sales and earnings growth through traditional marketing channels, the sudden jolt of an illiquidity crisis probably will unsettle you and require an outsider or another member of management to take over the leadership and form the crisis management team. At the other end of the spectrum, if your management style is innovative — entrepreneurial — and you are the kind of person who thrives on the daily "chase" and on management by improvisation, then you probably will not be able to build and lead a crisis management team either.

Neither the traditional manager nor the improvisational manager is suited to pull the company through an informal reorganization. The former is likely to be too unsettled by events, and the latter too intent on the creative process of developing a new product to have the patience necessary to accomplish a workout.

The optimum management style to lead a workout team is that of the crisis manager, a person who is a downside planner, a defensive strategist and a tireless seeker of cash. This management style involves locating the leverage points within the company to get the trapped cash out of the assets and overhead, then paying down debt and generating multiple cash flow channels. The crisis management approach focuses on slashing expenses, raising cash and leveraging others, while preventing others from inversely leveraging the company. It is an approach that requires clarity, a devotion to the core business and a relentless curiosity as to how much a vendor, lender or customer can be leveraged.

The Economy's New Hero

If the 1990s bear witness to tough economic times, the crisis manager will emerge as America's new business hero. My definition of "hero" is someone who has achieved an authentic instance of greatness. A hero is someone who has intentionally taken a step far beyond the capabilities of most people in solving a problem that affects a large number of people. A hero brings about something that is unlikely to have happened by the mere force of events. The economy's new heroes are distinguishable by the fact that their intervention makes the highly improbable happen.

Crisis managers are essentially shy and imprisoned within driven, fanatical personalities. In this involuntary confinement, they have developed an independent outlook. They know they are stronger, more imaginative and more effective fighters than the managers they replace and the creditors they fend off. They are fearless, understanding and indifferent to praise or blame.

Our heroes build groups of followers within the companies they help by convincing the followers that the managers' views of the future will become reality. Crisis managers have immense natural authority, dignity and strength. These qualities stem from a delight in being alive at "the right time" and in control of events at a critical moment in history. With so many companies self-immolating, the time for crisis managers has arrived. They thrive on change and instability.

The infinite possibilities of the unpredictable future offer endless opportunities for spontaneous improvisation and for bold, imaginative strokes that change the course of a company, an industry or a region. Strength comes to crisis managers from their clear vision of a reconstructed future and a faith in their power to mold it. They know where they are going, by what means and why. This strength enhances their energy and drive as it did Winston Churchill's during the Battle of Britain when he said: "It is impossible to quell the inward excitement which comes from a prolonged balancing of terrible things."[2]

These new American heroes usually are in their late forties or fifties, casual in their appearance, with an ease of dress. They wear no jewelry and disdain lace-up shoes that require time. They usually are married or divorced; the latter if the spouses were too frequently left out of things. Their language is rooted in strength and individual imagination. They are excellent communicators who can convince people to do things that they never intended to do before meeting them. They have a good sense of humor, some of it of the gallows variety. After all, they perform their duties on the bottom rung of the economic ladder. They have an ironical awareness of the short-comings of all people.

Crisis managers deal with the minds of the opponents and the minds of those who might put cash into the troubled company. They focus their knowledge, determine how to use it, then drive toward their turnaround goal. They do not strive childishly for wealth or power or to overcome the fear of failure. They have grown out of experiences where these strivings once were important. Now they have a single-minded purpose: to save the patient.

It is unusual to find these characteristics in an owner or manager, but not out of the question. To become heroic, the owner or manager of a crisis-riven company must recognize from the outset that he or she no longer is in the widget business, but now is in the workout business. Once that transformation is made, and it is a difficult one, the owner or manager can effect a turnaround without the assistance of a workout consultant.

Contrasting Management Approaches

While the traditional manager and the entrepreneurial manager always are planning for the upside, the crisis manager always is concerned with avoiding the downside. The crisis manager thinks defensively. In opposition to the entrepreneurial manager, the crisis manager is more sanguine about what tomorrow will bring but believes that it will bring more problems in need of solutions.

Figure 4.1 shows some other contrasts in management approach.

An Example of the Three Contrasting Styles

I recently worked with a troubled company that distributed products to hotels, restaurants and supermarkets in a large metropolitan market. It had annual sales of $12 million, an average gross profit margin of 20 percent, or $200,000 per month, and a fixed overhead of $230,000. The company owed more than $1 million in old accounts payable, in which it was unable to make a dent. All of its assets except $200,000 — the liquidation value of refrigerators and equipment — were pledged to a factor that was charging 21/2

FIGURE 4.1   Comparisons of Management Approaches

Traditional Manager	*Entrepreneurial Manager*	*Crisis Manager*
The objective of business is to maximize return on stockholders' equity	The objective of business is to develop and convey innovative solutions to consumers who will pay more than cost.	The objective of business is to generate maximum cash flow from the core product or service for a minimum expenditure.
The means to achieve this objective is capital investment to build a base, hire qualified people and create demand through mass marketing.	The means to achieve this objective is to fire in all directions and if something falls run toward it.	The means to achieve this objective is to find the leverage points within and without the company and squeeze them.
The teammates selected to deliver the objectives are experienced and qualified managers who think and act linearly.	The most important people are those who can clean up after the entrepreneur and implement his or her improvisational ideas.	The teammates are strategic thinkers and careful implementers who can think and act both linearly and associationally.
The ultimate plan for our company's product is to capture a significant market share in every developed country in the world.	The ultimate plan for our company's product is to develop a better one in two or three years that outsells the current one.	The ultimate plan for our company's product is to find a niche and sell it through five or six channels to avoid reliance on any single means of distribution.

FIGURE 4.1 Comparisons of Management Approaches (Continued)

Traditional Manager	Entrepreneurial Manager	Crisis Manager
Ownership of assets and production capability is a measure of our success.	The minds of our creative people are the true measure of our success.	The control of distribution channels and the tollgates in front of these channels is the measure of our success.
To lick the competition, we must outsell them by pouring resources into marketing.	To lick the competition, we must bring more innovative products to market more frequently.	To lick the competition, we must survive in the face of all adversity and keep the pressure on those who would try to take any market share from us.

percent per month on accounts receivable, which added $15,000 per month to the overhead. The company was on a severe downward spiral, bleeding cash at the rate of $45,000 per month, when I arrived to effect a workout and turnaround.

The company had three managers: the father, who was relatively inactive because of ill health, but conservative; one son, the marketing manager, who was growth-oriented and for whom the company's size in the market was important; and an entrepreneurial son, whose idea of survival was to locate new sources of supply to obviate the need to pay the current trade debt. The father was the crisis manager at the company, but he did not have all of the facts. The marketing-manager son believed the solution to the illiquidity crisis rested with increasing sales. The entrepreneurial son downplayed the crisis by looking for new suppliers.

My task was to stop the bleeding and find cash to pay the creditors. My leverage was with the father, who owned 50 percent of the stock and whose personal guarantee was on the line. He did not want to go down with the company, so his focus on a rescue plan was intense.

I completed my diagnostic analysis in a day and discovered that one customer accounted for 10 percent of sales — about $100,000 per month — but had squeezed the company's gross profit margin to 12 percent. It took a refrigerator and eight employees to serve this customer's monthly needs. I recommended dropping the customer and laying off the eight people. The overhead savings were $18,000 per month, including health insurance, worker's compensation and the savings on interest expense, a significant reduction in the monthly loss of $45,000.

With a few telephone calls, we located a competitor that needed more refrigerator capacity. We rented it the freed-up refrigerator for $4,000 per month and charged $2,000 per month for in-and-out labor. This attenuated the monthly loss by another $6,000. Two of the company's trucks were turned back to the leasing company for an additional saving of $3,000 per month, bringing the monthly loss down to $18,000.

The father was positively gleeful. Even the two sons began to catch my drift. I asked the son who was devoting his time to finding new suppliers to turn his energy to convincing customers to pay faster. A factor earns interest on every account receivable that it buys and for every day the receivable is outstanding. By factoring fewer accounts receivable, or by factoring but collecting the bills in one week rather than in one month, interest expenses could be reduced by three-fourths. This took a little explaining and a few weeks to implement, but by the end of one month, interest expenses were slashed by $10,000. We were within $8,000 per month of break-even, which we found in two ways. The marketing-oriented son found a new $40,000-a-month customer that did not require additional overhead to serve. At a gross profit margin of 20 percent, or $8,000, break-even was reached. We then took a hard look at administrative personnel and cut three jobs. This put the company into the black to the tune of $5,000 per month.

While all this was going on, I found an equipment-leasing company to provide $150,000 with the equipment as collateral and a second lien on accounts receivable and inventories. One hundred thousand dollars was used to pay down old accounts payable, and the remaining $50,000 was put into a savings account to meet future bullets or emergencies or to engage a bankruptcy lawyer, if needed. The monthly profit of $5,000 also was applied to accounts payable. This amount became larger when the factor was replaced with a conventional accounts receivable lender. The suppliers will have to wait six years to receive all of their old accounts payable, but they are pleased to be receiving some payment for the old debt as well as current payments on the new debt.

To sum up the situation, the three conflicting management styles, in combat with one another, were overseeing the demise of the company. A new voice (mine), speaking for the father, whose support I won early on, was needed to focus management's energy on a crisis that was caused by three factors: (1) one large, unprofitable customer, (2) excess overhead and (3) excess assets.

The differences in the form and rhythm of the three overarching management approaches run through every activity within a company. In a troubled company, the traditional manager is too rigid and the entrepreneurial manager is too improvisational. The crisis manager strikes the right balance.

The Workout Team

The closest approximation of the crisis manager's approach is that of the workout specialist. One reason that the best of the bunch are expensive, indeed ask for fees plus equity, is that they can get the job done when traditional or entrepreneurial managers cannot. Because of the short supply of workout specialists and the long supply of companies in trouble, workout fees are at all-time highs. They will level off as more people learn the process by hiring onto a workout team in their own companies.

The leader of the fire-fighting brigade within your company probably will be the manager — not necessarily the CEO — who has the wholehearted support of the board of directors and whose approach is most like that of the crisis manager. The chief executive officer may have to step back, as did Jerry Geist, the CEO of Public Service Company of New Mexico, who spent the utility's spare nickel on expansion of its delivery capacity, real estate development and venture capital investing. The workout business requires an entirely different mind-set from that typically found among company builders.

Whether hired from within or without, the leader will need a small band of warriors to find cash, defend the company from enemies, manage operations and develop and implement the redirect and grow plan. If the teammates' qualifications were sought in the animal world, the workout leader might choose the following creatures:

- *Ferret.* To find cash in assets, overhead expenses and other areas.
- *Lion.* To defend the company against creditor attacks.
- *Bulldog.* To guide operations through the rocky shoals of the workout period without losing anything of value.
- *Beaver.* To build a new and better operating plan once the debt is pared down and a stretchout plan is negotiated.

Pulling the Team Together

When I go in as a workout consultant (surrogate chief crisis officer, if you prefer), I establish with the CEO or the board of directors in advance that my role is consultative rather than decision making, except in those instances where the CEO or the board authorizes me to commit the company. I ask to interview the heads of finance, marketing and production to determine whether or not they have the stamina to contribute to and survive a workout situation. I also can learn during the interview process if the problem is a Pirandellian complex. I might advise the CEO or owner to yield some responsibility to senior officers and to me if he or she is too rigid or too improvisational to contribute to the turnaround process.

Notice that I do not consider heads of engineering or new-product development — managers within the company who spend its money today for an uncertain payback tomorrow — to be important members of the workout team because their departments will be scaled back. In addition, at least half of the administrative staff probably will be cut, with the remaining personnel in those departments carrying double loads. The core team that will steer

FIGURE 4.2   The Workout Team

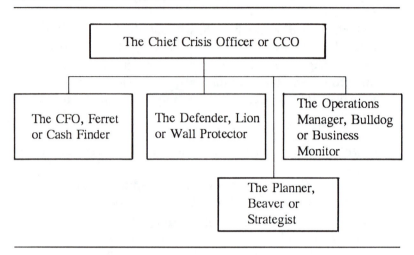

the company through the mine field will include perhaps five people (see Figure 4.2).

This is not your typical organizational chart, but a military operation is not, after all, a typical business condition. The Lion is monitoring the core operations while he or she and the Ferret sell, liquidate and spin off every division, hard asset and off-balance-sheet asset that will produce cash in a hurry. The Lion is speaking with, visiting, cajoling and passing a few coins to the creditors and maintaining the bullet list. The Beaver is maintaining the weekly cash flow statement projections and informing the Ferret, the Lion and the Beaver when they are ahead or behind schedule. The Beaver is also gathering data from these lieutenants to keep the road map as accurate as possible. When the worst of the crisis is passed, when the debts are compromised, settled or stretched out, the Beaver will provide strategies for financing the redirect and grow plan.

The Bulldog has the interesting assignment of trying to run the business in the face of adversity to keep cash coming in from operations. It is his or her task to operate the business for cash flow purposes, which means transaction by transaction, and not on a relationship basis. Some employees may be let go and called back when needed to provide consulting services. This saves payroll and insurance expenses. Customers will be asked to pay when the products are shipped. Suppliers will be paid as slowly as possible, unless they are bullets. Discounts will be sought from all suppliers. The Bulldog is aptly named, for this person must sink his or her teeth into the problem of running the operations on a cash flow basis to provide a constant stream of dollars to the Ferret and the Lion, while holding back from the rapacious Ferret any asset or expense item that is essential to operations. The leader selects the best people within the company to handle these four assignments. If they do not exist, they are brought in from other companies and other turnarounds. It isn't unlike a classic Western movie such as *Gunfight at the O.K. Corral* where Burt Lancaster pulls in an expert rifleman, a highly regarded six-shooter, the retired sheriff who joins the team for one last great shoot-out and a skilled horseman to head up the retreat, if needed.

Workout consulting companies run their businesses with very few permanent employees. Practically all team members are freelancers on call to the company for an hourly wage. What does this tell you about cash flow management?

Four Key Psychological Characteristics

In addition to the skill areas that must be covered capably, the small band of teammates must possess heart, courage, the ability to cooperate and an understanding of leverage. These traits are pretty rare in the homogenized culture of the corporate world. Once again, if senior officers and middle managers do not possess these characteristics, the team leader must hire from the outside.

- *Heart* is the inner drive that impels a person to make sacrifices to save the company.
- *Courage* is the internal strength to stand up to the most severe attacks without backing off.
- *The ability to cooperate* is the awareness of when to push and when to pull back in negotiations.
- *An understanding of leverage* is an internal sense that the company needs time, cash and supporters, coupled with a divining rod for locating all three.

I have written elsewhere[3] about how to identify these qualities during the interview process and when selecting your teammates. You may not think the inception of a crisis is a good time to curl up with a book, but if you have never been someplace before, you need road maps to help you steer the course until the workout consultant arrives.

There are two conditions to manage in a troubled company: the emotional distress and the battle to survive. In *The Business Bible for Survival,*[4] I provide an in-depth description of the former, including tests for the qualities you will need in your teammates. I underscore the importance of carefully selecting your teammates at the outset because your enemies are larger and better financed than you, and they are able to hire the best creditor-advocate lawyers in the country.

Authority To Commit the Company

It must be determined up front with clarity and complete under-standing how decisions on who gets paid will be handled. For example, if the workout team is composed of the four individuals I have suggested, plus the chief crisis officer (CCO), do they as a team have the authority to commit the company? Or does the CCO have sole authority to act with the advice and consent of the workout team? Another possibility for establishing authority is that all decisions involving a certain level of money — perhaps, up to $10,000 — can be approved by the Lion, who is the team member charged with deflecting attacks. Then, from $10,001 to $100,000, a unanimous vote of the workout team members is required. Alter-natively, the CCO, with the approval of the workout team members, can authorize payment of or commit the company to purchase or borrow assets between $10,001 and $100,000.

Then there is the board of directors. Does it remain intact throughout the battle, or are its members permitted to resign? Obtaining board approval is cumbersome, particularly when sev-eral members live out of town and lead busy lives.

At the time the company was incorporated or reincorporated, bylaws were written by company counsel. A company's bylaws prescribe the limits and extent of responsibility for members of the board. Normally, this includes the power to hire the CEO and to vest in him or her the authority to hire others to carry out the goals and objectives of the company. Bylaws also set forth the number of board meetings to be held and their location.

Bylaws could be cumbersome to a company involved in a rancorous workout. How do you obtain board approval, for instance, to repay a lender who has sent a U.S. marshal to remove the company's assets — desks, file cabinets and telephones — if the bylaws assign the responsibility for borrowing and repaying loans to the board of directors? The bottom line is this: The CCO should ask the board for emergency powers, even though they may contravene the bylaws, to commit the company to the best of its ability in times of crisis and to report its progress at board meetings that may, of necessity, be telephonic and impromptu, rather than held at regular intervals.

Board members could be blindfolding themselves and sticking their hands in a hornets' nest if they relinquish control to the workout team without first examining their liabilities, especially unpaid withholding taxes. The board member with the deepest pocket could end up paying all of the company's liability to the IRS.

There are two ways to seal off this liability. The first is to have the workout team sign letters to each board member absolving the board members of any responsibility for payments made or not made by team members. The second is to purchase directors and officers errors and omission liability insurance, known as D&O insurance, so that if the company's workout team causes economic injury to a third party, such as the IRS, the board of directors is absolved of blame. D&O insurance must be purchased before the liability is incurred; otherwise, it will not protect the board members.

The principal carriers of D&O insurance are listed in Figure 4.3.

Litigation Is a Weapon

As if the cash crunch, personnel defections and injuries to your image in the marketplace aren't enough to damage your company, the volley of creditor lawsuits will sail over the parapets of your company's walls and explode in the center of your office like a

FIGURE 4.3 Principal Underwriters of D&O Insurance

Aetna—Executive Risk Management Associates
Agricultural E&S Insurance—Executive Liability Division
ALC Insurance, Inc.
Alexander Underwriters General Agency
All American Agency Facilities, Inc.
All Risks, Ltd.
American E&S Insurance Brokers CA, Inc.
American Insurance Managers, Inc.
American International Global, Inc.
Aon Entertainment Inc.
Babcock Underwriters, Inc.
F.B. Beattie & Co., Inc.
Bolton & Co.
Russell Bond & Co., Inc./Environmental Liability Managers, Inc.
British-American Insurance Group Ltd.
Brokers Surplus Agency, N.A., Inc.
Burns & Wilcox, Ltd.
Casualty Underwriters Inc.
Centurion Corp.
Cooney, Rikard & Curtin, Inc.
Crump E&S of Atlanta, Inc.
Crump E&S of Boston Insurance Services, Inc.
Crump E&S of CA Insurance Services, Inc.
Crump E&S of Dallas, Inc.
Crump E&S Financial Services
Crump E&S of FL, Inc.
Crump E&S of Houston, Inc.
Crump E&S of IL, Inc.
Crump E&S of Memphis, Inc.
Crump E&S of NY, Inc.
Crump E&S Northwest, Inc.
Crump E&S of San Francisco
Crump E&S of WI
Dearborn Insurance Co./Virginia Surety Co., Inc.
Delaware Valley Underwriting Agency, Inc.
Eastern Shore Corp.
E&S Facilities, Inc.
John W. Fisk Co.
Harry W. Gorst & Co., Inc.
Gray-Stone & Co.
Great American Insurance Co.—Executive Liability Division

FIGURE 4.3 Principal Underwriters of D&O Insurance (Continued)

Hanover Excess & Surplus, Inc.
L.E. Harris Agency, Inc.
Horan, Goldman Cos., Inc.
Hull & Co., Inc.
Insurance Innovators Group
International Excess & Treaty Managers, Inc.
Interstate Insurance Management, Inc.
R.L. Jarrett Risk Services, Inc./Jarrett Specialty, Inc.
Jensvold & Le Fevre, Inc.
M.J. Kelly Co.
Lexington Insurance Co.
D.B. Linden & Associates, Inc.
LoVollo Associates, Inc.
Markel Corp.
Market Finders Insurance Corp.
G.A. Mavon & Co.
Mile High Markets, Inc.
NAS Ltd.
National Union Fire Insurance Co. of Pittsburgh
North Island Group
Pennock Insurance Agency
Phoenix Excess & Surplus Lines, Inc.
Princeton Risk Managers, Inc.
Preferred General Agency of the Midwest, Inc.
Professional Excess Affiliates Corp.
Professional Indemnity Agency Inc.
Professional Managers Inc.
Quaker Agency, Inc.
R A & MCO Insurance Services
RISC Inc.
Risk Specialists Cos.
Janet Schaeffer & Associates
Victor O. Schinnerer & Co., Inc.
Seaboard Underwriters
Special Program Management Inc.
Stewart Smith West, Inc.
Swett & Crawford
Tennant Risk Services Inc.
Tudor Insurance Co.
U.S. Risk Underwriters, Inc.
Weakley and Co.

SOURCE: *Rough Notes*, The Insurance Marketplace Edition, 1992, p. 57.

thousand sticks of dynamite going off in tandem. The objective of litigation, particularly in the early stages of crisis, is to weaken the opponent. Workout consultants call the early round "cannons," and their first objective is to tear down the defenses of the already shell-shocked company and to force a settlement with the creditor company on extremely unfavorable terms to the debtor.

Some of the litigation will likely charge the company with fraud, racketeering and other malevolent acts. Although these are civil offenses, dischargeable in court or by settlement by the payment of money, some creditors will reconstruct the events that induced them to ship goods, provide services or lend money to the company as acts of criminal fraud and urge the attorney general to bring a criminal action against the company. I can report from firsthand experience that it takes certain kinds of people to stand up to the battering ram of litigation, to pursue a survival plan and to thrive amidst the chaos.

Fraud Is Not Dischargeable in Bankruptcy

The second objective of litigation is to prevail with a cause of action that, should the debtor company seek protection under the bankruptcy code, will not be discharged by the court for cents on the dollar but must be paid in full in an amount to be determined by a court of law. If a company borrows $20 million from financial institutions several months prior to hitting the wall, the financial institutions in many instances will examine the books of the borrower, uncover some transactions in the checking account that seem questionable and bring 20 to 50 counts of fraud and racketeering. If the company cannot develop a survive and thrive plan outside of Chapter 11, then the $20 million claim for fraud stays with it through the bankruptcy proceedings, and the plaintiffs are not treated like other unsecured creditors. Indeed, if racketeering is added to the causes of action, Congress has determined that the plaintiffs, should they prevail, are entitled to treble damages plus legal fees. If the debtor company loses the racketeering case at trial, the plaintiffs may be awarded more than $60 million while the unsecured creditors receive, perhaps, 20 cents on the dollar.

Racketeering

"Civil filings under the Racketeer Influenced and Corrupt Organizations law have increased more than eightfold over the past five years to nearly a thousand cases in 1988," wrote William H. Rehnquist, Chief Justice of the Supreme Court. Chief Justice Rehnquist continued:

> Virtually everyone who has addressed the question agrees that civil RICO is now being used in ways that Congress never intended when it enacted the statute in 1970. Most of the civil suits filed under the statute have nothing to do with organized crime. They are garden-variety civil fraud cases of the type traditionally litigated in state courts. Why does the statute work this way? In part, because it creates a civil counterpart for criminal wire fraud and mail fraud prosecutions. It does this by stating that acts indictable under those provisions, as well as many other types of criminal acts, are capable of establishing the "pattern of racketeering" that is the predicate for a civil RICO action.[5]

Notwithstanding the Chief Justice's plea to reform civil RICO legislation, it probably will remain a burden that some debtor companies must carry. Some creditors have learned the military aspects of collecting the full amount owing them: Drive gaping holes through the walls of the debtor company, smear its management with charges of fraud and racketeering and force them into financial despair with the most expensive litigation the law will permit.

Who within your company has the heart and courage to stand shoulder to shoulder with you when the walls come tumbling down? If these people do not exist, find the workout consultants who can join you in battle.

The Damage Trail

Among the assignments to be given to your Lion — the defender of the walls — is to maintain a damage trail: a chronological listing of the damaging events that result from aggressive litigation. Lawsuits are filed with public courts, and anyone, including reporters, has access to them. In fact, many newspapers station people full-time in the courts to collect stories of disputes that become news a day or two later. Other self-appointed watchdogs then photostat the stories and send them to the defendant's customers or vendors and to national publications. Before the debtor company knows it, the inability to pay a vendor or lender becomes a RICO lawsuit described in minute detail in trade journals and national newspapers.

A national or trade publication usually will investigate a local dispute more thoroughly and telephone a spokesperson for your company as well as for the plaintiff. The Lion should be the person who fields those telephone calls, and he or she should be trained in the appropriate response. Many libel lawyers will advise not to contribute to the article. It only makes it worse, they say. The plaintiff or its counsel is likely to make a statement to the trade journal or national publication. It would be hard-pressed not to answer the question, "What is the substance to your claim of racketeering?" Its response might be something like, "We found several instances of misappropriation of money and accounting irregularities."

That is a damaging statement, and the Lion should enter it in the damage trail notebook. A large customer may read the article and tell the debtor company that it cannot do business with it any further until the charges made by the plaintiff are cleared up. The Lion should ask the customer for a letter to that effect to provide a direct causal relationship between the plaintiff's statement and the loss of business. The customer's letter is filed in the damage trail notebook.

Other companies may recoil from servicing the company on reading the article. Credit-card companies may send cancellation notices on their cards; banks may shut down the company's accounts; other vendors may stop shipping except on a COD basis. The Lion should dutifully record all these events in the damage trail notebook. They will form the basis of counterclaims for damages related to the plaintiff's statements to the press. These counterclaims may take the form of libel, tortuous interference, business interference and more. Pursuing the counterclaimant will require expensive, litigation-experienced lawyers and months of work compiling depositions and documents, but it puts litigants on notice that their cannons did not knock out yours.

Whether or not you pursue your causes of action to trial depends on the merits of your case, the predilections of the judge and the amount of cash you can raise to stay the battle. In many instances, if the debtor company can build a hefty litigation war chest, it can negotiate a settlement and withdrawal of the damaging litigation with a powerful counterclaim. If the company doesn't have the cash to pursue litigation and sustain business operations, its enemies may prevail. In the litigation battlefield, soldiers march on cash.

Overzealous Creditor Lawyers

There are approximately 700,000 attorneys in the country in 1991, and the nation's law schools are graduating 35,000 new ones a year. With so many lawyers needing to justify their existence and feed their families, litigation in Western civilization is skyrocketing. That's the bad news. The good news is that there are ways to bring overreaching lawyers to their knees.

The Federal Rules of Civil Procedure is pretty much the bible of how a lawsuit must be conducted in the federal courts (each state has its own version of *Fed. R. Civ. P.*, as the lawyers refer to it). Any lawyer who violates these rules without justification may be sanctioned by the presiding judge.

Remember that if you overreach and misstate facts in seeking sanctions against an opposing attorney, you may be subject to the same penalties for which you are seeking redress. Furthermore, your attorney may not wish to file a motion for sanctions against another attorney, as they belong to a professional fraternity and tend to respect one another notwithstanding aggressive behavior that is tantamount to lying. Thus, if you feel strongly that a creditor's attorney has caused you economic injury, you may have to file the motion for sanctions in your own name, or *pro se*.

The federal rules that you must measure the violations against to see if they are sanctionable are as follows:

Rule 11. Any attorney or other person admitted to conduct cases in any court of the United States or any Territory thereof who so multiplies the proceedings in any case unreasonably and vexatiously may be required by the court to satisfy personally the excess costs, expenses and attorneys' fees reasonably incurred because of such conduct.

Rule 11 is used primarily when opposing counsel causes you to spend time and money needlessly by requesting multiple documents and multiple depositions or by making false statements that you must spend time and money to correct.

Rule 37. This provision places the burden on the disobedient party to avoid expenses by showing that his failure was justified. . . .

Rule 37 may be invoked if the court issues an order that the opposing counsel disobeys. Penalties are stiffer under Rule 37 than under Rule 11 because a court order has been violated. It could arise in a situation where a creditor sues your company for nonpayment of a credit, and you seek through the court to determine if the amount owing on the creditor's accounts receivable ledger is actually the true amount owing. Differences could arise where there is a service contract involved or where goods or parts were shipped back because of defects. If the creditor refuses to allow access to its records, you can request them in a deposition. If the creditor blocks the deposition, or gives insufficient information at the deposition, you then can seek an order to have the information provided to you forthwith.

A motion for sanctions brought under this rule would be appropriate if opposing counsel were repeatedly contemptuous of the court by making false statements under oath.

Rule 26(g): Provides for sanctions against an attorney if he seeks to increase your costs of litigation "for any improper purpose, such as to harass or to cause unnecessary delay or needless increase in the cost of litigation." False statements, improper motions filed against you for harassment purposes, and other actions by opposing counsel that increase expenses needlessly, are plausibly actionable under Rule 26(g).

Pro Se: **The Benefits**

Because your counsel is unlikely to throw bricks at a colleague, perhaps you should think about representing yourself. By acting *pro se*, you will save thousands of dollars and probably do as well as if you hired counsel. (This is not true in bankruptcy. A debtor *must* be represented by counsel in Chapter 11.)

Another reason for representing yourself in the litigation aspects of a workout is that it renders creditors' counsel somewhat helpless, or at least uncertain as to how you are likely to respond in certain circumstances. They know how lawyers relate to one another, but they do not know how a businessperson will respond in every circumstance. Acting *pro se* is a Sun Tzu–derivative strategy: You get inside the opponent's head and upset the form and rhythm that the opponent typically follows to collect a debt. General Norman Schwarzkopf followed the strategy of Sun Tzu in leading the Allied forces against Iraq in the brief and brilliant Persian Gulf war of 1991.

A third reason for a *pro se* defense is that any lawyer you are likely to hire will think within the constructs of his or her legal training, but probably not strategically. Assume, for example, that a creditor hires the law firm of Jones, Smith & Doe to represent it in collecting a $1 million debt your company legitimately owes but cannot pay without a standstill agreement of 90 to 120 days, followed by a four-year stretchout. The creditor wants its money now, and Jones, Smith & Doe comes at the company with all guns firing at once. They are sure to gain the upper hand because they have more money to fight a sustained battle.

In the course of your company's many years in business, however, you have used Jones, Smith & Doe to represent your company in another matter. To interrupt the $1 million collection process, you raise the firm's alleged conflict of interest with the disciplinary commission of the state bar association (in some instances, the State Supreme Court) in the state in which the company has been sued, asking that the disciplinary commission remove the Jones firm

FIGURE 4.4   Legal Referees

Some lawyers occasionally cross the line between bold advocacy and breaches of ethics. Some overprescribe, misdiagnose or underperform. When this happens, ask your state's bar association or disciplinary commission to intervene. Neither can grant monetary relief, but here is what they can do, in descending order of severity:

Disbarment: The lawyer may be disbarred and prohibited from practicing law in the state. Disbarment usually is imposed for criminal actions or gross misconduct bordering on crime.

Suspension: The lawyer may be suspended from practicing law for a period ranging from one day to several years, depending on the nature of the improper conduct.

Public Reprimand: The lawyer may be sanctioned by the highest court in the state, and the sanction may be cited in the newspaper.

Private Reprimand: This is the lightest of wrist slaps, intended only to establish a record for reference in the event of further misbehavior.

A word of warning, however: The law firms in the state pay fees to these two referees, fees that provide them with the wherewithal to hire staff and serve the public. Like most regulatory agencies, the referees of legal disputes follow Milton Friedman's law, which states that regulatory agencies, to justify their existence, will support the industry they are empowered to regulate. Just remember — the layperson is *not* the client of the bar associations and disciplinary commissions.

SOURCE: American Bar Association.

because it represented you in the past. You may win the argument; but in any event, the creditor is forced to back off until the matter is resolved. The disciplinary commissions of the various states are empowered to resolve disputes between clients, defendants and their lawyers. Their revenues are derived from payments made by the law firms, which tells you right up front that your company is unlikely to obtain a balanced ruling. But I have found that the disciplinary commissions try to be fair as long as the alleged infraction that you bring to their attention is legitimate.

The degree to which they can punish the offending law firm is shown in Figure 4.4.

You need not feel vulnerable in a *pro se* proceeding. On the contrary, if you can read, you can follow the *Federal Rules of Civil Procedure.* If you need legal advice, you can obtain information from Nolo Press, 950 Parker Street, Berkeley, CA 94710 (800-992-6656), a publishing firm that assists people in representing themselves in legal matters.

A backup to Nolo Press is the local law school. It will refer you to local attorneys who have recently hung out their shingles and who will advise you, but not represent you, for a modest fee. The money you will save by operating *pro se* will be sufficient to part with one or two thousand dollars for books, tapes and software and for occasional legal advice.

SELL ASSETS TO RAISE CASH

The second step in the workout process is raising cash. This is the principal assignment of the Ferret. Read chapter seven of this book for additional cash-generating strategies.

Most companies are bloated with assets and overhead expenses, which is one reason they get into trouble (or become takeover targets) in the first place. The crisis management approach is to sell assets, slash expenses and generate multiple cash flow channels to maximize liquidity and cash flow and build a pile of free cash to apply to flash points during the workout. It is traditionally managed and entrepreneurially improvised companies that get into trouble, yet they generally do not have anyone with Ferret skills on staff. The skill is brought in when the team is formed. If each of the four skill areas — the Ferret, the Lion, the Bulldog and the Beaver — must be hired along with a workout consultant to replace the CEO, is it any wonder that the average informal reorganization is 12 months in length and costs more than $100,000 in consulting fees?

The Ferret's task is to raise cash quickly. Here is where the Ferret should go first.

Have Customers Supply Raw Materials

If your company manufactures equipment, machinery or a product sold under contract to a vendor that resells it to industrial or individual consumers, you may be tying up cash in raw materials, which is a service that does not earn your company a dime. Change your manufacturing process to that of a value-added manufacturer that provides the labor content only. Have your customers purchase the raw materials and deliver them to you just in time for producing their goods. You can charge for labor, plus a profit markup and delivery. For a $25-million (revenues) company with a cost of goods sold of 65 percent, half of which is raw material, you will free up $8.1 million in cash.

Sell or Lease Back Fixed Assets and Office Space

One of the most common ways to squeeze cash out of fixed assets is to sell them to a leasing company and lease them back. The most customary assets that investors are comfortable in purchasing and leasing back to companies are buildings, warehouses, equipment, trucks and vans. This tactic is called the sale-leaseback, and it is routinely done by traditional corporations whenever the wolf is approaching the door.

To find sale-leaseback investors for your office building or warehouse, begin with investors who seek high-quality buildings. Run through the field down to investors who seek low-quality buildings, and along the way you should find the right match. Insurance companies are the premier real estate investors.

In addition to insurance companies as sale-leaseback candidates, there are corporate pension funds, college endowment funds and association or small pension funds. At the lower end of the quality spectrum are wealthy individuals herded into syndicates by investment bankers. Individuals die, get divorced and want special reports sent hither and thither. Thus, there is a risk in selling your asset to individuals and leasing it back from them, but it frees up cash.

Spin Off Nonessential Assets

The Ferret's cash-generating skills must include knowing how to spin off assets that are not essential to the company's core. What is novel is the mechanics of the spin-off, the different kinds of spin-offs and the ability to profit in several ways from the spin-off while giving up risk and costs.

Selling a manufacturing subsidiary that never was part of the company's core is a simple judgment call and should be done quickly. The Ferret also will have to make tougher calls, such as: spinning off divisions that service the company (data-processing, human resources, advertising) not because they do not fit, but because spinning them off raises cash. These three spin-offs are seldom done by traditional managers, or, if done at all, not too well.

The optimum facilities management spin-off is of a precocious service department that manages an internal generic activity extremely well. Other corporations that have a need for these services would hire the department to provide services to them if it were freestanding. Most facilities management spin-offs have involved the data-processing departments of large and medium-sized corporations. Some commercial banks are spinning off their data-processing departments into stand-alone companies to raise cash.

In the facilities management spin-off, the budget of the department leaves the parent, thus freeing up cash, and the spun-off division contracts with the parent to provide its usual services on a contract basis. The spun-off division incorporates, and the former employees of the parent become employees of the new entity. It is free to provide services to other companies, and the endorsement of the parent assists the new company in obtaining contracts. Working capital for the spun-off division is provided by service contracts from the parent company and others. Smart Ferrets will hold onto some equity in the spun-off companies because these companies occasionally have a way of becoming valuable. For example, Oryx Energy Corporation, which was spun off by Sun Oil to manage its depleted oil reserves in the Austin Chalk area of west Texas, found oil using a new technology known as horizontal drilling. Oryx's market value in two years vaulted to more than $2 billion. This is a case of the foal becoming a better runner than the sire. Would that Sun had held onto some of Oryx's stock.

The Ferret should review the various divisions carefully to determine which have the most spin-off possibilities. Successful facilities management spin-offs must provide a service that other companies can use, must be made up of an enthusiastic, high-energy entrepreneurial group of employees and must be willing to take the risk when the umbilical cord is cut. The trust department of Chemical Bank became a successful management spin-off under the name Favia-Hill & Company, Inc., the names of its senior managers. The data-processing department of Uniroyal, Inc., was spun off as a stand-alone, Computeristics, Inc., in a transition that I worked on several years ago. McKesson-Robbins, the largest drug and health and beauty aids company in the country, spun off its pharmaceutical services company and held onto a chunk of its equity, which became valuable when the stand-alone company achieved an initial public offering.

Sell Slow-Paying Accounts Receivable

Your company's slow accounts receivable may be millstones to you, but they are diamonds to someone who knows how to leverage them. If you have a large enough cache of paper, perhaps more than $10 million, it may pay for you to form a captive finance subsidiary, put some key personnel into it with equity incentives and help them finance the subsidiary with bank loans or private placements. This is known as *securitizing* your assets and selling an interest in them to public investors. But securitizing your company's accounts receivable takes time, and you have precious little of that.

If your accounts receivable staff has been unable to collect accounts receivable efficiently, sell the paper for whatever you can raise. Interview several collection agencies to collect the receivables and select one of them. You may raise only five cents on the dollar for paper more than 180 days old but as much as 50 cents on the dollar for receivables 90 to 180 days old.

Sell Obsolete Inventory

Every industry has its liquidators and barter companies that are listed in trade journals as well as in the yellow pages. They provide the flotsam and jetsam of products that we see in flea markets on Sunday mornings. The liquidator in the B. Altman bankruptcy paid 50 cents on the dollar for the retailer's inventory. Of course, the purchase included saleable as well as slow-moving items. If your intent is to sell only slow-moving items, look for a price nearer to 30 cents on the dollar.

Several well-known consumer-electronics catalogs and direct-mail merchandiser firms, including JS&A (for Joe Sugerman & Associates) and DAK (for Dean A. Kaplan), buy discontinued and overstocked items from cash-poor manufacturers at distress prices. They buy cheap — but pay cash — then advertise the products heavily in their direct-response ads or catalogs and sell them at 25 to 30 percent off retail list. The strapped manufacturer can generate $10 quickly for an item that it might otherwise sell for $50 in time.

Rent Out Freed-Up Space

The process of generating cash from languid, slow-moving and peripheral assets can be accomplished completely in 45 to 60 days, and the Ferret can be reassigned to gathering cash from operating expenses. Before moving on, the Ferret should be assigned to rearranging the office and warehouse space. I have not gone into detail about the sale of peripheral divisions and subsidiaries because it goes without saying that as the company metamorphoses into the workout business from whatever business it was in, the peripheral operations are the first to be sold.

If the data-processing department has been spun off via a facilities management contract, the fleet-management department shrunk to a few people when the vans and trucks are sold, the maintenance staff let go when the buildings are sold, the purchasing division shut down when the company becomes a value-added labor provider and half the administrative staff terminated as peripheral divisions and subsidiaries are sold, there is a considerable amount of freed-up space that can be rented to other companies to generate additional cash flow.

SLASH EXPENSES

The third step in the workout process is slashing expenses, and this job also falls to the Ferret. This is an all-encompassing task because no expense item should be safe from the Ferret's scrutiny. The line items to be cut include the following:

- Management salaries
- Management perks
- Space
- Administrative personnel
- Vehicles
- Lawyers
- Auditors
- Health insurance
- Commercial insurance
- Telephone
- Postage
- Courier
- Travel and entertainment
- Advertising

The fundamental question that the Ferret must ask is: Can I pay less? Surprisingly few managers ask for discounts, lower prices, installment payments or barter. But people who live in humble circumstances do, and a company teetering on the edge of bankruptcy is in humble circumstances. You always can get something for less money, and there is always a less-expensive vendor. You just have to ask.

Salary Reductions

Across-the-board salary reductions are a mandatory first step for all personnel. The biggest cuts should be made in the largest salaries. Salary cuts for key people should be discussed one on one and not be announced with an impersonal form letter. Some people may be at the most expensive years in their working lives, with children in college, while others may be in less-expensive years. Some may be able to endure 33 percent cuts, while for others a 20 percent cut may be the maximum endurable limit. Cuts at the production-worker level cannot be impersonal because these people tend to feel, and rightly so in most instances, that they are like mushrooms kept in the dark and covered with manure from time to time.

A tactic I found useful in the workout of a manufacturing company was to go into the factory for a shirtsleeve meeting with the head of production, explain the situation and request everyone's extra effort. The head of production and I fielded questions for an hour and then asked for a voluntary 20 percent pay cut. A few hands were raised from the first volunteers, and then, when all hands were up, we pulled out a wad of crisp 50-dollar bills and passed them around to everyone. "You see," the head of production said, "we're going to pull through these dark days if we all pull together."

We routinely passed out 50-dollar bills whenever the production workers came in on Saturdays or did an exceptional job at getting out an order without flaws or providing warranty and repair work in record time. Some workout consultants recommend spreading shares of the company's stock around to all employees to compensate for longer hours and lower pay.

Health-Insurance Expenses

One could argue that in a crisis, the managers and employees should be willing to forego their health-insurance costs. After all, the proponents of this line of reasoning contend that this is a luxury the company can ill afford. The counter-argument is that employees will be putting in longer hours during the difficult months of a crisis and their families will object to a simultaneous reduction in both pay and benefits.

A middle-ground solution is to self-insure the medical needs of employees and their families by buying only catastrophic medical insurance, which is much less expensive. This sometimes works, depending on the hazards of the job itself, when coupled with a wellness program that includes smoke-ending and exercise. But crises cause physical stress and fatigue. Some people convert stress into motivators, while others fall prone to illness.

Nonetheless, if your company is paying $120 a month per employee (or $360 for the employee and his or her family) for health insurance, and if it employs 250 people after cutbacks, the monthly bill is $73,800. The Ferret's job is to slash expenses and raise cash, and no expense item is safe.

If health-care actuarial tables can be retrieved rapidly from the carrier, the Ferret may be able to determine that the actual cost of employee medical care for the preceding 12 months was only $45,000 per month, or 61 percent of out-of-pocket costs. He or she could recommend to the crisis management team that the company cancel its health-insurance plan and self-insure by setting aside $45,000 per month in a savings account. The cost would drop from $360 a month per employee-family to $180 (or $60 per person), and interest would accrue on the savings. If the company's back were ever thrust against the wall with no options, it could use the health-care savings to keep the doors open, as long as the employees approve the emergency measures.

But a self-insured program requires at least one full-time employee to monitor it. Some employees have extended families who try to use the company's insurance plan. Others have medical treatment on organs or tissues that were removed years ago. Others visit providers that add multiple diagnostics and treatments that are not called for. Can the company afford the time of an in-house health-maintenance person? Once again, it depends on the overall fairness of the workers and for the community of employees to pull together for a win-win situation.

Employee Leasing

These innovative companies are capable of lowering health-insurance costs to $60 a month per employee. They take all of your employees on their payroll and rent them back to you. The employees will receive improved health benefits, and when you want to terminate them, the leasing company will find them other jobs. You can save the payroll costs of your human resources department — at least $20,000 per person. The employee-leasing company will fill out all of the government and insurance forms for the employees and handle all terminations, giving you more time for other management tasks. Thus far, roughly 20,000 U.S. companies have begun using the services of employee-leasing companies. The leasing companies charge their clients the sum of payroll plus benefits plus a fee. They make an additional profit by negotiating substantially less-expensive benefit packages for their employees. The fee charged to clients is small, however, in comparison with the savings in management time and employee hassles.

Following are the services that employee-leasing companies provide for your people:

- Process payroll checks
- Provide weekly payroll and billing reports
- File and pay all state and federal employer taxes
- Prepare W-2 forms at year-end for all employees
- Provide a comprehensive employee health-insurance program
- Process Section 125 benefits deductions
- Process all insurance claims
- Offer and administer COBRA (Comprehensive Omnibus Benefits Retirement Act) benefits
- Provide coverage for workers' compensation; issue certificates and administer claims
- Administer state employment claims
- Provide a credit union
- Provide an in-house human resources consultant
- Provide in-house legal counsel

GTE, Holiday Inn Corporation, Greyhound, Hospital Corporation of America and thousands of other companies are leasing some or all of their employees from the 400 employee-leasing companies trolling for clients in the United States. The average size of company leasing its employees is 30 people, and many of them are rapidly expanding companies whose managers are too busy steering their companies' growth to pay attention to government and insurance compliance forms.

One of the largest employee-leasing companies, Action Staffing of Tampa, Florida, has revenues of $100 million. It leases the 19,000 employees on its payroll to 650 companies. Larry Jones, the ex-military man who runs Action Staffing, likens his company to a "collection agency for the IRS." Some companies with chronic withholding-tax problems must be assigned a tax auditor to monitor them on a weekly basis. Clearly, it takes fewer IRS auditors to observe the payroll records of one company with 11,000 employees than it does 450 companies of 25 employees each.

Insurance companies also are fans of employee leasing for two reasons. First, they can bill one company for their services rather than several hundred, and they can monitor the insurance records with far fewer auditors. Second, they need fewer salespersons to call on 400 employee-leasing companies than on the approximately 20,000 companies in the U.S. that now lease their employees. There are two primary savings to the lessee: an elimination of the salaries and related costs of its human resources department and a huge savings in management time.

Marvin R. Selter, chairman of National Staff Network, Inc., the nation's largest employee-leasing company, with approximately 35,000 employees, says that its typical client had been spending about 28 percent of its revenues on payroll, benefits and employee administration costs, and that it now spends 22 percent on employee leasing.

Other Insurance Expenses

The Ferret has several options in reducing employee health-insurance costs, and that applies to the company's commercial fire, casualty and product-liability insurance costs as well. These policies should be reviewed by local agents with two questions in mind: Do we need all of this coverage? Can we get the coverage that we need less expensively? The agents will doubtless bring in lower rates, particularly if they know they are in a competitive bidding situation. Then, when the best deal is struck, the Ferret should tell the agent that the company would like to pay for the policy on a monthly basis. Finally, the workout period is an excellent time to cancel management life-insurance policies paid for by the company. If the managers want to continue paying for them by themselves, they should be given that option.

Professional Fees

The second highest overhead burden after insurance expenses usually is professional fees. These include accounting, legal and consulting costs. The workout specialist and bankruptcy lawyer, if you retain one, will be expensive but necessary costs, but line items to reduce are the professional costs of the accountants and lawyers who failed to warn you that trouble was just around the corner.

Has your company competitively bid these services in the past? Did you ever examine what you were getting for what you were paying in the way of accounting and legal fees? A workout is an ideal time to have a serious discussion about fees with your lawyer and accountant. Tell them that you no longer will pay for lawyers fresh out of school to sit in on meetings. Tell them that you no longer will pay for bad advice.

A friend of mine who comanages one of the nation's largest and most successful multiple venture capital fund management companies told me how his firm has begun to deal with excessive legal fees. "We don't pay them," he said. "If the lawyer has advised us poorly, and if we followed that advice and lost money, we tell the lawyer to eat the bill — even if it is more than $100,000, which it has been on some occasions."

Accounting Charges.   Here are some questions to ask your company's accounting firm in order to lower its audit fees:

1. What is the price of this year's audit?
2. Does it include the tax filings?
3. Who is assigned to it?

FIGURE 4.5   Computation of Accounting Costs

	Accounting Firm's Cost
33 × junior accountant × $16 =	$ 528.00
33 × senior accountant × $24 =	792.00
34 × partner × $50 =	1,700.00
100	$3,020.00

4. What are their billing rates?
5. Are they experienced in this kind of business?
6. Does the audit price include the management letter?
7. What work can we do on the books internally to lower the audit cost?
8. Does the cost include the defense of your work in the event of an IRS audit or litigation?

Let's look at what is behind these questions. Accounting firms sell their time. They hire intelligent young people, train them and mark up their cost two to five times. Let's assume that one junior accountant, one senior accountant and one partner are assigned to perform your company's audit, that they respectively earn $40,000, $60,000 and $125,000 per annum, and that they each work 2,500 hours each year. Accordingly, their "raw material" costs are $16 per hour, $24 per hour and $50 per hour, respectively.

For the accounting firm to bid your job intelligently, it must estimate the number of hours the job will take. At the preaudit meeting, ask for an estimate of the number of hours the job will take. Then you will have a pretty fair idea of the markup factor, which will help you negotiate the fee. For example, if the accounting firm bids $40,000, estimates 100 hours, or $400 per hour, and if you assume 33 hours per auditor, then you probably are being high bid. (See Figure 4.5.)

Rather than a 500 percent markup, the accounting firm is trying to achieve a 3,300 percent markup. You have room to negotiate all the way down to $16,000.

Another way to cut audit expenses is to ask how your accounting department may help to reduce the time involved in data collection. Some companies, particularly those in which the chief financial officer was formerly with an accounting firm, do such an extensive audit prep that the accounting firm actually only performs a review. Leaving a detailed paper trail for all money transfers in and out is one of the best ways to cut audit expenses.

Legal Charges. The same type of analysis is required when negotiating the cost of legal services. Lawyers and accountants sell their time at markups above the actual cost of the skilled labor that is employed. If your law firm routinely brings three lawyers to its meetings with you, your company is being triple-billed, and the Ferret should put a stop to it.

The scope of the legal services needed can be determined by one member of the firm in less than 30 minutes. But lawyers frequently fill the conference room when it obviously is unnecessary. Most companies do not put their legal requirements out for bid or interview lawyers at different firms, but your company should.

Discuss rates at the beginning of the engagement. Discuss the manner in which you wish to be billed — contingency, hourly rate paid monthly or when an event occurs. Many lawyers prefer that you pay a retainer up front — bankruptcy lawyers quite properly want 90 percent of their expected fee up front — and then work the retainer off in hours. This is an appropriate arrangement for a complicated lawsuit or for a matter that has an uncertain ending, such as bankruptcy. It is inappropriate for the drafting of a contract.

Be sure to specify that you want fully itemized bills that break down how each hour or fraction thereof was spent. Question items in the bill that you do not understand. Your lawyer does not have to travel first-class, for example. If the lawyer does not work for you while traveling, he or she should not bill you for travel time. Prepare a budget with your lawyer before the task begins and monitor the budget frequently.

Paper Recycling

In one troubled company that I worked with recently, I instituted an employee stock-ownership plan to capture everyone's attention about small costs that add up. Here's what I told the stock-owning secretaries: "You're a cost center, you know. But you can become a profit center by combining the incoming paper trash such as magazines, catalogs and third-class mail with waste paper such as first drafts and bad photostats and by shopping for the best recycling price on this category of paper known as 'mixed paper.'"

Most paper recyclers will put several gaylord boxes on pallets outside your back door at no charge. A gaylord is a four-by-four-by-four-foot box that holds 600 to 800 pounds of paper. Four full gaylords make up approximately a ton. The range of value for your paper trash is approximately as follows (these prices vary between metropolitan areas and with economic conditions):

- Computer printer paper $150/ton
- Photostat paper   90/ton
- Colored paper (catalogs)   20/ton
- Newspapers   10/ton
- Corrugated boxes   5/ton

After you presort the paper trash into categories, make certain you keep it dry. Once paper becomes wet it loses its value.

Computer printer paper is recycled into the highest-quality stationery. Photostat paper is recycled as medium-grade bond. Mixed paper, your incoming mail, is recycled as inexpensive paper. And, in some markets, corrugated paper boxes and newspapers have a second life as cardboard and napkins. The recyclers in Miami, Florida, no longer are picking up newspapers because there is an excess of it.

Depending on the size of your company, its paper consumption and its volume of incoming mail, you might be able to generate $3,400 to $6,800 annually through paper recycling. That's about the volume that several heavily computerized firms of 250 to 400 employees are generating each year.

Aluminum Recycling

Aluminum cans are worth 56 cents per pound in most cities across the country, and there are 28 cans to the pound. If your company has 280 employees who swig one soft drink per day, their sugar addiction is worth $5.60 per day, or nearly $1,600 per year, to the company. For some companies, that is a meaningful savings.

DuPont Company and Waste Management, Inc. recently formed a joint venture to recycle plastic waste at a plant that opened in 1991. Americans discard 11 million tons of plastic trash each year. The joint venture pays 8 cents a pound for plastic bottles. A new savings area is around the corner.

Paper Usage

One of the largest savings in paper costs can be generated by photostating reports on the front and back of each piece of paper. At $15 per pound of photostat paper, by using both sides your company might save $1,000 per year or more.

Most fax messages are sent with a cover sheet that has your company's logo on it, the recipient's name and number, the date and time of the message, the sender's name and number and the total number of pages being faxed. This entire gaggle of information can be put on one-half of an 81/2- by 11-inch piece of paper. This represents a triple savings: 50 percent on cover sheets, 50 percent on storage space for used cover sheets (to be reconciled against the monthly telephone bills) and 50 percent on fax charges. Assuming that one full page costs 17 cents to send in the United States, and that your company sends 5,000 fax messages per year, each with its own cover sheet, by using half sheets, you can save $425 per year. Double that number for the value of the paper and storage savings.

Rental Expenses

The Ferret can cut office, plant and warehouse rental expenses by reviewing the company's real estate leases. You probably are paying for *rentable* space when you should be paying for *usable* space. The difference between the two is the *common area factor*. Common areas include tenants' pro rata share of the lobbies, corridors, restrooms, janitorial and electrical closets, vending and other areas that are shared by all tenants. If you are on an upper floor, your pro rata usage of the lobby is less than that of a first-floor tenant, so your firm should pay less for the common area.

Rentable area includes the entire finished interior of a building's floor, including common areas. Usable area is the entire interior square footage of office space available for the private use of the tenant. The Building Owners and Managers Association (BOMA) has established standards for measuring usable space. These standards state that usable space should be calculated by measuring from the inside surface of the dominant portion of the permanent outer building walls to the office side of the corridor or other permanent walls to the center of partitions that separate the office from other usable areas.

Landlords typically calculate a pro rata share of the common area for each tenant and add that amount of space to usable area to create a number for rentable area. Then they base the rent on the larger number. The landlord's loss factor, which should be called the "excess profit factor," arises from charging tenants for the janitor's closet, the air-conditioning equipment room and other common areas that tenants never use. You want to absorb as little of these costs as possible.

The second problem is that the measurement of the space your company is occupying for its office, plant or warehouse probably is inaccurate. The landlord more than likely took measurements from a blueprint or from the outer walls. Remeasure the space from the inner walls; carefully go around the buttresses with your tape measure; exclude the electrical and telephone boxes. Then compare your total square-footage number with the number in the lease. Your number probably is smaller.

Postage Costs

If your business uses direct mail as a common advertising medium, wasted postage costs can add up to several hundred thousand dollars per year. Here are some tips to save postage costs:

1. Use an electronic scale to avoid the need for adding extra postage "just to be safe."
2. Use a postage meter rather than stamps to limit your expense to the exact amount required.
3. Use "Forward," "Return Postage Guaranteed" and "Address Correction Requested" on all mail. This is a relatively inexpensive way to keep your mailing lists current.
4. Save unused postage stamps that were printed in error. They can be redeemed at 90 percent of their face value.
5. Use first-class presort when possible. For those mailings that qualify, savings can be as much as 25 percent. (More information on presort will appear later in this chapter.)
6. Third-class bulk rates can save more than 60 percent for mailings of 200 pieces or more. In addition, sorting by carrier routes eliminates three United States Postal Service handlings, allowing faster delivery.
7. Include promotional pieces in your regular mailings of invoices and statements. Most letters mailed at the one-ounce rate weigh much less, so take advantage of this.
8. Keep a variety of envelopes on hand and always use the smallest possible size. This will lower weight and avoid postage surcharges.
9. Use registered mail only when insurance is necessary. Certified mail is less expensive.
10. For promotional mailings, use a first-class postcard rather than a first-class letter. A 41/2- by 6-inch single-fold piece will double your message area and can even accommodate a business reply card.

Presorting Services. Major mailers, such as credit-card companies and mail-order houses, sort their mail by zip code before taking it to the post office. The postal service offers them a 25 percent discount, or 7 cents off of a 29-cent mailing. The 350,000-member American Postal Workers Union argues that its members could do the job just as well, and they would like to see 3 cents of the discount in their paychecks. An independent government commission that reviews postal rates says, however, that the presorting discount is a bargain.

FIGURE 4.6   Rate Comparison for Overnight Air-Freight Service

Weight (lbs.)	UniShippers	Federal Express	DHL Express	Emery Express
Letter	$ 8.50	$ 14.00	$ 14.00	$ 14.00
Pack	14.00	20.25	25.00	23.00
1	14.00	20.25	25.00	23.00
2	15.00	23.00	25.00	23.00
3	18.00	25.75	28.00	25.75
4	21.00	28.50	31.00	28.56
5	23.00	31.25	34.00	31.25
50	68.00	95.00	89.00	95.00
90	103.00	145.00	129.00	145.00

But what about companies that generate 500 pieces of mail per day or less? If that is your situation, you can call on one of 250 privately owned presorters located throughout the country. These innovative companies save your company most of the seven cents, which can add up to several thousand dollars per year, depending on volume.

Overnight Couriers.   The average cost to send a one-pound package overnight is $14.00. Federal Express charges $20.25 for the same package, but it guarantees delivery by 10:30 the following morning. The air-freight companies offer discounts of up to 40 percent to AT&T and other large corporations.

The Ferret can achieve the AT&T-size discount by using a repackager, UniShippers Association of Salt Lake City, Utah. Figure 4.6 is a comparison of UniShipper's rates with three of its competitors.

What does this mean to your company? Let's say your company ships 200 packages per year, or about one every other day, and that the average weight is two pounds. If you use one of the carriers mentioned previously, you will pay $4,600 per annum. But if you ship via UniShippers, you will pay $3,000, a savings of $1,600 per annum. The real savings occur with big packages.

Another way to reduce courier expenses is to ask the recipient for his or her courier credit-card number. There are circumstances in which the receiver needs the contents of the package more than you need to send them.

Be especially aware of lawyers, advertising agents and other company agents who add a surcharge above conventional courier rates. A public relations firm that one of my client companies used briefly added a 17.5 percent surcharge to communications costs. You should insist that these "handling charges" be rolled back. Then introduce your agent to UniShippers.

Telephone Costs

There are several means to reduce telephone costs. As you know, there are alternatives to using AT&T as your company's primary carrier. Your company can purchase lease interconnect telephone systems that offer a feature known as *least cost routing.* (AT&T will provide equipment that is competitive in most areas with those of interconnect or competitive telephone-equipment manufacturers.) This feature relies on a microchip that automatically selects the least costly carrier for a particular long-distance call — WATS, AT&T, ALC, MCI, Sprint or Telenet. If you are in the service business and your telephone calls are billed to a client or customer, you can select an interconnect system with *call accounting/cost accounting* that assigns each call to a specific telephone.

There are 125 repackagers of telephone services in the country. They buy hundreds of trunks of telephone lines at a reduced price each month from the major long-distance carriers, which the carriers sell for eleven cents per minute. The repackagers pay a price of five cents per minute and resell them for eight cents per minute. You can use a repackager and buy (or lease) interconnect systems that offer cost-saving features. Let your Ferret consult the yellow pages for repackagers in your area to slash the cost of long-distance calls.

Interconnect systems also offer the ability to block certain telephones from calling certain area codes. This restriction could block, for instance, the accounts receivable department that calls the West Coast from making calls to the other regions of the country to check in with Aunt Tillie and Uncle Mel. Codes toll restriction will slash another 5 percent off the monthly telephone bill.

Advertising versus Public Relations Costs

Your company does not have to advertise at its current level. Leads can be generated inexpensively, customer response can be measured using customers' money and sales can be achieved through word-of-mouth or testimonial selling. The important distinction to bear in mind is between finding potential customers — lead generation — and selling the prospects — marketing. Advertising generally is assigned to the former task. In certain instances, such as where a product's utility cannot be easily distinguished from the utility of its competitors, advertising has its role. If that situation occurs with some of the products or services of your company, you can supplement advertising with public relations or video news releases.

The function of marketing is to persuade the customer that your product is a substitute for all competitive products, but that none of the competitive products is a substitute for yours. It is foolhardy to think that an advertisement in a trade journal can put this message across, unless you have a one-in-a-million ad, such as Avis's brilliant "We Try Harder" campaign. Don't be afraid to slash your advertising budget to the bone during a workout. Among other things, it will lead you to consider less expensive, more creative ways to obtain orders.

Generating interesting articles about your product or service in national media is more effective and far less expensive than advertising. A magazine or newspaper article is read and passed around by many people, and the information is retained more than that in an advertisement. What will this kind of consumer research cost you? Perhaps a $1,000 retainer paid to the public relations agent, and postage and handling costs to mail your story to reporters.

Other Ferret Targets

Once the Ferret gets the hang of finding cash in the company's selling, general and administrative expenses, nothing will be sacred. Travel, business entertainment, sales commissions, utilities — all will be examined, lowered and, when possible, paid for over time. It is a challenging assignment, and one that the Ferret should work out of in 120 days. It then can be used by one of the other lieutenants to monitor the cash function through a well-organized management information system.

IMPROVE EMPLOYEE MORALE

You can see that the Ferret's assignment is an exciting one that produces daily victories — some in the tens of thousands of dollars. But other employees may not be having that much fun. The key to the turnaround is spreading the excitement of the chase to save the company. When all the employees become as involved as the Ferret, the workout and turnaround may cause one of the more humorous employees to say, "Hey, boss! That was fun. Let's get into trouble again."

Crisis as a Turning Point

The social psychologist Erik H. Erikson said that in charting development through crisis, a heightened vulnerability signals the emergence of a potential strength, creating a dangerous opportunity for growth, which Erikson calls "a turning point for better or worse."[6]

Another student of crises, Hans Selye, provides the following three basic rules for adapting to stress:

1. Find your own purpose in life, that fits your own personal stress level — separate leisure from work — "if work is what you have to do then leisure is what you want to do."

2. Control your emotional level by recognizing situations as being either life-threatening or nonlife-threatening — anger results from threatened values; due to low self-esteem.
3. Collect the goodwill and appreciation of others —persuade others to share your natural desires for your own well-being.

The third Selye dictum must be shared with the less directly involved employees. Share with them some of the company's wins, involve them in the turnaround mission and interject some humor into the turnaround process.

The proper response to crisis is threefold: (1) take the impact head-on, (2) recoil from it and (3) begin energizing solutions. When a company does not respond properly, solutions do not materialize and the company begins to disintegrate. Following are three steps necessary for responding to a crisis effectively: The first is an inner-directed move that will help you put the problem into perspective. The other two steps will help to involve your employees in the workout process, turning a crisis into a positive, team-building experience.

1. *Perception.* Further the correct perception by seeking new information and by keeping the problem in front of you.
2. *Nomination.* Manage the effects on personnel by giving names to the crisis provokers.
3. *Delegation.* Develop procedures for seeking and using help outside the company and assign tasks to these outside helpers.

Perception

Working your way through a crisis requires correct perception of the crisis-producing events. Sometimes, it is as simple as a production layout problem causing delays, downtime and defective products. Other times, it is a criminal indictment. Perception is based on what is known as *directed remembering.* You hear or see a particular fact, absorb it into your memory bank, relate it to other experiences and then say, "Aha!"

For example, if the crisis-provoking event is in the area of cash flow, apply directed remembering to everything you know about cash, banks, wire transfers, letters of credit, selling assets, speeding collections, discounting accounts receivable and the like. But that's not all. You must use visualization and imagination techniques. Relate your need for cash to a tank of water. How many ways can you get water (cash) into the tank in the shortest period of time? Do you need more nozzles? Hoses? More water carriers? Go to a thesaurus and look up words for *fill*. You will see the nouns *pudding*, *stuffing*, *filler* and *fullness*. And you will see the verbs *load*, *shoal*, *fill up* and *silt up*. One of these may provide you with a visual key to the correct perception of the crisis.

Sometimes perceiving is inexact. Like the artisans in Plato's cave, you are chained in place staring at shadows on the wall. You cannot see the shadow casters, but you must make judgments about them based on the shapes of their shadows. Once again, you rely on directed remembering. Much as the movie viewer recognizes that "the villains wear black hats," so the businessperson may interpret shadows on the wall to mean, "Our deficits are running too long to convince our bank to loan." Be careful not to interpret or second-guess others. Perceptions become distorted under pressure.

Nomination

Give names or assign symbols to the crisis-provoking events to make them memorable or important. For example, buy small statues of Greek wrestlers and put them on the desks of your controllers and salespeople. Label the first, "Florence (your controller) Battling Jim (the company's banker)." Label a salesman's figurine, "Bill Chokes an Order from Valued Customer."

Put an appropriate Peanuts cartoon on your production manager's bulletin board, perhaps showing Snoopy's gritty management of the little birds that interfere with his daily regimen. In doing this, you are discharging tension. This is a first step to mastering the problem.

For the person you assign to lay off 100 people in administration, label a stuffed rhinoceros "Mike the Merciless" and put it in his office. You are saying, "I know I stuck you with a tough job, and you are a softhearted guy who did it well."

Give nicknames to your enemies. Call your toughest bill collector the most ridiculous word you can think of, like "Al, the Anteater" or "Godzilla Gorilla," or better yet, have your accounts payable clerks choose terms of endearment, with the winning nomination receiving a 50-dollar prize. Sounds ridiculous? Believe me, humor is a superb morale booster, and you can make the crisis seem both real and manageable by using it pointedly.

Delegation

Michael Dingman, 58, chief executive officer of Henley Group, is known to his many fans on Wall Street as a "Class-A Schmoozer." Dingman knows how to work through his managers: He delegates everything and then strokes his managers by laying on the charisma. Their ability to get the job done is enhanced by what Felix G. Rohatyn of Lazard Freres & Company calls "schmoozing." This literally means sitting with people, talking to them, laying it on thick and charming the pants off them. It breeds loyalty, and if it is genuine friendliness, it works.

Do not delegate without staying in touch. Keep close tabs on and demonstrate your concern for the task you have delegated. You are dealing with many personalities. You may have a personality tailor-made for crisis, but your teammates may need reassurance.

When you delegate to people outside the organization, visit them frequently. If an outsider is assigned the task of selling your headquarters building and leasing it back, stay on top of him. Take him to dinner and review his progress. Go over the details again and again. Then schmooze him with your compliments. Convince him that his sale-leaseback is the heart of your survival strategy. Raise his self-esteem. Ask him to report on the progress of his mission every day. Give him your private telephone number or home number. Encourage his speed. Let him know that an entire company, perhaps a whole region, turns its anxious eyes to him. It will work.

Ethics

Following is a humorous event that occurred when I was advising a company in a workout situation a few years ago and I got into the picture a little late. The creditors were enraged, and many of the obligations had been turned over to lawyers. We needed all the creditors to back off for two months so that management could develop and implement an informal plan of reorganization. How do you buy two months?

We installed a new controller, who was in her seventh month of pregnancy. She introduced herself on the telephone and very appropriately said that the invoices would have to be pulled together so that within a week or so she would know the accounts pretty well. There were 400 individual obligations.

"By the way," she added, "I'm going to have a baby soon."

There is no credit manager, collection agent or commercial lawyer on earth who does not revere the miracle of giving birth.

"A baby? And you're doing this job?" they asked.

"Yes, my first."

"When is it due?"

"In two months."

The die was cast. The creditors realized they were not going to hassle this young mother-to-be. Many stopped calling. A handful hung in there and scratched away for nickels and dimes; but, for the most part, the company bought the two months it needed.

When the controller left to have the baby, another voice handled the calls. More questions were asked about the controller's condition than about payment dates. By the time the baby was born, the company was well on its way with a stretchout plan.

Do you invent a pregnant controller if you do not have one? Do you invent a recovery plan if you do not have one? What are the ethics of dealing with creditors?

The Golden Rule and the Ten Commandments provide the ethical baseline. If you are trying to convert suppliers and lenders to long-term partners, convince them to own your stock or convince them to take ten-year notes, there is no way to succeed unless your ethics are of the very highest order. A lie or misrepresentation will be transparent to your creditors. The only solution is to be perfectly honest. Never promise anything you cannot deliver. Stay with the truth; it is easier to remember.

On the other hand, just as you would not tell the referee in a hard-fought basketball game that you walked or fouled an opponent, so you would not reveal every nuance of your crisis to your creditors. As in any sport, you are playing to win, and you can play as hard as you like as long as you play fair.

The company must change the voices that talk to creditors in order to buy time. You have put several cash-generating plans into play, but they need time to light up the scoreboard. You have designed a stretchout plan, but you need time to sell it to creditors and their lawyers.

SUMMARY

Nothing succeeds like success. If the Ferret jumps right into his or her job and begins finding cash, then quite a few bullets are going to be paid and some trouble that could have mushroomed into expensive and perhaps disastrous litigation is going to be mitigated. The company might save a couple of credit cards, preserve several key-supplier relationships and keep its lights on. Some worried employees may start to feel a little more relaxed and recall their hastily prepared resumes. Coming to work will not seem like the drudge it once was. The crisis will begin to appear more like a turn-on than the certain death knell of the company.

Endnotes

1. Arthur Miller, *A Death in the Family* (New York: Viking, 1949), p. 133.
2. Isaiah Berlin, *Personal Impressions* (New York: Viking, 1981).
3. A. David Silver, *The Entrepreneurial Life* (New York: John Wiley & Sons, Inc., 1983).
4. A. David Silver, *The Business Bible of Survival* (Rocklin, Calif.: Prima Publications, Inc., 1989).
5. William Rehnquist, "Get RICO Cases out of My Courtroom," *The Wall Street Journal*, May 19, 1989, p. A-9. Reprinted by permission of *The Wall Street Journal*, ©1989 Dow Jones & Company, Inc. All Rights Reserved Worldwide.
6. Erik Erikson, *Insight and Responsibility* (New York: Norton, 1964), p. 139.

■ CHAPTER FIVE ■

The Workout Process

GEEKS BEARING GIFTS

The company in trouble always is accosted by a variety of strange people offering palliatives to ease its distress. But isn't this, after all, the law of the jungle? In the Mara in Kenya, you can watch the lion attack the wildebeest and satiate himself. Then the hyenas strip the meat off the bone, and when they are finished, the vultures arrive. Some companies bring these liniment salespeople on themselves by advertising in *The Wall Street Journal* and other widely used publications under the "Capital Needed" heading. Let's pull the sheets back on some of these so-called life rafts to see what's really behind the offers.

The Factor

Of all the assets on a company's balance sheet, accounts receivable are the most like cash. Within days or months, they will be collected for cash. There are two ways to borrow on accounts receivable: via a revolving line of credit or via factoring.

In a revolving-line-of-credit arrangement, the borrower makes a sale and faxes a copy of the invoice to its lender, who wires 70 to 85 percent of the amount of the invoice into the company's bank account. When the customer to whom the invoice is directed pays for the items, the lender receives the 70 to 85 percent, and the company receives the difference. As sales rise, advances under the revolving line of credit rise. As sales decline, advances decline. The line keeps revolving and never is repaid, unless the company stops sending its invoices to the lender. The interest rate on revolving lines of credit is charged only when the lender actually advances money and typically ranges between prime plus 2 percent and prime plus 5 percent.

When an accounts receivable line is set up, the borrower pays a one-time loan origination fee of 1 percent of the face amount of the maximum amount of credit established for it, and in some cases a $10,000 loan administration fee. As we have discussed, personal guarantees or other forms of side collateral may be requested.

In a distress situation, accounts receivable are the preferred collateral on the balance sheet because they generally are paid directly to the lender. This is known as *assignment*. It means that should the borrower be forced into Chapter 11, the cash the customers pay to the lender becomes the borrower's collateral as well, and no creditor can attach either the accounts receivable or the cash. Notice in the directories in the appendixes at the back of this book the large number of lenders that are willing to finance a troubled company, in or out of Chapter 11, if they can secure a lien on the accounts receivable.

Factoring accounts receivable works the same way as a revolving line of credit. The difference is primarily in the cost. Typically, a factor charges 1 percent per month for the maximum line of credit it establishes for the borrower, but then charges (fasten your seat belts) up to 3 percent per month for each account receivable that it "purchases." The toll can run in the 48-percent-per-month range if customers pay in 30 days or so. If they pay in 15 days, the 3 percent is reduced to 11/2 percent and the total cost of the money is 24 percent.

Who can afford these rates? Companies with gross profit margins in excess of 50 percent and operating expenses lower than 20 percent can survive an interest rate of 30 percent, particularly companies that have an accounts receivable collection staff to pull their customers' money into the house in less than 30 days. But if you can collect your accounts receivable in less than 30 days, why bother factoring? Factors and accounts receivable lenders will disallow accounts of more than 90 days' duration (and sometimes

60 days'); thus, the principal argument in favor of factoring is the initial injection of cash. The second-best argument is that in pledging its accounts receivable, the company puts itself in the Bobby McGee condition, which dissuades creditors from rushing to judgment and presages an informal reorganization.

I was called in to a distressed company that was factoring and paying 27 percent interest on accounts receivable that averaged $2 million per month. The factor's advance ratio was 70 percent — not a sign of confidence. Worse yet, the company's gross profit margin was 25 percent and its operating expenses were $3.5 million per annum. Look at what the cost of the factor's money was doing to the company's bottom line (see Figure 5.1).

The company was losing money on every sale. It would continue losing money at practically every level of sales because factoring charges are a variable rather than a fixed cost. Although I had not even begun the diagnostic stage of the workout, I knew my first task was to replace the factor with an accounts receivable lender and bring the cost of capital down into the teens. It took some doing, plus the pledge of inventory as backup collateral, but within three weeks I found an accounts receivable lender that was willing to advance prime plus 5 percent, or an interest rate of about 14 percent, which had two immediate effects:

1. An initial injection of $180,000 when the accounts receivable lender paid off the factor:

80% × $2,000,000	=	$1,600,000
Less: 70% × 2,000,000	=	1,400,000
Less: loan origination fee	=	20,000
Net to borrower		$ 180,000

2. The company was not losing money on every sale but operating at break-even.

The factor did not charge a breakup fee because the borrower had been a customer for more than 12 months. Most asset-based lenders, however, make it very expensive to divorce them within the first year of a relationship. It is not uncommon to see breakup fees equal to the number of months remaining under the borrowing contract multiplied by the percentage interest rate that the lender would have earned in those months.

FIGURE 5.1   Hypothetical Cost of Factoring

	Annual Operating Statement
Sales	$24,000,000
Cost of goods sold	18,000,000
Gross profit	6,000,000
Operating expenses	3,500,000
Net operating income	2,500,000
Interest expense (a)	4,500,000
Net profit (loss) before taxes	$(2,000,000)

(a) $24,000,000 × .70 = $16,800,000 × 27%
= $4,536,000.

Factors are *transaction lenders*. They are not seeking relationships. They do not visit the client and look for additional lending services or depository relationships. They expect to provide the borrower with emergency financing on a short-term basis until the company is bankable. Consequently, factors charge a high price for their money because they do not have multiple cash flow channels. To a borrower that needs cash coming in every day from its sales, factoring can be important life raft. On the other hand, it generally is too expensive to rely on for more than a few months.

Arab Lender Seeks Guarantor

The classified ads generally turn up this unusual source of financing, which never amounts to anything. A loan finder, which usually sports a high-toned name like "International Finance & Credit, Inc." and an impressive address in a major banking center, will offer to provide a distressed company seeking $2 million with four times that amount via a long-term loan at somewhere near the prime rate. The lender, you will be told by a spokesperson for International Finance & Credit, Inc., of Church Street, London, is an Arab sheik seeking to export capital to the safe climes of the United States. He has committed to make the loan subject to a guarantee by a well-known U.S. bank. That is the story you are supposed to swallow.

The scheme works like this (on paper): The U.S. guaranteeing bank receives the $8 million and loans $2 million to the borrower at 10 percent interest, with 9 percent paid to the Arab sheik and a 1 percent override paid to the Intergalactic Finance & Trust Ltd. The U.S. bank then slaps a 2 to 5 percent loan guarantee fee on the borrower for the full $8 million and puts the $6 million plus the annual fee of $300,000 into safe securities, such as governments, to make certain that it can return $8 million to the Arab sheik at the end of 15 years or at the end date of the loan.

Sounds like it should work, but there are a few hitches. I know because I pursued one of these offers to its source a few years ago. The loan is really from an unnamed source with a Swiss bank account, which could mean drug laundering or illegally earned money. Finding a bank willing to guarantee is not difficult today because so many commercial banks need an injection of capital but cannot risk being involved with Swiss bank accounts of unnamed origin.

But the deal breaker is frequently the loan application fee. The Cosmological Fiduciary Loan & Trust wants the borrower to pay $25,000 to $150,000 up front to obtain a signed loan agreement to enable the borrower to photostat a dozen times and send it to a dozen potential guarantors. Without the approved loan, the deal cannot march toward a closing. When asked for the application fee, the borrower should ask for names of other borrowers to contact for references on the bank. There will not be any.

Loan Insurance

The Arab sheik ploy begs the question: Is there loan-repayment insurance? The answer is, happily, yes. The distressed borrower generally can find an insurer of a term loan if the insurer can mitigate its risk by collateralizing its position with hard collateral. Surety bonds are the principal kind of loan-repayment insurance, and they cost anywhere from 2 to 5 percent per annum. The surety insures payment to the lender and takes a lien on an asset equal to at least 150 percent of the amount of its loan guarantee. Lloyd's of London, which prides itself on insuring virtually any risk, was a major player in this market for many years, but it has had its wings clipped by buying some bad risks recently.

For a list of some of the more aggressive surety companies, see Figure 5.2.

To obtain their addresses, check the telephone directories in major cities. Visit your local library to research the companies in *Best's Insurance Company Review.*[1] A. M. Best rates insurance companies according to their financial strength. Try to deal only with A-rated companies or better — Best's highest rating — because only those companies have the net worth to meet their obligations as they come due.

Vulture Capitalists

The distressed company may be contacted by a workout consultant who says he or she wants to help turn around the company for an hourly fee plus success bonus, but who then swallows the company in one quick gulp. This deceptive practice is not condoned by 98 percent of the workout consultants in the country and is not practiced by the legitimate vulture capital funds who announce their intentions up front as seeking a significant equity position in exchange for a meaningful investment. But it is that 2 percent that you have to watch out for.

The first thing the owner or manager should know about workout consultants is that they have different views of troubled companies. Some owners and managers have hired workout specialists without investigating how they work and have been bought or thrown out of their companies without a legal leg to stand on. Others have hired workout specialists on the recommendation of their senior secured lender, only to find their companies set up for an asset strip by the lender while the business is laid waste and the stockholders are left holding an empty bag. Beware the workout consultant who says he has come to aid you, but in reality is a cathartida, a turkey vulture that feasts on carrion.

FIGURE 5.2 Leading Surety Companies

Name	Total Annual Direct Premiums ($000s)
St. Paul Group	$312,437
Reliance Insurance Co.	306,138
Aetna Life & Casualty	227,836
United States F&G	188,752
Accredited Surety	121,267
Safeco	90,530
Fidelity & Deposit Group	89,877
American Country Insurance	87,128
First Indemnity of America	71,637
Westfield Companies	53,535

SOURCE: A. M. Best Company. Reprinted with permission.

It does not require a financial genius to come to the aid of a struggling company, make a deal with its distressed owner to trade a cash infusion for equity and then take control, kick out the owner and change the locks on the door. Some workout specialists are new to the game. Peter Uebberroth, who ran the profitable 1986 Olympic Games, bought Hawaiian Airlines via a leveraged buyout. When it got into serious trouble, Uebberroth formed a workout consulting firm to come to the aid of troubled companies.

Cathartida vulture capitalist transactions happen all the time, and they are sometimes based on financial sleight of hand. I will explain how it works through an example of a hypothetical company called Meathead, Inc., owned by Phil Putz and managed by him and his children. The firm's balance sheet is displayed in Figure 5.3.

The balance sheet of Meathead does not suggest a deeply troubled company, although it is heavily leveraged. The debt-to-worth ratio is approximately 19.0x. On the other hand, Meathead's current ratio is a positive 1.2x. To create a little tension in the atmosphere, assume that $700,000 of the company's $1.4 million of accrued expenses represents unpaid employees' withholding

FIGURE 5.3   Balance Sheet of Meathead, Inc.

Assets		Liabilities and Stockholders' Equity	
Cash	$ 200,000	Notes payable— bank	$2,000,000
Accounts receivable	5,000,000	Accounts payable	6,000,000
Inventory	6,800,000	Accrued expenses	1,400,000
		Current portion long-term debt	800,000
Total current assets	12,000,000	Total current liabilities	10,200,000
Plant and equipment —net	3,000,000	Long-term debt	5,000,000
Other assets	1,000,000	Total liabilities	15,200,000
		Stockholders' equity	$ 800,000
		Total liabilities and Stockholders' equity	
Total assets	$16,000,000	equity	$16,000,000

taxes. The Putz family elected to use the government's money a few months ago to pay some bullets, and it hasn't been able to put the toothpaste back into the tube thus far.

The precursor of Meathead's difficulty is a prolonged decline in sales. You see some indication of this because inventory exceeds accounts receivable on the balance sheet. Meathead is a manufacturer of industrial parts — that is, products that normally turn over six times a year and with average accounts receivable outstanding of 45 days, or 9x turns. You can see in Figures 5.3 and 5.4 that the accounts receivable are turning a little more slowly, about 6.6x or 55 days, the inventory has slowed to 4.3x or 85 days, which indicates that customers aren't ordering very fast or, even worse, that Meathead's product line is becoming obsolete.

The 12-month operating statement does not tell the whole story. The monthly cash flow statement is more prescient because it shows

FIGURE 5.4   Operating Statement of Meathead, Inc.

	Percentage	*12 Months*
Sales	100.0%	$45,000,000
Cost of goods sold	65.0	29,240,000
Gross profit	35.0	15,760,000
Operating expenses	30.7	13,800,000
Net operating income	4.3	1,960,000
Interest expenses	2.4	1,120,000
Net profit before taxes	1.9	840,000
Provision for taxes	.8	380,000
Net profit after taxes	1.1%	$ 560,000

how much cash comes in each month and how much goes out. For example, Meathead's monthly "nut," or fixed cost, is the sum of operating and interest expenses divided by 12 or, in this case, $16,880,000/12 or $1,400,000 per month. Add to this the cost of producing the goods shipped in a particular month — that is, labor and materials — which in the case of Meathead is a little more than $2.4 million per month. Thus, $3.8 million in cash is going out of Meathead each month, or *less* than the anticipated accounts receivable collections. Compounding the problem is that about $1 million of accounts payable are growing whiskers, several hundred thousand dollars of withholding taxes are in arrears and the wheels could come off the bus if only one of the following events happened:

1. A key supplier stops shipping until its account is paid in full, an immediate need for $1,000,000.
2. The bank calls the $2 million note payable.
3. A customer with a $700,000 account receivable owing the company goes out of business, leaving the debt uncollectible.
4. The IRS demands immediate payment of the withholding tax arrearage, perhaps $600,000.
5. A production jam creates a week's delay in shipments; and $800,000 worth of orders are canceled after they are produced.

Legal Vultures

Meathead may appear profitable, but in reality it is a heartbeat away from serious trouble, particularly if one of the triggering events pulls its monthly cash receipts below its $3.8 million monthly nut.

If Meathead's owners have personally guaranteed the loans, what typically follows is that one of the family members telephones the company's accountant or lawyer and asks for advice.

When Phil Putz calls his lawyer to say, "I have run into a serious cash crunch and I am beginning to lose credibility with some of my suppliers," Phil's lawyer probably will recommend a consultation with a bankruptcy specialist in the lawyer's firm or in another firm that has a reciprocity understanding with Phil's lawyer. It also is likely that Phil's lawyer and an associate in the firm will sit in with Phil and the bankruptcy lawyer to sell some hours. If Phil is persuaded to put Meathead into Chapter 11 based on the circumstances I have described, a great disservice has been done because Meathead is not a Chapter 11 candidate.

Bloodsuckers

Let's look at Meathead from another vantage point. This time we will perch on the shoulder of Cathartida Capital Corp., a $35-million venture capital fund, so its brochure reads, "that invests in distressed companies with the objective of turning them around via the implementation of skilled management, fresh capital and leverage, and selling them at a higher price." Assume that Cathartida hears of the Putz's distress through his accountants and asks to be sent current financial statements and a brief description of the operations.

A Cathartida partner telephones Phil and arranges an appointment to visit the company. The partner persuades Phil that Meathead's problem is a shortage of capital. With capital, the partner explains, Chapter 11 can be avoided (or Cathartida will fund the company's plan of reorganization if its lawyer has misguidedly filed for protection). Phil is delighted that the company's problems can be wiped away so quickly. He agrees to a due-diligence analysis by Cathartida, which is done quickly, and the Cathartida partners ask to meet with Phil and his family privately.

The next scene is so rapacious that it belongs in the National Enquirer under the heading: "Business Managers Eaten Alive by Pin-Striped Investors."

"Phil," the Cathartida partner says in his most solemn voice, the one used when paying condolence calls, "the problems at Meathead are larger than I thought."

"How large?" Phil asks.

"Phil, you could lose everything," the partner croaks inaudibly. "The whole company could be liquidated for the benefit of creditors and you and your family may not get a dime out of it. Not a dime," the vulture capitalist adds for effect.

The melodrama goes on with spreadsheets, due-diligence reports and financial mumbo jumbo that confuses Phil and his family until finally one of them asks what Cathartida can do to help. The trap is sprung. Cathartida will invest the necessary capital to save Meathead from certain death, but it must have voting control of the company's stock.

"Why do you need voting control to make an investment?" Phil asks astutely.

"Because you have damaged Meathead's relationship with certain vendors and possibly your bank and others. Cathartida must be prudent with its money; after all, we are fiduciaries of the money provided by our investors. We need to roll up our sleeves and follow our investment with some hard work to turn your company around," the partner argues.

Phil protests, but his family is less concerned with 49 percent ownership if the company, their meal ticket, can be saved. The meeting drags on until the wildebeest becomes exhausted and the lion goes for its throat.

Phil caves in and sells Treasury stock to Cathartida equal to 51 percent of its total issued and outstanding shares of voting common stock for $1 million. A couple of days later, Cathartida refinances Meathead's $1 million note payable with a $3 million revolving line of credit. It uses the $2 million net cash to pay withholding taxes and accounts payable, and swings its $1 million capital investment back out to itself via 12 monthly consulting fees of $83,333 each. Phil, who is still on the board, protests that the capital should have remained in the company, and arguments erupt at a series of board meetings. Eventually, Phil agrees to sell his family's remaining 49 percent interest for a distress price paid out over time. Or, as Phil will tell the story months later, to eliminate his distress.

The moral of the story is that greed lurks around the corner of every troubled company. Vulture capitalists posing as workout consultants prey on the distress of companies whose owners or managers perceive their difficulties as insurmountable. The principal factor that the worried manager overlooks is inertia: the tendency of an object in motion to remain in motion. Troubled companies have a community of allies that may go down if the company goes down. Vendors will lose a customer. Lenders will lose a borrower. Customers will lose a source of supply. The troubled company has more people who will stretch themselves to keep the company afloat than it has adversaries who will seek its liquidation.

But to many owners such as Phil Putz, the hassle factor is too much. They toss the keys over to a bankruptcy lawyer or a vulture capitalist and walk away with a few dollars and injured pride.

The Utility of Vulture Capital Funds

The function of capitalism is to weed out the losers from the winners in the marketplace. But this does not mean that all companies that are losing market share or that are in a liquidity crisis should die. The death of companies has more to do with the management than with the company's strengths or weaknesses.

Most vulture capital funds are staffed by men and women who have turned around some desperately troubled companies. They have developed unique skills in the boneyard of American industry. They invest in and purchase distressed companies with the agreement up front that new management will be installed with complete authority to commit the company. These vulture capital funds raise their capital from the same sources that have invested in venture capital and LBO funds since the early 1970s. Their investors — Yale University Endowment Fund, Rockefeller Foundation, General Motors Pension Fund and Warner-Lambert Pension Fund among others — have invested in one or more of the 30-plus vulture capital funds that have put together capital pools in the past two years. They are seeking annual returns of 30 percent, which is a typical venture capital return, according to Ann Johnson, president of Tremont Partners, Inc., of New Canaan, Connecticut, which organized a pool of capital to be managed by several vulture capital funds. Unlike venture capital and LBO funds, however, vulture funds occasionally must maneuver their portfolio companies through the rocky shoals of bankruptcy, which can stretch the actual return of capital to the funds' investors and reduce the annualized rate of return.

At least 30 vulture capital funds have raised $1.5 billion in the past two and one-half years, with another $1 billion in capital sought after by a like number of vulture fund managers. *Buyouts*, a Needham, Massachusetts, newsletter, keeps score on the nascent industry's new formations and investments.

The funds come in two breeds: control buyers and small-chunks buyers. The former take over control of troubled companies and install their own handpicked management. The latter take small bites of many troubled companies, usually publicly held, and sometimes assume board or creditor committee seats, but do not operate the companies. They prefer to bet on the skills of the workout specialist hired by the board.

Institutional investors such as the University of Michigan Endowment Fund spread the risk and invest in several vulture capital funds with different operating styles.

TAKE A LOOK AT YOUR CONDITION

The workout is an intellectual process performed under fire. All the difficult moments in your life have trained you for this particularly stressful point in time. It is a multiple-choice test in which you get the right answers by eliminating the wrong ones and then carrying out the instructions of the right answer. To succeed in the workout, you have to do the right thing, rather than do that thing right. We reviewed some of the wrong things in the opening section of this chapter. We looked at several palliatives and placebos. Now let's consider some of the right things to do.

STATE YOUR OBJECTIVES

Is your objective to preserve the company as it presently exists, doing what it has been doing but in a liquid condition and without crushing debt? Three things will determine whether or not your company can be restored to its historic business plan:

1. The company's economic viability or demonstrable economic justification
2. The company's access to capital
3. The degree of damage done to the company by creditors, the press and internal dissension

A viability assessment should be performed during the early stages of the workout to determine what business the company is going to be in when it solves its current dilemma. The test must be objective, however, and must avoid the bias of trying to remain in the existing business. Why fight the inevitable, particularly when the alternatives may be healthier? Several companies that we proudly hail today as shining examples of corporate achievement went through workouts as brunets and were rehabilitated as blonds. Penn Central, Itel, J.I. Case, General Motors and General Electric come to mind. If you fight to save the existing business, you could end up holding a corpse. The key is *product obsolescence.*

PRODUCT OBSOLESCENCE

There are numerous examples of companies being broken on the rack by product obsolescence, but the one most thoroughly exposed in published documents is Itel Corporation.[2] A less well-known and altogether happier story is that of Moldex/Metric. Each company faced a crisis caused by product obsolescence. One survived.

Itel Corporation

Itel was founded in 1967, and its primary business was purchasing IBM 360 computers and leasing them to others under two- to five-year operating leases, which were cancelable on 12 months' notice. Initial financing included a $10-million investment by Fireman's Fund Insurance Company (later acquired by American Express), a bank credit line of $105 million made available through Bank of America and an initial public offering of Itel's common stock in October 1968. In 1969, the company earned $3 million on revenues of $40 million, which grew in ten years to adjusted earnings of $48.4 million on revenues of $688.7 million. There were "infirmities in the structure of Itel, its business, management and professional support, which led to its collapse."[3] On January 19, 1981, Itel filed for protection under Chapter 11 of the Bankruptcy Act, resulting in hundreds of millions of dollars in losses to its public stockholders. The *Examiner's Report* cites several reasons for the fall of Itel, but its failure was precipitated by IBM's introduction of new computers in 1977 and by the simultaneous cancellation of lease insurance by Lloyd's of London. Itel's senior management had wisely diversified into marketing computers through its Data Products Group, which had achieved revenues of $170 million by 1977. But when Itel senior management turned to that division for cash flow, it came up empty. What happened?

The Data Products Group's inventory records in 1978 were "in shambles."[4] The records did not reflect the group's inventory, its location or its condition. The company's internal auditor believed Data Products Group's inventory was grossly overstated, and he recommended a reserve of $8 million to $13 million. Even though Itel was a publicly held corporation, managers of the Data Products Group reported the overstated inventory to senior management, which made erroneous filings with the Securities and Exchange Commission (SEC). Moreover, the group's basic management information system, which was supposed to control billings and receivables, was inefficient. Although overblown financial statements were given willy-nilly to stockholders, lenders and investors, Data Products Group management knew that their numbers were inadequate and that the division would crash the following year.

While the crisis was swept under the rug, Itel maintained its lavish life-style. "Persian rugs on the floors and Perrier water in the office refrigerators greeted visitors to Itel's San Francisco headquarters at One Embarcadero Center. Executives, successful salespeople and deal prospects were ferried about the country in a company jet airplane. The successful Itel performers, in addition to high compensation, were invited to the annual meetings of the 'Itel Club' and entertained and motivated during a shipboard cruise or a week's stay at a first-class resort."[5]

A more appropriate response to Itel's losing its computer-leasing business and relying on its Data Products Group would have been a recognition of the bloated inventory records, a downsizing and refocusing of the business, a termination of the "no problem" guys who ran the division and a public recanting of the errors in Data Products Group's financial reporting. Apple Computer Corporation and others have survived product-obsolescence problems via changes in both management and operating methods. But that is not what occurred at Itel.

According to the *Examiner's Report*, incompetence at Itel was only one facet of management's character; there was another, more serious flaw. Members of Itel's management team "were aware near the end of 1978 that Itel's computer-leasing business was in serious difficulty and that Itel's computer-sales business was slowing and was threatened by new IBM technology."[6] With this knowledge, Itel's senior management — Peter S. Redfield, John H. Clark and Joe D. Foster — sold thousands of shares of Itel stock to the public at prices ranging from $26 to $32.50 per share (the stock later fell to less than $1 per share). The *Examiner's Report* stated that such sales probably violated Section 10(b)5 of the Securities Exchange Act and could result in fines and imprisonment. Itel's management has gone unpunished.

After filing for bankruptcy protection and settling with creditors, Itel (under more enlightened management) has rebounded, becoming a highly successful and diversified company. Its crash, as explicated in the *Examiner's Report*, is a classic example of corporate murder by a management unprepared to address its problems head-on and thus unprepared to protect its shareholders.

Moldex/Metric

In contrast, Herbert Magdison, president of Moldex/Metric, addressed his company's product obsolescence with readiness and intelligence, and he came out of it with his integrity intact. Moldex/Metric grew to sales of $60 million over 20 years of manufacturing molded bra cups for such swim-wear makers as Jantzen and for such foundation-garment makers as International Playtex. But fashions — and fortunes — change. By the late 1970s, big busts were out, and foundation-wear companies began making bra cups in-house.

Magdison recognized that he desperately needed a new product. Through problem formulation and opportunity analysis, he found it: disposable face masks for industrial workers. Against bracing competition from 3M Corporation, which dominates the $75-million mask market, Moldex went after the higher end of the market — a 75-cent mask versus 3M's 65-cent model — and offered greater durability and comfort. The Moldex mask features a plastic mesh that holds the mask's shape, a cross between the old bra cup and a fighter pilot's mask.

By 1987, Moldex/Metric had captured 10 percent of the disposable face mask market, and with a related safety product (foam earplugs), its sales grew to $265 million. Magdison, who was 29 when the hammer fell, met the enemy of obsolescence head-on, with the happy result that Moldex/Metric is four times larger and more profitable than it was before the cup crisis.[7]

Thus, two companies in the same state were drawn onto the battlefield at the same time by that devilish enemy, product obsolescence. One management team denied the problem, presented false financial statements to the public to support its stock price (which is more than mere denial) and then dumped shares on an unsuspecting public by using insider information. The other management team was forthright, identified its crisis as potentially devastating and found new products for its technological capability as well as a market segment that it could conquer.

The apparel industry, centered on Seventh Avenue in New York, has witnessed thousands of business failures because of product obsolescence. If a garment manufacturer believes short hemlines will come back when, in fact, customers prefer a midcalf look, there is no way to get rid of 12,000 miniskirts. The gallows humor of Seventh Avenue suggests that it is never too late to implement a plan to avoid the crisis of product obsolescence, that there always is time enough to think up a solution. If you plan ahead cautiously, however, you will survive to see the results of your labor.

THE COMPANY'S ACCESS TO CAPITAL

While the Beaver is developing a viability analysis, let's check in with the Ferret to analyze the company's options for raising cash and accessing the capital markets. If the Ferret has succeeded in generating a meaningful amount of cash, what do you do with it? If the company is not viable in its present business, the free cash generated by the Ferret can be used for bullets and then saved to implement the redirect and grow plan. But if it is decided to remain in the same business, the free cash can be applied to bullets and accounts payable. In either event, the creditors will have to be notified at the end of the standstill period, or in about 60 days, as to the direction the company is taking and how the company intends to pay them. The announcement to the creditors is made via a formal letter and promissory note, as shown in Appendixes I and II of this book.

Each Monday morning during the workout process, the crisis manager should meet with the Ferret, the Lion, the Bulldog and the Beaver to review the workout status. The Lion provides the bullet list first.

The bullets that must be paid this week are the following:

1. Monthly installment to the IRS on back withholding taxes $ 8,500.00
2. Quarterly payment of withholding taxes to the IRS   21,023.67
3. Quarterly payment of withholding taxes to the state   4,560.24

4.	Stipulated judgment on a monthly workout of overdue credit-card payables	1,500.00
5.	Utilities: telephone, electricity, gas and water bills are due this week with shutoff notices on Thursday. We need cashier's checks.	3,876.25
6.	Payroll is due on Friday, but if we pay at the end of the day, we can cover the checks by next Monday by 10:00 A.M.	24,000.00
7.	A bullet reserve for payouts that I am negotiating this week. If I can stretch about $75,000 in accounts payable, I'll need to pay 10 percent this week or next. But let's say this week to be safe.	7,500.00
	Total bullet list this week:	$70,960.16

The Lion's weekly bullet list is higher than usual because it is a payroll week and a quarterly withholding-tax payment week. Typically, the weekly bullet list is in the $40,000 to $50,000 range. But the seriousness of this week's needs does not escape the crisis management team. They will have to put in 16-hour days to survive the week. Each list, by the way, should be typed and distributed to members of the crisis management team at the beginning of the weekly meeting.

The Ferret reports next:

We begin the week with approximately $17,000 tucked away in our "war-chest" bank account. We generated that by asking the landlord for three months' free rent during the standstill period. So, one month's rent of $5,000 went into the war chest. The rest came from selling the delivery vans and leasing them back.

Here are my places to generate cash this week:
- *Accounts receivable.* We have $88,500 tied up in over-90-day receivables from three customers. Each cus-

tomer is important to us if we remain in business, but each one is having its own cash flow problems. If we plan to leave our business, we can sell the receivables to a collection firm for 30 cents on the dollar and raise just under $30,000. If we plan to stay in our business, we can offer six-month installments to these three customers and raise one-sixth of the amount this week, or about $14,000.

- *Inventory.* We have about $65,000 in obsolete inventory. I have spoken with several firms that buy old goods and sell them in catalogs and at auctions to customers we would likely never call on. The best offer is 15 cents on the dollar. We could raise $9,750 this week.
- *Equipment.* When we laid off half of the personnel in the administration department during the past two weeks, we freed up six personal computers, twelve desks and chairs, four file cabinets, five calculators, one fax machine and a water cooler. A used-equipment firm has offered $9,000 for the lot. We could sell them ourselves with classified ads and at flea markets, but that might take time. I recommend that we take the $9,000.
- *Operations.* The Bulldog may have another number to report, but cash flow from operations this week, before bullets, should bring in $20,000 give or take. Let's assume $15,000 to be safe.
- *Subtotal.* To this point, we're looking at $52,750, or call it $50,000 to be safe. So, we're $20,000 short of our need.

The crisis manager then will review other cash-raising strategies with the Ferret to try to find the critical $20,000 piece. Without it, the company might not live another week. Here are the questions he or she might ask the Ferret:

1. We have freed up about 2,000 square feet of office space. The design and engineering firm on the floor above us needs more space. Have you considered rent-

ing them the 2,000 square feet? If not them, try some of the other tenants. If you can get $1,500 per month with two months prepaid, I would say go for it. Be sure to tell them they will need to provide for desks and chairs, but we have telephones and two free lines that we can dedicate to them. If they need to use our conference room, see if you can rent the space for $1,750 per month, with a first and last month deposit plus a security deposit.

2. You can have the company car that I have been driving to sell. I checked with a dealer in town, and the bluebook on it is $9,800. See what you can do. I'll use one of the family cars.

3. Can you get some advertising money refunded? We bought 12 insertions in the trade journals, but we don't need the remaining nine. That could bring in more than $15,000 if you can get the money back. Take $10,000 in a heartbeat.

4. What about scrap paper? Have you looked into selling our junk mail and unusable computer print-outs? It should bring in $1,000 per month. It may not stop a bullet, but it is good to see every employee saving incoming junk mail, paper clips, spring clips, used paper and soda cans for resale.

5. Last, but not least, how have you done on renting out our customer list and our noncustomer list? We have about 1,500 in one and 11,000 in the other. If we could get seven cents a name from ten renters, that would bring in about $8,750. Again, not a bullet stopper, but once we have survived this week, it is something to think about for next week.

6. My subtotal from the car, subtenant and advertising rebate comes to $9,800, plus $3,000 to $4,000 for the sublet, plus $10,000 from the magazines, or $23,300. If you can do half of that this week and the other half by the first part of next week, we probably can live through the week and have a much smaller hill to climb next week.

The crisis management team does not mention the $17,000 war chest. It is sacred, to be used only when a creditor has burst through the walls. But the war chest must be added to, because the company owes more than $400,000 to creditors and suppliers, and $17,000 won't begin to make a dent in that total. The Bulldog may have some ideas on restocking the cash trough:

- *Suppliers*. Of course, we're on COD with 90 percent of our vendors, and matching receivables with payables reasonably well. The accounts receivable lender wires money in on receipt of fax copies of our orders, and we notify our vendors to ship or not based on what is wired into our account. We try to keep a positive balance of about $10,000. The standstill agreement has helped, but we are one month into it and I have a list of vendors who need reassurance telephone calls from you that we are working on a plan to get them paid.
- *Sales*. We owe three months of commission checks to our sales force, and although the salespeople are unrelenting in their efforts, if we can cut into that obligation next week, by paying at least one month's back commissions, I think it would pay off. The total would be around $5,000, but it might bring in $30,000. Our sales are above break-even by $24,000 this month, so you can count on us for that contribution to bullets and the war chest. Two large sales of $12,500 and $15,000 each could pop next week, each of which could vault us to $20,000 above the $24,000. If you could make the closing sales calls with the sales personnel, I believe we could pick up the orders.
- *Employees*. We lost a couple of good people who have filed unemployment claims. I can protest the claims because we have been late on a few payrolls and pleading poverty. Otherwise, employee morale is fairly good. If we make these two large sales, I would recommend giving 50-dollar bills to the people who have been coming in on Saturdays — about 40 people, or $2,000.

- *Summary.* I can't help with bullets this week, but I can produce, with your help, about $20,000 to $25,000 next week.

The weekly meeting concludes with a summary by the crisis manager of who will do what and the reporting mechanism. The team agrees to meet on Wednesday to see how the bullet payments are being handled and to redirect the plan if something has gone awry.

DAMAGE CONTROL

The crisis management team is working well together in its fifth week. The teammates know their jobs and they are carrying them out efficiently. But the plans could go amiss if the company becomes severely damaged by negative publicity, a writ of attachment or a blistering lawsuit that charges it with heinous crimes. Caution is the watchword. Only the crisis manager can speak to the press or make public statements. And those are made with Sun Tzu's warning:

A skilled general must be master of the complementary arts of simulation and dissimulation; while creating shapes to confuse and delude the enemy, he conceals his true dispositions and ultimate intent. When capable, he feigns incapacity; when near, he makes it appear that he is far away; when far away, that he is near.[8]

COURAGE

The crisis manager must remind his or her teammates that what they are achieving at this stage of the workout process is only a beginning. If the company survives the workout, it still will have to raise capital to finance its turnaround. The rehabilitation process may be even more difficult than the fight to save the company. It looks like only $20,000 to $30,000 per month in free cash is being generated; and with 60 days until the standstill period is up, the company will have to find at least $200,000 *plus* a plan to pay the $400,000 in debt.

After all, if an informal reorganization does not get the creditors paid in full, or three-quarters paid, they are likely to opt for Chapter 11 or, perish the thought, Chapter 7.

Your war buddies will need moral courage. If your survival plan calls for an informal reorganization followed by a redirect and grow plan, as does the example in chapter ten of this book, then your company will lack the sueproof safety net afforded by Chapter 11. As a result, you and your company are going to get sued quite a bit because your survival plan is unconventional — you want to preserve your creditors' and investors' values, rather than trash them by filing for bankruptcy protection.

Your largest creditors, who can afford the biggest law firms, will sue you for everything they can think of that you might have done. If your company has been unable to pay for a shipment of raw materials, your supplier's lawyer may claim fraudulent inducement, hoping that if your company is forced into bankruptcy, it can make the fraud charge stand and receive the full amount of the shipment plus interest and legal fees. Fraud claims are not dischargeable in bankruptcy.

Regrettably, lawsuits are public documents, and the local newspaper may have a stringer who sits in the courthouse copying the juicier lawsuits for publication the next morning. It takes courage to face the news of your company's lawsuits in the local newspapers or, worse yet, to see the story reprinted in the trade journals. It is primarily when your opponent is a creditor's lawyer that you will need to train your troops in back-to-the-wall street-fight tactics.

The mention of courage brings to mind the shipping entrepreneurs of earlier years. It must have taken enormous courage to invest one's life savings in a cargo that had a good chance of sinking to the bottom of the sea or of being seized by pirates. Because the early merchants had that kind of courage, they became wealthy while providing the goods that other people needed.

Cecilia Danieli of Italy provides a more contemporary example of that kind of courage. When she assumed control of the Danieli Company in 1980, the construction firm was in serious financial trouble. It had suffered losses of 1.7 billion lire ($1 million), and profit margins were getting thinner and thinner on large construction jobs. She took three bold steps that not only saved the company, but turned it into an enterprise that did $200 million in sales in 1985.

Her first step was to rewrite the company's business plan, a move that meant rethinking the very basis on which the Danieli Company was built. Once that was done, she began bidding on mid-size projects only. She also put her company's energy into turnkey projects in which it became responsible for designing, managing and commissioning entire factories. The third step in her strategy was to move boldly beyond Italy, seeking jobs in other European countries and even in the Soviet Union and the Eastern Bloc nations. To obtain the quantity of revenue she was seeking, Danieli made the sales trips herself. The results included contracts to build a rolling mill in Sweden and to build a 750,000-ton-a-year steel mill and a bundling plant in the USSR.

Because she had the courage to make moves that no one else had dared to try, Danieli built her company into a world-class operation that now locks horns with Mitsubishi, Hitachi, NKK and Krupp, and that also requires the courage of a lion.

The wellsprings of courage seem to generate a kind of vision that allows people to look at an insurmountable problem and see directly through it to the only right solution. At age 16, in the depths of the Great Depression, Jeno Paulucci, who was to found Chun King Corporation, worked in a grocery store in Duluth, Minnesota. One warm day, the store's refrigerator broke down, causing 18 crates of bananas to develop brown-speckled skin. The bananas were otherwise undamaged, but because of their unusual appearance, the store owner told his young employee to take them outside and sell them at bargain prices. Jeno was a man of courage and vision, even at that young age. He took the fruit outside, made a sign saying "Argentine Bananas" and began shouting about the shipment of exotic fruit. Within three hours, he sold all 18 crates at a price four cents per pound higher than that of ordinary bananas.

In selecting your workout teammates, look for people who understand that winning is merely getting up one time more than you have been knocked down.

SUMMARY

On the road through workout and turnaround, you are going to meet some amazing characters. Some will say they can help you but intend to take your company from you. Some will say they can help you but intend to take your money and leave your company in a more desperate condition than it was in when you met them. Still others can help you only if you step aside.

In *The Divine Comedy*, the poet Dante finds himself wandering astray in a dark wood. After a night of anguish, he sets out toward a hill illuminated by the sun, but three wild beasts — a leopard, a lion and a wolf: symbols of lust, pride and avarice — bar his path and force him back toward the darkness of the wood. Virgil, sent by the Virgin Mary, St. Lucy and Beatrice, appears and helps Dante out of Purgatory and to the supreme vision of the divinity.

A successful turnaround is a divine experience, but it is difficult to achieve. There are innate problems in effecting turnarounds because most managers are not trained in crisis management. And there are leopards, lions and wolves in the path of the turnaround manager that keep the company tied down on fruitless searches. Beware of the simple solution. Beware of anyone who says you are in worse trouble than you think. And, above all, beware of geeks bearing gifts.

Endnotes

1. A. M. Best Company, Park Avenue, Morristown, NJ 07960.
2. *Examiner's Report: Itel Corporation*, United States Bankruptcy Court, Northern District of California, March 1991.
3. *Ibid.*
4. *Ibid.*
5. *Ibid.*
6. *Ibid.*
7. Lisa Kirk, "When You Lose Your Market," *Forbes*, April 20, 1987, p. 105.
8. Sun Tzu, *The Art of War* (circa 500 B.C.), translated by Samuel Griffith (New York: Oxford University Press, 1963), p. 41.

CHAPTER SIX

The Rules of the Road in Chapter 11

"All bankrupts, of whatsoever denomination, ought to be hanged," wrote Charles Lamb, a nineteenth-century man of letters and noble upbringing. We have come a long way in two centuries. Today, bankrupts are forgiven the error of their ways and creditors do a lot of hanging out for some of their money.

FORMAL VERSUS INFORMAL REORGANIZATION

Chapter 11 is an option. It is not the preferred structure in which to rehabilitate the company, but a backup. Your creditors, if they are knowledgeable, will prefer an informal reorganization to a Chapter 11 because they will get paid more in an informal reorganization than in a formal one. If your company is in the Bobby McGee condition, a Chapter 11 will benefit the secured creditors handsomely but might leave the unsecured creditors with less than ten cents on the dollar. You want to avoid Chapter 11 because it is longer and more expensive and because it could tumble your company into Chapter 7 if a plan of reorganization cannot be agreed to by a majority of the creditors.

That which your company can accomplish in an informal reorganization it can accomplish in a formal reorganization. But a formal reorganization is more expensive, takes much longer and is done in a courtroom under guidelines set forth by the Bankruptcy Act of 1978 and enforced by 286 bankruptcy judges throughout the land. As you know, a Chapter 11 filing generally is required or chosen (1) if you do not know how to rehabilitate the company outside of Chapter 11, (2) if the first person you call for advice is a lawyer, (3) if your credibility is completely shot with creditors and they join hands to force you into Chapter 7 or (4) if you are unable to persuade the creditors to accept the plan of reorganization and you see no option other than letting a bankruptcy judge force the creditors to accept it or a version of it.

Because you may end up in Chapter 11, even with the best of intentions and the most highly skilled crisis management team at your command, you must understand some of the fundamentals of the act.

LEGAL FEES — THE LAW OF SUPPLY AND DEMAND

One reason that there are approximately 20,000 annual corporate Chapter 11 filings in America is that there are very few skilled crisis managers to catch the falling objects, fix them, wind them up and send them back into the stratosphere. On the other hand, there are more than 700,000 lawyers. Not all of them are trained in bankruptcy law, but they each know of one who is, while few of them know or choose to recommend a workout consultant. Thus, it is high cotton time for bankruptcy lawyers.

Until the early 1980s, the major U.S. law firms were content to leave bankruptcy law to smaller firms that specialized in the area. But they have changed their minds. Fees from bankruptcy work are enough to turn the heads of lawyers who used to regard members of the bankruptcy bar as holding the dirty end of the stick. You can expect to pay a major city debtor-advocate bankruptcy lawyer $300 to $450 per hour and his or her associates $150 to $200 per hour.

The leading debtor-advocate bankruptcy law firms in the country as voted on by the nation's workout consultants are listed in Figure 6.1.

It isn't just the fat fees that are attracting lawyers to bankruptcy work. Bankruptcy court is a remarkable arena in which to troll for

FIGURE 6.1   The Country's Best Debtor-Advocate Bankruptcy
Law Firms

	Firm Name	Home Office
1.	Weil Gotschal & Manges	New York
2.	Stroock & Stroock & Lavan	New York
3.	Stutman Triester & Glatt	Los Angeles
4.	Winston & Strawn	Chicago
5.	Latham & Watkins	New York
6.	Murphy Weir & Butler	Los Angeles
7.	Levin Weintraub Crames & Edelman*	New York
8.	Jones Day Reavis & Pogue	Cleveland
9.	Skadden Arps Meagher Slate & Flomm	New York
10.	Steinfield Maley & Kay	Houston

*Recently merged with Kaye, Scholer, Herman, Hays & Handler, a
firm 25 times its size.

SOURCE: A. David Silver, *The Bankruptcy, Workout and Turnaround Market Directory and Sourcebook* (New York: HarperCollins, 1991), p. 15.

new clients. At a typical hearing in bankruptcy court, there may be 50 creditors present, including banks and vendors. A bankruptcy lawyer can display his or her skills in front of a very receptive audience.

Rare is the debtor-advocate bankruptcy lawyer who doesn't do creditor-advocate work as well. That isn't at all bad for debtors because their lawyers bring fresh news and views from the opposing perspective.

The key is to interview several debtor-advocate bankruptcy lawyers to see how they regard your company's chances to emerge with a confirmed plan of reorganization. If you hire one, make sure it is the one most highly regarded and respected by creditors. You will need to pay an up-front retainer of at least 3 to 5 percent of the amount of your company's debt before the firm will represent you.

THE RULES OF THE ROAD IN CHAPTER 11

As Yogi Berra told reporters who asked him what it was like to understudy the legendary catcher Bill Dickey, "He learned me all his experiences." In this section, I am going to give you guidelines to follow if your company files for protection under Chapter 11. I don't talk much about the rules of Chapter 7 in this book because, as you know, that is a liquidation scenario in which a trustee is appointed to sell the company's assets. The trustee acts unemotionally and with dispatch because he or she earns a fee of 3 percent of the amount of money collected from the sale of the assets. There is not much in the way of process to say about Chapter 7.

Restriction on Payments

If its assets are collateralized in Chapter 11, the debtor company is not permitted to pay for services unless it obtains court approval. The debtor's counsel asks for a retainer up front because he or she may not see another payment until the end of the case, when his or her bill is tossed into the priority payment basket called "administrative costs of the estate." These costs include, in addition to legal fees, income tax obligations incurred after the filing.

A company faced with the prospect of a Chapter 11 filing should stop paying nonbullet creditors and start stockpiling cash. The bank that has a lien on the company's accounts receivable might argue that the cash belongs to the bank. If it wins the argument, cash must be found elsewhere in addition to accounts receivable and stowed away because the company will need cash (plus a redirect and grow plan) to come out of Chapter 11.

Payments before Filing and After

Payments made to creditors within three months prior to filing can be reversed by the court. Payments made to managers or significant stockholders, such as a large management fee, within 12 months prior to filing can be reversed by the court. The latter is a good law because it prevents self-dealing in a manner that injures creditors, but the former can harm the company in Chapter 11. The creditor might demand that the reversed payment be made good before it will pick up the company's garbage or service its computers.

If the company pays a prepetition debt to one or two creditors, but not all, it commits a criminal act. Therefore, all of the small but important bills should be paid in full before filing; all credit cards should be paid down to zero because, after filing, the prefiling bills cannot be paid and charge privileges will be shut down.

Due Process

The U.S. Constitution provides that no person shall be deprived of life, liberty or property without due process of law. Unfortunately, the judicial process in this country is extremely backed up, and these delays can work to the detriment of the debtor company. Assume that the debtor company has been injured by another company. It sues the other company, but the damage is so great and the case is so long in coming to trial that the company must file for protection to avoid further damage. Then, once in Chapter 11, confirmation of the plan of reorganization depends on the previous case and it drags further, until the company's creditors give up and file for Chapter 7.

Personal Attacks on the CEO

The CEO is the lightning rod who takes most of the shots from creditors and the press for the company's problems. Many CEOs have to change their home telephone numbers to avoid nasty calls from angry creditors and insidious people unrelated to the case.

The smaller the community, the greater are the personal attacks because the filing can cause disruption and unemployment throughout the community. Even hairdressers and service station owners are affected, and sometimes these people are not afraid to tell the beleaguered CEO what they think.

Raising New Capital in Chapter 11

A bankruptcy filing does not dim the debtor company's prospects for raising new capital. Asset-based lenders, in fact, frequently prefer lending to a Chapter 11 company than to a company in an informal reorganization because it cannot be surprised by a blitzkrieg from an angry creditor. In a Chapter 11 filing, the creditors are backed off in a court-mandated standstill. Thus, new lenders make loans secured by postpetition receivables and inventory, which then finances the plan of reorganization. Equity investors are not dissuaded from investing fresh capital in a Chapter 11 company. They typically rely on the strength of management and, in most instances, they will not back the management team that caused the company to become insolvent.

Debtor-in-Possession

Yes, you can manage your company in Chapter 11, which is known as debtor-in-possession, unless the creditors become so angered that they file a motion with the court to have a trustee appointed. This happened to Frank Lorenzo in the Eastern Airlines Chapter 11 proceeding.

Creditors may become angered if the management of the debtor is dilatory in filing a plan of reorganization, or if the plan calls for significantly smaller payments than the creditors expected to receive.

Unpaid Payroll Taxes

If your company files for protection owing federal withholding taxes — and cash-deprived companies frequently fail to pay these taxes — there is no compromising with the Internal Revenue Service. The full amount is owed when you emerge from Chapter 11; the IRS, however, allows six years to repay the debt.

You are liable for these unpaid taxes if your name is on the signature card for the payroll account and if you were in direct control of that account. Thus, a CEO who does not sign the payroll checks and who does not directly control those people who do probably is not liable for unpaid federal and state withholding taxes.

The worst scenario is when a company goes into Chapter 7 (liquidation of assets rather than reorganization) unable to pay its obligation to the IRS, and the IRS comes after the CEO, the chief financial officer and members of the board of directors. In this instance, there is bad news and good news. The bad news is that the IRS will garnishee 10 percent of your salary for the rest of your life, or until the obligation is paid in full. The good news is that you can have only one garnishment at a time. So if you see this event coming, remember that the IRS will have to wait in line if another garnishment is filed ahead of it.

For example, you are in Chapter 11, your business heads south and you are unable to pay postpetition payroll taxes, in addition to prepetition taxes. How do these get paid? The rule is that the plan of reorganization, to be acceptable to this class of creditor, must include payment in full of postpetition taxes on emerging from Chapter 11 along with other "administrative costs," while the prepetition payroll taxes may be paid over time. Quite simply, lacking cash to pay administrative claims, a company may not emerge from Chapter 11 and indeed may be forced into Chapter 7.

Cram-Down Provision

The creditors of a company in bankruptcy are arranged into classes according to the priority of their claims. The priority class of creditors includes the IRS and administrative claims — that is, legal bills from your bankruptcy lawyer and others who have been approved by the bankruptcy court to do work for your Chapter 11 company, plus postpetition taxes. These must be paid in full to emerge from Chapter 11. Fully secured creditors are next in line, and lenders usually fill this category. Partially secured creditors, or those with "impaired" collateral, represent the third class; it is important to have an ally among the creditors in this class because one impaired creditor who accepts a plan of reorganization enables the judge to effect a cram-down. Finally, there is the unsecured class of creditors, those without any collateral.

Fifty-one percent of all creditors and two-thirds of each class of creditor must approve the debtor's plan of reorganization before the company is permitted to emerge from Chapter 11. It is the nature of some creditors to continually reject the plans of reorganization submitted by the debtor. They feel that if they keep leaning on the company, it will improve its plan. They are right in some cases; they are nitpicking nuisances in others.

The authors of the 1978 bankruptcy code introduced the *cramdown provision* to keep recalcitrant creditors in line. If at least one impaired creditor — that is, a partially secured or unsecured creditor — accepts the plan of reorganization, the bankruptcy court can cram it down the throats of all creditors. Thus, virtually any reasonable plan of reorganization will be approved by the court if the debtor persuades one impaired creditor to accept. You can do this by paying a creditor promptly while in Chapter 11, showing your good faith and your attention to its needs.

Go Public

Yes, you can go public via a Chapter 11 filing. The expression once applied to companies that save their lives by an initial public offering — "Go broke *or* go public" — has become obsolete. It now is possible to go broke *and* go public. The 1978 Bankruptcy Act provides that creditors may be offered stock in settlement of their claims. The stock is exempt from registration under the Securities Act of 1933, which means that the stock is *free trading* (the holder can sell it through a broker the minute he or she receives it). This creates an extraordinary opportunity for troubled companies to raise cash.

Why might you want to issue stock to creditors? First, it saves cash and enhances the company's liquidity. Second, if debt is replaced with equity, the company's net worth increases. Third, much of the stock will be dumped at distress prices and you or your key employees might be able to buy up stock (issued as one share for each one dollar of debt) at 16 cents or less per share. Fourth, upon the company's emergence from Chapter 11, the stock will rise in price, and in two years, the insiders — you, your key employees and your investors under 10 percent — can sell some stock to create personal wealth.

Compumed was founded in 1983 by Robert O. Stuckelman, a former Litton Industries executive, and by Howard S. Mark, M.D., to rent electrocardiograph (EKG) machines to physicians. More than 2,600 EKG machines were installed throughout the country and tied to Compumed's central computer in Los Angeles. Compumed charged its clients a rental fee and a processing fee. By 1985, the company was very profitable but highly leveraged because of $8 million in borrowings to buy the EKG machines. To alleviate its debt, Compumed filed a registration statement with the SEC for an initial public offering, but the SEC told Compumed that it had violated the law. The SEC claimed the EKG rentals were franchises, and Compumed was selling them to the public without filing a prospectus with the SEC. The initial public offering was derailed, and Compumed filed for protection under Chapter 11. It was a classic Bobby McGee Chapter 11 — three large creditors and hundreds of unsecured creditors. Rental fees were sufficient to pay interest and operating expenses, but the company was prohibited by the SEC from placing more units in the field; thus, Compumed had to change the nature of its business.

Because their clients' rental payments would run out in three years, Stuckelman and Mark felt that they could grow only if the company acquired other medical devices to sell or rent to its 2,600 physician clients. To make acquisitions, Compumed would have to be public because it had no cash. To do this, Compumed paid all unsecured creditors with stock, creating a net worth sufficient to obtain a NASDAQ listing, which means a daily listing of its stock price in the newspapers. Moreover, because its expansion story was pretty well accepted by its new stockholders, there was not much selling of the stock. Compumed has roughly 8 million shares of stock outstanding and was trading over the counter at about 13/16 to 1 1/4 cents per share in late 1991.

Compumed is a perfect example of two axioms:

- When you're broke, buy something.
- Go broke to go public.

The Tax Loss Carryforward

Even though it has been diluted, the tax loss carryforward still is an effective way to shelter the earnings of the company your loss company acquires. Prior to the Tax Reform Act of 1986, if the buyer had accumulated losses over the past few years and was acquiring a company that had earnings, the seller's earnings could be sheltered for five years by carrying the buyer's losses forward. For example, if the buyer had a $1 million loss in 1989 and acquired a company that produced a combined income of $1 million in 1989, there would be no tax payment on 1989 combined earnings.

But this privilege has been removed and in its place is the following: The buyer multiplies the interest rate on seven-year government notes — for instance, 7 percent — by the acquisition price, and if the buyer has losses it still can carry them forward, but to a smaller degree. For example, using the previously mentioned case and assuming an acquisition price of $4 million, the annual savings would be $280,000 per annum, or 7 percent of the acquisition price. If the seller owes $400,000 in taxes on $1 million of profits, it will pay only $120,000 if acquired by a loss carryforward buyer.

SUMMARY

If you have to take your company through a Chapter 11 proceeding to rehabilitate it, then it is important that you know the rules of the road to avoid surprises. First of all, there are many bankruptcy lawyers for you to interview. They will ask to be paid in advance, and the amount will be about 3 percent of your company's total indebtedness. Do not make payments to creditors or try to move assets out of the reach of creditors prior to filing. These actions are fraudulent and will be reversed by the bankruptcy judge.

You will need cash to emerge from Chapter 11. Thus, begin looking for it immediately within the company and from outside sources. You can speak with sources of capital in the directories in the appendixes at the end of this book to determine their interest in financing your company. A public offering is not out of the question either. Bottom line: Find cash quickly and preserve it for use in negotiating a plan of reorganization with creditors.

■ CHAPTER SEVEN ■

Get the Cash before You Crash

A WORLD WITHOUT CASH

You are beginning to get the picture by now that raising cash is critical to a successful workout, whether it is done informally or in Chapter 11. Cash is king!

Think for a moment what it might be like to operate your business in a world without cash. This is every businessperson's worst nightmare. If a large number of insurance companies and commercial banks collapse, cash could vanish from the economy. Consumers will hoard cash under their mattresses. Suppliers will ship only on COD terms. Banks will shut down by the hundreds, and the FDIC will be too broke to bail them out. The economy could gasp and wheeze for several months without cash. How do you survive this scenario, particularly if your company is in crisis? You get busy generating cash. Make this your goal beginning today, because soon we could be living in a world without cash.

You don't believe it? Reread some history books on the Great Depression. Read about the Irish potato famine of 1836 to 1840, when Ireland had no cash for nearly five years. Read about the South during the Civil War or Japan following World War II. You will learn how people trade, barter, exchange and invent new means of survival to exist in a world without cash.

Many of you cannot conceive of a severely depressed economy and intensely illiquid economy where all the world is for sale, but buyers are nonexistent. But it could happen, and in this chapter I will give you several strategies to help you create genuine liquidity.

As a first step, take a personal inventory of your company's assets and sell everything that is not needed in the business. Then consider the following immediate cash-generating actions. Some may be appropriate for distribution businesses, others for retailers and a third group for manufacturers.

- Maximizing credit
- Bartering
- Schlepping
- Licensing
- Off-balance-sheet assets
- Sale-leasebacks
- New distribution channels
- Shared mail marketing
- Cable TV marketing
- Franchising
- Users groups
- Crazy ideas to get you thinking

TAKING PERSONAL INVENTORY

When you have been slammed against the wall by a severe cash crisis, you must quickly pass through the stages of denial, anger and blame. Forget that you are in the whatever business, because you aren't in it anymore. You're in the survival business. You must take an inventory of the things you can sell to generate cash. There are no sacred cows in your company. Your mission is to raise cash.

My first suggestion is borrowed from the yard sales that you see in the country. Have employees comb through their desks, file cabinets and closets for accumulated bric-a-brac. Have the plant manager clear out old parts, tools and components. Then put up a tent in a vacant lot and hold a weekend flea market. Invite other companies to join you. Put signs up two weeks in advance. If the housecleaning turns up 25-year-old calendars or nostalgia items, take those to an antique dealer. They might be worth more than you think.

Then examine your company's physical needs. Do you need all of your office and warehouse space? If not, rent out some space to small companies. When hospital occupancy rates fell in the early 1980s, unoccupied rooms were rented out to ice-cream-parlor operators and rug-shampoo equipment firms, to name two examples. Find several compatible companies that will pay you rent in consideration for space, a receptionist, conference room and warehouse or production space.

Take a hard look at your company's inventory. If it is turning six times a year, can it possibly turn eight times a year? Ten times? Twelve times? Sure it can. If your company is a manufacturer, ask your suppliers to purchase raw materials and deliver them to you; then you can add the labor component. You will save cash and dramatically increase inventory turns.

Do you carry finished goods inventory from one season to the next? That is cash-intensive as well. Stuart Bagus, the CEO of Union Hall, an Illinois discount retailer, stopped recycling seasonal inventory. Clearance sales meant *all* unsold inventory must go at the end of each season and not be carried for 12 months.

Your company probably has accumulated a lot of extra desks, chairs, lamps, calculators, computers, file cabinets, rugs, vases, coatracks, containers and other relics from your tycoon era. Turn them over to the junk dealer for cash.

Your machinery and equipment probably are being used less than full-time. Offer contract manufacturing services to other manufacturers in your region or in your community. Instead of one shift per day, schedule two shifts, and offer contract manufacturing on the free days. If you make a product for the domestic market, offer contract manufacturing services to foreign companies and offer other facilities such as advertising, market research, sales, customer service and accounting.

If you own and operate vans and trucks, get into the moving business and let your rolling stock stay full all the time by moving other folks' goods. If this can't happen for you, then sell the fleet for cash and hire out the moving services to an independent carrier.

A pizza delivery company in Albuquerque, New Mexico, recently got into the home video business to increase its revenues per driver trip. The company began a new service: stocking home videos on consignment and offering one free home video rental or two for one dollar with each pizza over $5. Its vans picked up the videos on their trips the following day. The skin-grafted business is doing so well that the company may begin selling and delivering rapid turnover food products to save people a trip to the store.

If someone in your firm becomes proficient at selling off used equipment, ask that person to see if there is an opportunity to broker used equipment for other companies. You may identify a small but meaningful profit center. Fred Herdlick, president of Electro-Rep in St. Louis, Missouri, a battery distributor, found a niche in cleaning and restoring used batteries for utility companies and forklift truck operators.

Then there are people. You always can get along with one or two less accounting clerks or administrative personnel. Three sales-persons can share one secretary. The accounts payable department can get by with fewer bodies if you reduce your purchases of raw materials. In a scaled-down business, fewer people will be needed.

MAXIMIZING CREDIT

If your company is carrying accounts receivable without a receivables line of credit, contact a commercial finance company and arrange credit. For accounts receivable from corporate customers, you can borrow up to 85 percent of the invoice when you generate the sale. For existing accounts receivable, you can raise 85 percent on amounts less than 90 days of age. If your accounts receivable are from individuals or governments, you might not be able to borrow on them at all unless you can document a historical record of consistently good collections. In any event, the advance rate on these less-desirable accounts receivable will be less than 80 to 85 percent. Certain insurance companies will guarantee the collectibility of most accounts receivable for a fee. This is important if you have noncorporate or foreign accounts receivable.

Factoring is a more expensive means of generating cash from your company's accounts receivable. A factor buys, rather than loans against, accounts receivable and in so doing assumes the collection risk. The price of factoring can be as much as 40 percent per annum, and the customer sends its payment to the factor rather than to you.

If you establish a line of credit with a commercial finance company for your accounts receivable, ask the lender if it will be willing to provide credit against your inventory. Finished goods and raw material inventories are considered acceptable credit. The advance rates are rarely higher than 60 percent and can be as low as 30 percent. Commercial finance companies will calculate the liquidation value of your inventory — that is, the price it will bring at auction, or "under the hammer," as they call it — and advance you at a discount from that value. If, however, the advance rate is 35 percent, for every dollar of acceptable inventory on hand, you can raise 35 cents; the same applies to purchases. Then, as you sell the finished goods, your invoice is submitted to the factor or commercial finance company and you receive 75 to 85 percent of the sales price, repay the 35 percent advance and end up with cash in your pocket.

If your company has machinery and equipment on its books that is debt-free, you can raise cash by borrowing long-term loans against it, or selling it to an equipment-leasing company and leasing it back. The advance rate is typically 60 to 75 percent of the liquidation value of the asset. More on the details of this will appear later in this chapter. The same applies to your buildings or property.

Furthermore, in most states, there are funds available from state agencies to provide job-saving or job-creating loans. These loans range from $10,000 to $20,000 in cash for every job your company *projects* it will save or create over the next two to three years. Collateral for the loans generally is the equity remaining in the company's assets after they have been pledged to conventional lenders. The interest rates on state loans generally are in the 6 to 8 percent per annum range, and the term is 10 to 15 years, substantially longer than conventional loans. You have to make a "but for" case to state lenders; that is, you have to convince them that but for their loan, your company would lay off 50 people or create 50 new jobs in three years.

If your company's balance sheet resembles the one in Figure 7.1, notice the amount of cash you can wring out of it via conventional and state loans.

FIGURE 7.1   Cash Availability from Conventional Lenders

($000s) Asset	Book Value	Acceptable or Liquidation Value	×	Advance Rate	=	Initial Drawdown of the Loan
Accounts receivable	$1,000	$900	×	.80	=	$ 720
Inventory	800	600	×	.50	=	300
Equipment	1,200	750	×	.75	=	565
Plant	300	750	×	.75	=	565
Total	$3,300					$2,150

The balance sheet in the case in Figure 7.1 will generate $2.1 million in immediate cash. But you have left some money on the table if you have not approached the economic development director in your county. Let's look at the availability for a long-term state loan at a below-market interest rate (Figure 7.2).

To justify the additional $850,000, your redirect and grow plan must show the saving or creating of at least 85 jobs over three years. Some states — primarily those in the sunny, tourist-welcoming Southeast and Southwest — do not provide these "but for" term loans.

Needless to say, your cash flow statements and projections must demonstrate an ability to service the interest and principal repayments of the debt. To service $3 million in debt at an average interest rate of 9 percent per annum in "normal" times, you will need to generate earnings before interest and taxes (EBIT) of $270,000 per annum, plus at least twice that amount to repay a portion of the term loan each year plus interest. Remember to add back noncash expenditures such as depreciation and amortization in calculating the ability to service debt.

If you need an annual EBIT of $540,000 to service $3 million of indebtedness, you can figure on needing 50 percent more in troubled times, if your borrowings are tied to the prime interest rate. If they are, and if your cost of money doubles to 18 percent per

FIGURE 7.2   Cash Availability from State Loans

($000s) Asset	Acceptable or Liquidation Value	×	Inverse of Advance Rate	=	Additional Loan Value
Accounts receivable	$900	×	.20	=	$180
Inventory	600	×	.50	=	300
Equipment	750	×	.25	=	185
Plant	750	×	.25	=	185
Total					$850

annum, you will need more than $800,000 per annum to service debt.

In negotiating new loans at the precipice of what you consider a stormy economic crisis, try to put a ceiling on the interest rate if it is tied to prime, try to avoid personal guarantees and try to provide in the loan agreement a "cure period" of as much as 90 days in which to correct a default. The first two points may seem obvious in their intent. The third point is to allow you three months to turn your company around in the event that you default on the loan covenants and find the sheriff at the door.

There is a question of how greedy one should be at the loan window prior to a serious recession. If you were raising equity capital, there is no upper limit to how many chestnuts to gather to keep the family fed during the long, cold winter. But bear in mind that loans must be repaid.

Xicor, Inc., a Milpitas, California, semiconductor manufacturer, ended calendar year 1987 with more than $45 million in cash. In March 1988, it raised approximately $20 million in equity from the public for a reserve. When asked by his underwriters why he wanted more cash, Raphael Klein, Xicor's CEO, replied that he remembered the severe recession in the semiconductor industry in 1983–1984 and didn't want to be caught short again.

But you cannot treat debt like equity. When borrowing money to avoid being caught short, you must do some downside planning so that you will be ready to pursue alternative plans to generate cash flow in the event that your sales turn south and your EBIT falls below debt service.

If your company is carrying a comfortable debt load prior to the onset of a crisis, try to restructure your loans now to make the bulk of them fixed-interest-rate term loans. You can do this via private placements with insurance companies or pension funds or via the sale of debentures to the public. If the U.S. market does not respond to your private or public offering, the U.K. market might be more receptive. Have your accounting firm or another international service agency that you use arrange introductions for you in London. You want to avoid having demand loans called when you are trying to keep your ship afloat in a crisis.

BARTERING

Virtually anyone can enter the barter economy and trade excess inventory for cost-saving services such as advertising space, airplane seats, hotel rooms, rental cars for company salespeople and more. Fred Tarter, founder of Deerfield Corporation, the world's leading barter company, tried to explain to me how Deerfield operates.

Let's say St. Tropez Cosmetics calls me and says they would like to unload 10,000 gross of lipsticks, 12 to a box. That's about 15 million tubes of lipstick, which is in St. Tropez's inventory for $7.5 million. Let's say I can find a home for the lipstick with various Latin American health- and beauty-aid distributors for $2.5 million. That's fine with St. Tropez, but the Latin Americans don't have $2.5 million in cash. They tell me they have various things to trade — airline seats, prepaid rental car vouchers and some credits from their government. The package is a little cumbersome, but I give my client some currencies, which it converts into dollars, then I go to work on airline seats and car-rental credits. I find that Hertz likes to buy the back page of in-flight magazines. So, here I am with a bunch of car-rental chits, which I barter with magazines to generate ads for Hertz, for which it pays the difference. Then I sell the airline seats to buyers of discount tickets for cash and pay my client.

Tarter's explanation shows that barter experts are creative cash generators. You can unload saleable inventory on them for cash or barter chits, and they will move the goods to distributors who need them. The barter companies do not pay top dollar. They are a port in the storm, a form of bailout insurance to the company drowning in illiquid assets.

If your company is in a service industry and it does not have excess inventories to barter, take stock of your underutilized service capabilities and barter them for products or services that can be converted into cash. Can your finely tuned receivables collection department provide similar services for customers in consideration for their paying you up front or ordering more of your services? Do you have more printing, telephone or computer capacity than you need? Radio and television stations frequently barter unused advertising time, or time created because of last-minute cancellations, to brokers who resell it at discount prices to large and frequent advertisers. Topol toothpaste is advertised almost exclusively in canceled space time slots.

If your company has incurred operating losses, these, too, can be bartered to a company that needs to shelter some of its earnings. This is done via an acquisition or by spinning off the loss-generating division to a limited partnership that will provide capital to the division in consideration for the losses.

As you comb your inventory of barterable products and services, remember that your weaknesses may be someone else's strengths, and your excesses someone else's weaknesses. The economic community runs smoothly most of the time because of its elegant mechanism for fitting needs with suppliers.

SHIFTING COSTS TO CUSTOMERS

Ask yourself: What tasks can my customers perform for themselves (without my losing any cash flow) that I am presently providing for them and, indeed, tying up cash to provide? Can I trade some of these services to the customer and free up assets or people?

Once there were only public zoos and wild animal parks in the United States. But in the mid-1970s, Lion Country Safari, Inc., discovered a means of operating them profitably with a small initial capital investment. It shifted the burden of paying for cages and energy costs to the customer. Visitors to Lion Country's wild animal parks paid for the cages (their cars) and energy costs (gasoline) and paid admission fees, while the company leased the land and paid for the animals — which, happily, reproduced — and their feed. A clever trade-off. Customers gained convenience and the added pleasure of seeing the animals in wild habitats. Lion Country conserved cash and generated a profit by leveraging the customers' needs.

Rethink your business in terms of customer leverage and laying off services on the customer. Furthermore, if you have an excess of anything, trim the fat, get to the bone, trade your excesses for others' needs.

SCHLEPPERS

"Schlepper" is Yiddish for a person with a couple of old shopping bags full of odds and ends that he or she has picked up somewhere and intends to sell somewhere else.

In the black community, the schlepper was the "rags 'n old iron" man who pushed a cart full of odd bits down the alleys selling junk, buying junk or swapping junk as he went along shouting out his song, "rags 'n old iron."

The modern version of the schlepper and the rags 'n old iron man is the discontinued, overstocked-item consumer-products catalog or direct-mail merchandiser. The best-known entities in the consumer-electronics industry are the Sharper Image, JS&A (for Joe Sugarman & Associates) and DAK (for Dean A. Kaplan). They buy unique products whose manufacturers lack advertising and marketing dollars from cash-constrained small manufacturers at distress prices, then advertise them in their direct-response ads or via their catalogs at prices of 25 to 30 percent below retail list. The strapped manufacturer can raise $10 per unit in immediate cash for a product that it normally would sell for $50.

I visited a manufacturer of one of the best-known business software products in the world in late 1987 — 50,000 units sold at $100 per unit — which recently had introduced an upgrade for $400 per unit with more than 30 additional features. The company was going to launch the new version with a big advertising campaign, and the capital was to be raised via a new issue of its common stock. Then came Black Monday. In two months, the company's sales fell from $350,000 to $15,000 per month. It had no users group. It did not have its customer names in list-rentable form. I devised an informal reorganization plan for the company and, to raise emergency cash to meet the payroll and the telephone bill, we sold 9,000 boxes of the Version I software product to software-industry schleppers for $10 per box. The $90,000 came in the nick of time and permitted us to take the informal reorganization plan instead of being forced into Chapter 7 and certain liquidation.

A number of successful businesspeople began in the pawnshop and schlepper trade. One of the most notable is Rose Blumkin, the 97-year-old founder of Nebraska Furniture Mart, which was acquired in 1983 for $60 million. She came to the United States from Russia as a little girl and helped her husband run a pawnshop until his death. With no cash and with children to feed, Rose began selling her own furniture out of her house. With her first cash receipts, she bought more used furniture, stored it and resold it.

LICENSES

If your product is more high tech than furniture, there usually are many opportunities to raise cash by linking up with a sister product manufacturer. A *vertical market license* is the sale of exclusive marketing rights to a product to a company that can resell it only to a certain industry. Cipherlink Corporation, a software developer, licensed Coopers & Lybrand the exclusive rights to use and resell Cipherlink's Automated Auditor package to the accounting industry. If your product is generic, you can license several vertical market applications. Enabling Technologies, Inc., a Chicago software developer, licensed its solids-modeling software package to the medical industry and to the printing industry. It sold original equipment manufacturer (OEM) licenses to computer manufacturers that bundle Enabling's software into the price of their hardware.

Another form of license is the *territorial marketing license*, in which you sell the exclusive rights to market your product in another part of the world, one that you cannot afford to create a sales and service organization to reach. U.S. manufacturers of medical-diagnostic equipment frequently do this because Europe and the Far East are large territories and foreign health-care equipment makers have sales forces in place but are seeking innovative new products to shove through their pipelines. With foreign-licensing arrangements, bear in mind that it is costly to audit the licensee's books and records. Therefore, you should insist on a payment up front representing at least 50 percent of the estimated first-year aggregate royalty, with the next 50 percent payable in six months. If the licensee questions you on this point, explain that you simply cannot afford to audit or sue if the company shortchanges you. Thus, for year one you will take one-half up front.

For example, if the minimum number of units that the licensee must sell in year one has been agreed to at 10,000, and if the licensee's selling price is $500 and the royalty fee is 5 percent of the first 10,000 units, then the licensee is obligated to you for at least $250,000. It is your prerogative to demand $125,000 in cash up front when the agreement is signed. Be sure that the licensee guarantees the second payment and that its guarantee is worth something. If the licensee has a net worth smaller than the guarantee, you have not been given anything of value. After all, you will want to discount the second payment with a factor or asset-based lender, and thus raise another $100,000 up front.

Precisely define the minimum annual sales and the territory encompassed by the license. Also, put an outside date on it — for example, five years — with renewal by mutual consent. You may want to regain the market that you have given up in a moment of weakness. The licensee probably will want to keep it, because it paid for its development. Thus, when it comes time to renew the license, there is a strong possibility that you can raise the ante or sell the territory outright for a large fee. For ideas on shrewd territorial license deals, look no further than the Coca-Cola Bottling Companies. The rights to sell Coca-Cola in bottles were sold in 1899 to two Chattanooga lawyers by Asa Candler who purchased the rights to Coca-Cola from its inventor for $1,200. Bottlers ordered the syrup from Coca-Cola, but the Tennesseans created one of the great family fortunes in the South by licensing the bottling rights throughout the country.

To obtain a panoply of licensing candidates, obtain the names of the corporate planning officers of the largest corporations in the United States and in major foreign countries — most of the latter group have New York or California offices — that are most likely to have a need or a resell desire for your product. The major business magazines frequently publish lists of these large corporations, and you can telephone them for copies of their annual reports. For fastest access, order 10-K reports filed with the SEC from Disclosure, Inc., which sends out reprints of 10-Ks via overnight courier. Many corporate planning officers belong to the Association of Corporate Growth. You might obtain a membership list by contacting them in New York.

FINDING OFF-BALANCE-SHEET ASSETS

A customer list, once appraised by a list broker, represents excellent collateral. A customer's name, if rented 20 times per year at five cents per name, is worth $1 per name; 100,000 names are worth $100,000 at market and $80,000 in loan value. If you don't have 100,000 names, pool your names with those of others in your community, and together contact a list broker.

Begin generating a customer list immediately. If your business does not lend itself to obtaining the names of its customers, then devise other means to build a list off their names and addresses. If you operate a cash-only restaurant, have your customers fill in their names and addresses to win a prize or to answer a questionnaire. The prize idea is best because it will generate more names. If you sell a product for cash, put a warranty card in the box and your customers will be delighted to tell you who they are and where they live. These names are much sought after by direct-mail marketing firms that are constantly seeking more responsive lists. In fact, if your customer list includes telephone numbers, it could be worth more than $1 per name to a list broker.

Technical know-how is also an off-balance-sheet asset. A computer software company does not carry the cost of developing source codes on its balance sheet, but the company owns it. A lender might find the source code, or the company's knowledge, as lendable collateral. In the same manner, purchase orders are not assets, but they represent collateral for certain factors and asset-based lenders.

Your company's plant and equipment may be fully depreciated and reflect a low value on the balance sheet. Have them reappraised to see if there is additional collateral in the bricks and steel.

If you lease retail space, you can assign your leases to a lender to generate cash. Manufacturers of consumer-electronics products rent lists of their warranty cardholders. If your logo is well known, it might be licensable to a clothing manufacturer, as McDonald's Corporation recently did with Sears to create the McKids line of children's clothing.

SELLING AND LEASING BACK

Many cash-starved companies sell their plant and equipment to leasing companies to generate money. The leasing companies generally advance 75 to 85 percent of the liquidation value of the equipment and 60 to 75 percent of the market value of the plant, and the company repays the leasing company over five to seven years on the equipment lease and seven to ten years on the building lease. Many large commercial banks and commercial finance companies have equipment-leasing divisions. You will require up-to-date appraisals, audited financial statements, precisely documented cash flow statement projections and a sound, overall business plan to obtain the financing. If your company tumbles into Chapter 11, however, the leasing company has title to the assets you sold it. Those assets then are not available for other lenders to attach. Because of their preferred position in bankruptcy, equipment-leasing companies will expose themselves to more risks than will conventional lenders.

Are there employees in your company whose services you need less than full time? If so, why not terminate them as full-time employees and rent their services as independent contractors on an as-needed basis? They are free to offer their services to others as well as to your company, and you have unburdened your operating statement of their payroll costs and benefits.

ADDING NEW PRODUCTS TO CURRENT DISTRIBUTION CHANNELS

Book publishers have a knack for pushing additional products through their primary book-distribution channels. T. George Harris, the founding editor of *American Health* magazine, recently acquired by Reader's Digest, can point to dozens of cash flow channels from a single product in addition to sales of the magazine itself:

- Advertisements
- Subscriber list rentals
- Sales of articles to domestic newspapers to run as health-and-fitness features
- Sales of articles to foreign newspapers
- Sales of audiocassettes based on a series of articles
- Sales of videocassettes based on a series of articles
- Sales of books based on a series of articles
- Product endorsement fees
- Sales of T-shirts, sweatshirts and tote bags bearing the magazine's logo
- Sales of related products such as dictionaries of health and fitness terms

Some of these channels may work for you right now. Run the numbers and see if they do. Once you apply some of the following ideas about the fundamentals of creating additional distribution channels, you will be on your way to tripling your company's cash flow.

When I launched my investment banking firm in 1970, it occurred to me that I had to generate additional sources of income to fill the cash flow valleys. Furthermore, I perceived that many of the clients who sought my services had no idea that I existed or how to find me. Thus, I discovered that there were secondary channels of distribution for my product: publishing and speaking. Readers of my books and attendees at my seminars could contact me at a future date to hire the services of my firm.

Other businesses that provide a service such as mine have carried the publishing and speaking channel to a higher level of sophistication. Howard Ruff, an investment counselor, offers week-long retreats for several thousand dollars. Joseph Mancuso founded several clubs, including the Chief Executive Officers Club and the Center for Entrepreneurial Management. They provide forums across the country at which Mancuso's books, tapes and newsletters are sold. Sheldon Adelson, producer of COMDEX, the largest industry trade show, and other computer industry conferences, publishes trade-show daily newspapers and sells tapes and printed compendia of the seminars given at COMDEX. Adelson recently formed a travel- and tour-management company as an additional cash-generating channel that brings people to COMDEX and the other conferences.

If you are in the service business, now is a good time to create this additional channel. You can launch it on customers' advance payments. The function of the publication is to index the myriad issues in the industry on a monthly basis, to generate advertising dollars and to locate new customers for your principal service.

USING 900 NUMBERS AND ONE-CALL POLLING

Several recent innovations in telecommunications can help you learn more about your customers' needs and wants. This market research is paid for by the customer, which helps your cash flow.

AT&T offers the Dial-It 900 Service (976 for local calls), which handles large numbers of simultaneous calls to your company at a flat rate of 50 cents for the first minute and 30 cents per minute thereafter. Newspapers such as *USA Today* use the 900 service to survey readers' opinions on burning issues; then they print the results of the polls the following day. Manufacturers enclose an announcement of the 900 service in the packages their products are sold in and encourage customers to call with their comments. Customers do call, and the manufacturers describe additional products and services, offer contests or ask preformulated questions to get more information about their customers. Ralston-Purina Company uses the 900 service for its Great American Dog contest, and Quaker Oats uses it so that children who eat its oatmeal can call to hear a prerecorded message from a well-known teddy bear.

One-call polling, a new service developed in 1987 by Creative Communications Associates (CCA) in New York, permits companies to tape 5,000 simultaneous outgoing calls to businesses and households. The calls are in the form of decision trees, and the respondents give touch-tone responses. Bedras Bedrusian, CCA's president, proclaims the value of the service for polling, market research and promotions. For CCA, the service is less expensive than sending out 5,000 direct-mail questionnaires.

You can use the Dial-It 900 service or one-call polling as entirely new distribution channels for locating new customers, asking them questions, determining their interest in your established products, taking their credit-card numbers and filling their orders, all without hiring any new sales personnel. Furthermore, with the 900 service, the customer pays for the connect time to your company's prerecorded message. For example, you manufacture Cajun and Creole sauces that are sold through supermarkets. Add a few lines of type to the labels describing your 900 dial-in service for cooking tips. Then prepare a prerecorded message that offers a Cajun/Creole cookbook for $9.95; a stockpot for boiling chicken and shrimp, as described in the cookbook, for $12.95; and a free tin of cayenne pepper or an apron with every order of $25 or more. Then ask the customer for his or her name, address and credit-card number. You have used the customer's money to generate a new source of cash for your company, and you did not pay for employees, advertising or postage. The Dial-It 900 service is an entirely new sales channel with immense cash-generating potential.

USING DIRECT-MAIL MARKETING

No other business is quite as easy to enter as direct-mail marketing, as demonstrated by all of the shop-by-mail catalogs you are offered. Printing and postage are basically the only start-up costs.

One of the best new businesses to launch in a depressed region is a direct-mail catalog firm that offers the unique products of the area to tourists who have chosen to stay away. Santa Fe, New Mexico, is a popular summertime and ski-season tourist area, but the artifact and art merchants have lean times from February to June. A direct-mail catalog that advertises their wares helps generate cash during those tough months. The local merchants provide color photographs of their products plus a list of sizes, colors and prices, and they often pool their mailing lists to reach thousands of prospects. The direct-mail business is going electronic as well, so that owners of personal computers can log onto hundreds of catalogs and order their products for delivery via mail, courier or United Parcel Service.

Direct mail or mail order is the fastest-growing segment of retailing. It is a $150 billion per annum business, and it represents about 15 percent of total annual retail sales.

USING JOINT VENTURES

Joint venturing is a frequently overlooked distribution channel and a method for creating cash quickly. A joint venture is a partnership of two or more entities formed to undertake a certain project. A joint venture opportunity exists when each partner brings to the project a property that the other partners do not have but regard as integral to the success of the project.

A business in search of cash must honestly confront the fact that more than money is necessary to launch a new project. Although the project may call for manufacturing or distribution of a certain product, merely obtaining capital does not make the company the most efficient manufacturer or the most successful distributor. You may have an elegant and innovative product ready to roll out to the marketplace but lack both the cash and the "feet on the street" to sell it. A large corporation may have manufacturing space available and a large sales force looking for new products. This situation beckons a joint venture: a fifty-fifty-owned enterprise wherein you manage the operation for cash up front and an ongoing management fee. We frequently see the joint venture arrangement in very large-scale projects such as mining, aerospace and telecommunications. Honda Motor Company introduced the moped through U.S. bicycle shops that later became its automobile dealerships.

USING SHARED-MAIL MARKETING

If you are currently mailing catalogs or direct-mail brochures to potential customers, you must be mindful of rising postal rates. To offset these costs, entrepreneurs have been popping up over the past ten years with shared-mail marketing schemes. Your literature gets to the intended recipient, but in a package containing other brochures as well. Not only do you cut your costs by two-thirds, but the other offerings often enhance the sale of your product. Shared mail marketing is a terrific cost saver, and the several shared-mail marketing companies presently in operation apparently are able to work more closely with the U.S. Postal Service to assure delivery.

Advo Systems, Inc., Hartford, Connecticut, founded by Jack Valentine in the late 1960s, was a lackluster direct-mail service company that put the addresses of all of the nation's homes in its computers and performed huge mailings for its customers. Slugging it out toe-to-toe with R.R. Donnelley, Dun & Bradstreet and other mass mailers was not Valentine's idea of a good time. He needed to do something more unique with Advo's 90 million addresses. His team came up with the idea of bundling up to ten direct-mail pieces in a folder to reduce the cost of the mailer per customer.

If your company is in the printing business or if it mails a great deal of material every day, it is possible that you could offer a piggy-back mailing service to other companies that wish to reach the same market but lack the money. They can contribute their mailing lists into a merged list, and for a small fee, you can print and mail their literature. If ten of you get together, the costs of direct mail will drop appreciably and you will have turned a cost area into a profit center.

USING CABLE TV MARKETING

Home shopping via cable is big business, aggregating $1.2 billion in 1989 and by all accounts rising. Syndicators buy blocks of time on the home-shopping cable channels and resell them to investment advisors, jewelry merchants, apparel manufacturers and hair-restoration companies. It might cost your company $40,000 per half hour to talk about your product line, but you can lay off part or all of that cost with advertisers.

The viewing audience for cable TV home shopping is similar to the readership of the *National Enquirer*. Although fascinated by the sensational, the audience is primarily interested in self-improvement, losing weight, regaining health and making money. They will purchase a unique cure, diet plan, penny stock gambit or how-to instructional tape that they see being discussed by satisfied customers on the home-shopping show. They wouldn't be watching that particular channel in the first place unless they were open to buying something. After selling some of the 30 minutes to noncompetitive advertisers, you might be able to reduce your out-of-pocket expense to $10,000. Then, assuming your product sells at retail for $40, you need to sell only 250 units to break even and 1,000 units to generate $30,000 in positive cash flow (excluding the cost of the product).

If the viewing audience is rated at 1 million households, a 2 percent response would be 20,000 orders. Before plunging into a $10,000 to $40,000 dice roll, however, ask the network's officers for references you can talk with to see how well this medium will work for you.

FRANCHISING

When your company is being backed into a corner by the force of events and must raise cash quickly, it may be too late to think of franchising. After all, to launch a franchising company properly, you need to hire counsel, draft a franchise prospectus and file the prospectus with the states in which you wish to sell franchises. That is the way it is supposed to be done. That is not the way it usually is done.

A case in point is Harold Otto, founder of the Wiks 'n Stiks chain of candle stores. Otto had an idea in 1976 that a small retail store specializing in freshly dipped, colorful, special-purpose candles might be a franchiseable concept. He decided to test the concept. While waiting for a Houston mall developer to prepare his first store, Otto heard that someone across town wanted to have a franchise. Otto took a franchisee check for $7,500 before he had built the model store. The Wiks 'n Stiks chain has grown to revenues of $61.3 million and net profits of $560,000 after taxes; in 1986, it achieved an initial public offering that valued the company at $36 million.

Franchising is first and foremost a financing method. It is not a particularly efficient product-distribution system, and most of the profitable franchises are acquired backed by the franchisor to enhance the value of the franchisor's common stock. The first franchise was sold by I. W. Singer, inventor of the sewing machine. A tool distributor in Ohio to whom Singer had granted a territorial dealership in 1886 was selling more sewing machines than Singer could produce. To switch the dealer's payments from after the sale was made to before the sale was made — so Singer could get the cash to produce the product — Singer sold the Ohio dealer a franchise. The dealer gained territorial exclusivity on a very popular product, and Singer gained up-front financing.

Your retail concept, if unique, is replicable in other markets. If your operations manual is complete, thorough and self-explanatory, and if you have an employee who can train someone in implementing the business, then you have something that will generate cash quickly. The legal blessing can come after you have generated some cash to stay afloat. However, avoid states with the stiffest franchising regulations, such as Virginia, California, Ohio and New York, until your legals are in order.[1]

If you do not want to franchise your retail business, you can possibly franchise or license parts of it, such as special foods, recipes, trade names. If you have a well-known branded salad dressing, such as Winn Schuler's of St. Joseph, Michigan, or a renowned cocktail sauce, such as Arnaud's of New Orleans, Louisiana, you might license other restaurants to use the product. They would have to buy it from you and pay in advance for the first shipment.

Franchising also can bring cash in a different way. You might consider the nation's 35 million franchise locations as potential customers for your product. They frequently run contests and offer premiums to bring in customers, and you can supply them.

USING DATABASE MARKETING

What better time than during a calamitous recession or a sales downturn to rethink your marketing methods? Do you really know much about your customers? Why do they buy from you? Who are they? If you knew more about them, you would be able to sell them more products and your customer list would become inestimably more valuable.

Companies such as Lexi International in Los Angeles are offering database research services. They employ artificial intelligence software to scan customer questionnaires that have been filled in by telemarketers, thereby generating answers to gut-level questions: Why does the customer buy your product but have it serviced elsewhere? Does a service customer trade up where he or she gets service, or does he or she return to you to trade up?

What are the problems your customer encounters with your service department?

The cost of marketing goes up inexorably, but database marketing can generate vastly higher response rates to mailing lists or to customer calls because you know more about the customer you are calling on. Furthermore, what if database marketing revealed that one-third of your product sales were to people — in businesses or households — who play tennis? You could share a catalog or videolog mailing piece with a tennis-products marketer. Or you could acquire a tennis-products supplier. You cannot catch black marlin with a worm hanging on a ten-ounce line. How you bait the hook will determine the size of the fish you catch.

LEARNING ABOUT USERS GROUPS

If the product or system that your company produces is proprietary, unique, has many applications and is used in multiple environments, as was the microcomputer when it first came on the marketplace, form users groups. These are regional groups of customers who come together every three months or so in a hotel conference room to discuss the product and how they are using it, to ask about applications they would like to do but require assistance with and to network with other users. Customers solve lots of problems by networking with other users, thus saving you personnel costs. Developers of peripheral equipment are invited to user-group meetings to demonstrate a feature of their product that expands the main product's capability. The advantage to you of forming users groups are several:

1. The users pay to attend the meeting.
2. The size of your service staff can be reduced.
3. Market research is gathered inexpensively.
4. New peripheral equipment is exposed, which you might be able to acquire or adapt.

Two other hints: Tape the users-group meetings and sell the audiocassettes for $12.95 each to customers who could not attend. You also might begin a users-group newsletter and offer it free to customers; fill it with applications news and solicit advertising from manufacturers and service companies that wish to reach your customers. Companies that could benefit from users groups include business-product manufacturers, telecommunications-systems companies, medical-equipment manufacturers, service fran- chises, dealership organizations, aerobics- and fitness-products manufacturers and recreational-products manufacturers. In the event of a cash crunch, you can think up a variety of payment schemes to implement through the users group by telling them that there is no time like the present to upgrade, add features, trade or introduce you to more potential customers.

BRAINSTORMING CRAZY IDEAS TO GET YOU THINKING

Generating cash by daring to try new things can be a real high. Thus, while your mind is buzzing with new ideas for selling everything that isn't nailed down, here is a crazy idea for you: the going-out-of-business business, which you can create out of thin air. I am perhaps citing an extreme example, but the message is not extreme. It is one of *readiness*.

The business is simplicity itself: You help merchants in a certain community unload slow-moving inventory by taking it on consignment, renting a downtown, street-level store for two months, arranging the merchandise on tables and racks and then plastering the windows with huge, handmade "going out of business" signs. The merchandise is sold for 33 percent off retail, or perhaps more toward the end of the sale, and you split the cash — no credit cards, please — fifty-fifty with your suppliers.

This strategy works very well with apparel, but it also could work for sporting goods, tools and home furnishings. You can move from town to town organizing 60-day going-out-of-business sales. Or you can remain in your community and do it there continuously. Shoppers forget the original business that was in the spot you rent, and when they see going-out-of-business signs, they walk into the store to look for bargains.

When companies face a cash crisis, they respond entrepreneurially by using primitive business methods that generate the most upfront cash in the shortest period of time. To do this, they place the burden on the customer to generate cash in advance of delivery. In this manner, crude though it may appear, the company makes itself ready to take the next steps to resolve its crisis.

SUMMARY

When I go into a company to do a workout, I tell the president and the senior officers, "Get rid of the sacred cows. You no longer are in the 'whatever' business. You're in the survival business. Here the rules are different. First, we sell everything that you do not absolutely need, and we sell it for cash. Second, we buy time. We need six months to reorganize and only cash will buy us time." If the management team has been backed by venture capitalists who have turned tail and run, they probably are in the denial or anger stage, but rarely are they in a realistic stage. They think that if they just had more marketing money, they could dig themselves out with cash from product sales. That will not happen.

Management teams not backed by venture capital usually are more realistic. Having bootstrapped themselves all the way, they never believed in the tooth fairy and have more street smarts and intuition about different ways to raise cash. While the manager backed by venture capital is talking to a Cayman Islands money finder who will deliver a commitment from a "prime international lender" for a $25,000 commitment fee, the street-smart manager is on the telephone with seven schleppers, six barter guys, five licensing candidates, four partnerships that do sale-leasebacks, three list brokers, two asset-based lenders and the ad manager for the users-group newsletter.

That is what it takes. Turn your energy from the business you were in to the survival business.

I have given you more than 20 ways to generate cash by selling something, all of which you can implement immediately, and some of which dovetail neatly while shifting the costs to the customer. For instance, by putting your products into a shared videolog and asking viewers to call you on a 900 number, you can (1) generate sales through a new channel, (2) generate a higher average sales ticket, (3) learn more about your customer via a touch-tone questionnaire and (4) generate a more valuable customer list to rent to others. This could permit you to lay off some sales personnel, thus freeing up space to rent to a complementary business. In this way, you will generate enough cash to carry you through your redirect and grow plan.

Endnote

1. Dennis Foster, *The Complete Franchising Book* (Rocklin, Calif.: Prima Publishing, 1988).

■ CHAPTER EIGHT ■

Raising Capital for a Distressed Company

THE PROSPECTS FOR RAISING CAPITAL

Once the crisis management team is organized and has stopped all immediate threats to kill the company, the crisis manager can begin searching for outside capital. You will recall that in chapter three we mentioned the prospect for raising capital as one of the nine key factors to consider in diagnosing a company's problems and its outlook for recovery.

The prospects for raising capital derive from the company's ability to provide appropriate answers to five questions that all investors or lenders ask when they are presented with a financing proposal:

1. How much can I make?
2. How much can I lose?
3. How do I get my money back?
4. Who says this deal is any good?
5. Who else is in the deal?

These are the five most important issues that investors in a "concept" seek answers to. The concept you are offering is that you can turn red ink into black using their money. You claim to be able to manage investors' capital more successfully than they can, notwithstanding prior mistakes that depleted early investors' capital.

Thus, in selling a concept, the management team must provide answers to tough questions in these key areas:

- Performance
- Protection from loss
- Liquidity
- Management's track record
- Endorsement

Although it is not impossible for the people who ran the company into the ground to raise the capital to turn it around, it is useful for the stockholders to replace the senior manager with a workout manager so that the person who claims he or she can deliver black ink isn't the same one who produced the red ink.

Raising capital for anything requires writing a business plan and carefully rendering 36-month cash flow and operating statement projections that provide the text in the business plan with its credibility.

HOW MUCH CAN I MAKE?

The essence of the business plan lies in the answer to this question. In financial terms, the answer is known as a rate of return on investment, or ROI.

Most high-risk investors have a target ROI of 45 to 60 percent compounded per annum over a three- to five-year period. For boneyard investment opportunities, or risky deals, the target is closer to 60 percent; for less risky deals, it is closer to 45 percent. Investors convert the ROI percentage to four to five turns on their money in three years, or approximately ten turns on their money in five years. They assume that the company will achieve a public market for its common stock within three to five years or sell out for cash or stock, thus producing the return. These rates of return may strike you as overly ambitious or as false targets thrown at naive managers to make them shelve their business plans and search for cash elsewhere. Not true. An investor who can achieve these ROIs in three or four investments out of ten is way ahead of market yields. By picking companies with favorable product niches in huge markets with good people, the investor can peddle even those that do not make it to large corporations at prices in excess of the investor's cost.

The first section of the business plan that investors read is the three- to five-year operating statement projections. They look at the third year's projected earnings and multiply by an appropriate price/earnings (P/E) ratio for similar companies, maybe 10 to 12 times. Then they multiply the amount they are being asked to invest by four or five and divide the resulting number by the first sum to determine the required percentage ownership. If it is too high, then the projections are too low, and the deal will be turned down. If the required ownership level is too low, they will ask if there is pricing flexibility and a willingness to negotiate before they go forward.

Operating statement projections are known as hockey sticks because most of them take that shape. The company's earnings are at the base of the hockey stick, but if it receives venture capital, they will move up to the handle.

In the hockey stick in Figure 8.1, the company projects third-year net profit after taxes (NPAT) of $2 million, or a market value at that time of $24 million using a P/E of 12. The investor multiplies $1.5 million by 5 and divides the resulting value of $7.5 million by $24 million to see how much ownership his or her $1.5 million should purchase — about 31 percent in this case. If the business plan offers an ownership percentage of about that amount, the investor will read the business plan in more depth. The valuation formula once again is as follows:

$$\frac{\text{Investment} \times 4 \text{ or } 5}{\text{Third -year NPAT} \times 10 \text{ or } 12} = \frac{\text{Ownership level necessary}}{\text{to achieve target ROI}}$$

Referring to Figure 8.1, the valuation formula translates as follows:

$$\frac{\$1,500,000 \times 5}{\$2,000,000 \times 12} = \frac{\$7,500,000}{\$24,000,000} = 31.25\%$$

FIGURE 8.1   The Hockey Stick

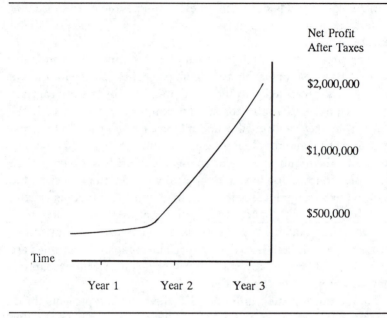

Net Profit
After Taxes

$2,000,000

$1,000,000

$500,000

Time

Year 1   Year 2   Year 3

Two red flags in this formula could result in a quick turndown, and they have to do with proportionality. If the company claimed that it could achieve the $2 million earnings level with a small amount of capital, perhaps $150,000, the deal would sound too optimistic. It would not appear reasonable to the investor that a fairly dramatic surge in earnings would result from so minuscule an investment. The steeper the earnings ramp, the greater the fuel requirement at the base. "Surely, you would not want to give this investment opportunity to a perfect stranger," would be the investor's initial reaction. Or "What's wrong with this deal that so little investment can create $24 million in market value in three years?"

Earnings in the third year are multiplied by ten or twelve to determine the company's market value. The investor's capital is multiplied by four or five, and the first sum is divided into the second to determine the investor's required ownership position. If the investor asks for that ownership position (the manager initially may offer less), he or she will make four or five times the investment, a 45 to 60 percent compound annual ROI (before capital-gains taxes) if the projections are met.

On the other hand, assume that the $24 million of market value required an initial investment of $6 million to achieve $2 million in third-year earnings. Four times $6 million equals $24 million, and the investor would have to buy all of the company to justify the investment. Or the projections should perhaps be extended a few more years, at which point they may begin to grow vertically and create a more attractive rate of return in the fifth year. A number of deals require years of laying pipe before the oil is pumped. MCI Communications took three rounds of financing. Federal Express, which raised $96 million on its first round, needed two more massive financings before it began to generate income. By the time of its third round, Federal was on death's doorstep and did a down-and-dirty financing at approximately one-tenth the price per share of its second financing. The investor also might look behind the $6 million to see if some portion of it might be done with debt to reduce the equity investment and increase the return on investment.

Boneyard investors are extraordinarily busy people for whom time is invaluable. Not only must they devote a big slice of each day to reviewing new proposals, but they have portfolios to monitor, board meetings to attend, tasks to do for portfolio companies and on-site inspections to make for new deals. In recessions, most of their time is spent nursing their portfolios rather than reviewing new proposals. Therefore, when a new business plan floats in the door, the first areas reviewed are the hockey stick, the amount required and the management team. If the hockey stick suggests the kind of ROI these investors are interested in, they will read management's track record to see if the projections were prepared by qualified managers or merely good hockey-stick artists. If the former, the package will get a thorough reading. If the managers have short track records in the turnaround business, the other aspects of the business plan must be extremely interesting, including the ROI, market size, growth rate and product niche.

Credibility of the Projections

What makes the projections believable? Normally, it is the credibility of the projection maker in concert with the facts. Lee Iaccoca had a combination of experience and management skills, plus bubbling enthusiasm, to convince the federal government to guarantee $500 million of loans to Chrysler Corporation in 1980. To their regret, John DeLorean, who had previously run the Chevrolet division of General Motors, convinced sophisticated investors pulled together by Oppenheimer & Company, plus the government of Ireland, to invest and loan $165 million to launch DeLorean Motor Company. Fred Smith, at the age of 29, on the strength of a paper he had written at Yale and no previous business experience, raised $96 million in venture capital and joint venture funds to launch Federal Express. Jeffrey Roloff, at the age of 23, raised $600,000 of venture capital from two funds and $600,000 in industrial revenue bonds to expand Central Data Corporation, a computer manufacturer that he began at the age of 19. The task of each of these entrepreneurs was to convince lenders, guarantors and investors that the projections would be realized.

Let us begin with the key line in an operating-statement projection — revenues. If declining sales were a precursor of the troubled company's problems, why do sales increase in the projections? The plan for achieving those sales must be carefully thought out and expressed in the business plan. If the company is manufacturing a product, the traditional channels for reaching customers may be added to. Perhaps the company plans to change from shotgun to direct-response marketing. Perhaps it intends to begin census-based telemarketing or other unique strategies such as air-space marketing — putting products near the cash register.

The boneyard investor is concerned with cash flow, not profitability. The owner or manager must provide cash flow projections to supplement the operating statement projections. These will describe the company's ability to service the creditors, who presumably will have been convinced to compromise the amounts owing them or to stretch them out. The investor wants to see if there will be cash available after all payments to new suppliers for operating expenses and to pay old debts. The numbers based on assumptions will be suspect. The prospects for raising money for a troubled company are based on the credibility of the projections, and that begs the question: Who is making the projections? Who is responsible for making these numbers happen?

HOW MUCH CAN I LOSE?

The answer to this question lies partially in the structure of the financing and partially in the riskiness of the deal. In regard to financing structure, the weakest instrument an investor can purchase is a limited-partnership interest and the second weakest is a minority common-stock position. A senior common-stock or preferred-stock position is the third weakest, providing preferences to the investor only in liquidation and in receiving dividends prior to any dividend payments on the common stock. The fourth weakest instrument is an unsecured loan, usually referred to as a subordinated debenture, and the strongest instrument is a secured loan.

In all of these securities, the investor and the company can enter into agreements that spell out how they will treat one another over the course of the relationship. But the investor can enforce his or her position if the investment vehicle is strong. The purchase agreement entered into between the company and the investor at the closing contains a litany of the things the company must do (positive covenants) and the things it must not do (negative covenants) to and for the investor. Failure to comply places the company in default, and the remedies in the event of default are the determining factor in measuring the risk of loss of the investment. One of the remedies that is useful in protecting an investor's principal is the ability to take control of the company's board of directors. This permits the investor to bring in new management to turn the company around.

Other remedies, which may include demanding immediate repayment of the investment, are difficult to enforce on strapped companies but serve as a threat to illustrate the lengths to which the investor will go to protect his or her principal.

The second measure of the downside of a deal is the inherent risk. There are three major risks in every troubled company:

- *Production.* Can the product be produced?
- *Marketing.* Can the product be sold?
- *Management.* Can the product be produced and sold at a positive cash flow?

For the troubled company operating at break-even or at a loss on a *cash flow basis* (profits are irrelevant in a workout situation), all three risks are relatively large; hence the projections lack credibility. When the workout specialist's capabilities are placed in front of the old management team's, the projections take on the sound of hard currency.

One very strong plus is going for the troubled company when it is seeking financing: More wealth has been created by investing in bankrupt or seriously troubled companies than in rapidly expanding ones for which the investment price is steep. Milton S. Petrie acquired roughly 10 million shares of Toys 'R' Us at prices below 50 cents a share when it was in bankruptcy from 1974 to 1978. The stock is worth nearly a billion dollars today.

Charles Schwab bought his discount stock brokerage firm back from Bank of America at a steal when the bank was coughing blood. He has turned it into a thrilling success story while overbuilt and overleveraged multinational stock brokerage firms cut back and look for dimes in the parking lot.

The overworked investment motto of the legendary Rothschilds says it best: "Buy when blood is running in the streets. Sell when the fatted lamb is lowing in the fields."

HOW DO I GET MY MONEY BACK?

The normal means of achieving liquidity in a venture or boneyard investment is by public offering or acquisition by a larger company for cash or stock.

The business plan should indicate that the owners are, indeed, interested in arranging for an exit route such as this for the investors. If they have another means in mind for achieving liquidity, such as participation in earnings, this, too, should be mentioned, but it is rarely as attractive as selling out at a high P/E ratio. Over the years, the research-and-development efforts of large industrial corporations have been poorer at generating valid new products (except in the pharmaceutical industry) than has the entrepreneurial process. Thus, the troubled high-tech company has more options than the insolvent manufacturer or distributor to take its investors out at a high P/E ratio.

If you plan to offer stock to creditors to compromise a portion of their accounts payable, it may be a practical idea to merge your company with a public shell. A little-known loophole in the Bankruptcy Act of 1978 makes their stock free-trading — that is, immediately exchangeable for cash. This unique tactic is described in chapter six of this book.

WHO SAYS THIS DEAL IS ANY GOOD?

Investors like endorsements and testimonials. Professional venture capitalists will call dozens of customers, suppliers and personal references before investing. Why did you buy the product? What do you think about it? Will you buy more? How was the service? are a few of the typical questions asked of customers. Personal references include bankers, previous employers and previous co-workers.

The reference checks on entrepreneurs are not always glowing. Burt McMurtry, a specialist in high-technology investments, says:

> Quite often when I check on a prospect, his former subordinates say they worshiped him. He was dynamic, the high-energy type. His peers, however, were often irritated with him because he was something of a prima donna, always trying to get his project funded first. And his former bosses? Some of them will say they like what he accomplished, but he nearly drove them crazy. Didn't take no for an answer easily, and had zero grasp of corporate politics.[1]

Some venture capitalists ask for seven personal references — five good ones and two bad ones. The business plan should offer to make these available, but they should be handed out only at meetings with interested investors.

The business plan should include product endorsements appearing in trade journals, letters received from customers and customer responses given at demonstrations and trade shows. Investors should be given a hands-on demonstration of the product or service by going to a trade show, visiting the company at its plant or, at a minimum, through product photographs. When attempting to convey enthusiasm about a business to an investor, the manager should bear in mind the plight of the first person who ate a lobster and tried to convince others that it was good. "You mean you ate that strange thing that crawls on the bottom of the sea?" they were likely to ask. "Yes, and let me explain why it was good." Clearly, the lobster eater could have used the endorsement of others who ate it and did not die.

WHO ELSE IS IN THE DEAL?

Investors like to have company in a deal. They want to know that other institutions or corporations are involved with the company in either a risk-taking capacity or as lenders, suppliers or customers.

When Fred Smith raised $96 million to launch Federal Express, he first got General Dynamics excited about selling him hundreds of Falcon jets. Then he hired an investment banker to endorse the business plan and himself. Then he showed that he was investing all of his net worth. Then he got Prudential Insurance to say they would supply a middle tier of long-term financing subject to the venture capital being raised. Then he went back to General Dynamics and improved the terms of their deal to signify to others an improved and improving relationship.

The investment bankers needed $26 million of venture capital to support the debt structure, and they landed some important names first: First National Bank of Chicago, Allstate Insurance and Citicorp. The rest of the financing came together quickly because of the endorsements. Endorsements ensure that if the company needs more capital in the future, there will be more than one person pulling the oars.

The business plan or the workout specialist's cover letter should indicate whether other institutions or corporations are financially involved with the company. Endorsements are very important in the rather small world of business where, with a few telephone calls, an investor can check out the credibility and integrity of an owner or manager.

SUMMARY

If the answers to the five questions raised in this chapter are satisfactory, your company's chances for raising capital are good. The prospects hinge on credibility — yours and your company's.

Before approaching investors, be sure to have in hand a carefully crafted business plan that includes accurate cash flow projections and operating statements for investors to analyze. Your personal reputation also will be under scrutiny as potential investors seek endorsements from customers, suppliers and bankers.

Finally, bear in mind that investors seek not only a favorable risk/reward ratio, but a means of achieving liquidity in the deal. Unless you include appropriate exit routes in your proposal, you will frighten off interested investors.

Endnote

1.   Thomas, P. Murphy, "Venture Capital," *Forbes*, August 3, 1981, p. 131.

CHAPTER NINE

Developing the Redirect and Grow Plan

In hard economic times, many of your closest competitors will be more frightened than you are. They will see the glass half empty when you see it half full. They will fear a personal nightmare that includes losing their homes, pulling their children out of college and pawning their jewelry. Your fortitude and your skill in forecasting crises will create opportunities for you to generate cash by buying out your competitors and other troubled companies. Here's a true story from the last deep recession to help you understand this strategy.

A COMPANY IN TROUBLE

Harry and Phil Goodman (not their real names) inherited an $84-million (sales) drug, health- and beauty-aid distribution company from their father in early 1974. They paid him $2 million, which their father borrowed from the company's traditional bank by pledging the company's assets. Then dad and mom retired to Miami.

Harry and Phil began making all the key decisions, and the business remained reasonably stable for about a year. When the recession of 1975 hit, the boys went down to the company's bank to obtain a line of credit. They unwittingly overcollateralized the line.

Accounts receivable and inventory, all of it in finished goods, aggregated $20 million, which normally would support borrowings of approximately $3 million. The building, trucks, vans, forklifts and other equipment would permit another $2 million of debt, using conventional borrowing ratios of the asset-based lending industry. But the boys did not know about asset-based lenders or commercial finance companies. Dad had always borrowed at one bank, and that is where they went to obtain a revolving line of credit. They came away with $5 million in loans, including the $2 million loan to buy out their father, by pledging the company's accounts receivable, inventory, buildings and equipment — the works. Dad's contacts had long since retired, and the banker was a young lady sporting a new MBA degree. When she asked Harry and Phil to sign personally and to provide their homes as side collateral, the boys willingly agreed. This is what Dad must have done, they thought. Then the 1975–1976 Khomeini recession hit.

By the time the prime rate had shot up to 21 percent, Harry and Phil had drawn the full amount of the line, and the company's profits were being used to pay $80,000 per month in interest fees. The boys began to panic. One night, Harry's wife awoke to hear her husband crying into his pillow. Harry explained that he had signed personally for $5 million in loans that he did not think the business would be able to repay. He looked at his wife and said, "I think we could lose everything." His wife responded immediately with a reflex solution: "In the morning, we're going to see my cousin George, the bankruptcy lawyer."

The next morning, George heard the story, saw the anguish in his cousin's face and, without analyzing the financial condition of the company, put the company into Chapter 11.

A smart businessman — let's call him Dan — had been routinely placing an advertisement in the *National Bankruptcy Journal*, a weekly newspaper that reviews changes in the bankruptcy code, rulings on important cases, changes in judgeships and other trade information. The advertisement read as follows:

Attention Bankruptcy Lawyers

Our team can rescue your client's company, turn it around, add capital, develop a workable plan of reorganization and bring it out of Chapter 11. No front-end fees. Contact P.O. Box ____.

George saw the advertisement, and with Harry's and Phil's approval, he contacted Dan. Dan asked to see the company's latest unaudited financial statements. Upon reviewing them, he smiled broadly and then telephoned George to say that he would be in the area on other business during the next week and would be able to drop by to meet Harry and Phil. Dan knew the company would support greater borrowings. He understood that asset-based lenders frequently preferred to provide secured loans to companies in Chapter 11 as part of their plan of reorganization because all other lenders were stopped from placing liens on the borrower's assets. What Dan did not know was how much debt the company's cash flow could support. He would have to see how badly Harry and Phil were managing things.

In George's office a few days later, Dan interviewed two terribly nervous men. Harry and Phil were unable to think of anything except the possibility of losing their personal assets. They had not spoken with any creditors, most of whom were shipping only on COD terms and were concerned because of a lack of information. The only secured debt in the company was bank debt. As a result, the company was a perfect candidate for a turnaround; that is, the company had a large number of unsecured creditors, no significant leases and only one secured creditor. A Bobby McGee! Federal payroll withholding taxes were current on a prepetition as well as a postpetition basis. Sales and income taxes also were current. The company was too healthy to be in Chapter 11, but so are many.

Dan interviewed Harry and Phil for several hours. Finally, he said in his most serious voice, "Gentlemen, you have gotten yourselves into a real mess. I don't know if I can bail you out, but let me change my schedule so I can stay overnight. I'll study your financial statements in my motel room and, if I find a way to rescue you, I will make a proposal in the morning."

Dan did not have much analytical work to do that evening. The bank could readily be replaced by an asset-based lender. Banks are cash flow lenders — they seek repayment first from the borrower's cash flow. Commercial finance companies and commercial finance divisions of commercial banks are asset lenders first and cash flow lenders second. If Dan could find an asset-based lender to replace the bank and to remove Harry's and Phil's personal guarantees and personal collateral, they might be sufficiently relieved either to pay Dan a large fee, to give him a large interest in the company or both. Dan drafted an agreement calling for majority ownership because he believed that the company could grow. The substance of the agreement called for Dan to raise $8 million for the company, repay the $5 million of secured debt, remove all personal guarantees and have $3 million in the bank. Dan's consideration would be a 51 percent ownership for raising fresh capital plus a 10 percent fee on all capital that he raised. Dan planned to locate a seasoned manager to run the company at a higher level of profitability, a level sufficient to pay interest and principal of $2 million per annum.

Dan studied financial statements that showed a company capable of earning $4 million per annum before interest and taxes, but it now was earning only $1.5 million. More than $2 million was being wasted each year on fat: too many employees, too many company cars, country club dues, vacations paid for by the business and excess inventories. Excess inventories provided an opportunity to improve profits. Distribution businesses have a typical percentage of "outs" — out-of-stocks. They typically can fill 94 percent of every order. To fill 96 percent of every order, which the company was doing, it had to keep another 2 percent of inventory. In other words, about $500,000 in cash could be saved by working the "out" ratio down to 94 percent and special-ordering those items to protect good customer relationships. Dan listed about 25 other operational changes, but he would save them for discussion with his chief executive officer candidate.

Dan returned to George's office in the morning and presented his proposal. He requested a 60-day exclusive option to rescue the company. If he succeeded, Dan wanted a 51-percent ownership, a 10-percent fee on all new capital raised and the ability to manage the company as chief executive officer (or to choose one), which included the right to reduce costs, the right to hire and fire personnel and any powers needed to generate cash flow sufficient to retire indebtedness under the plan of reorganization. George conferred privately with Harry and Phil and added only one change to Dan's contract: subject to the approval of the bankruptcy court. Dan accepted.

Four years later, Dan sold the company for $20 million, putting $10 million in the boys' pockets, before taxes. Harry and Phil joined their father in Miami, where all three men have gone into real estate development together. Dan made $8 million from the sale, and his chief executive officer made $2 million.

The knowledge of the distribution industry, the bankruptcy law and the lending requirements of asset-based lenders generated a significant profit and a happy result from a situation that began with two frightened inheritors of a sound regional distribution business. (To find salvageable companies for yourself, subscribe to *National Bankruptcy Journal*, published by Andrews Publications, 5123 Westchester Pike, Edgemont, Pennsylvania 19028.)

BUYING A COMPANY WITH YOUR TROUBLED COMPANY

"When you're broke buy something" is the clarion call of the workout entrepreneur. As Bill Tauscher and Richard Bard did when their insolvent Lag Drug acquired the thriving FoxVliet Drug to create the beginnings of $3-billion FoxMeyer Corporation, you, too, can use the carcass of your insolvent company to acquire your way to genuine liquidity. The assets you have to work with are the following:

- *Your suppliers.* They do not want to lose the money that your company owes them, and they will make concessions to get their money back.
- *Your tax loss carryforward.* Although diminished in value by the Tax Reform Act of 1986, you still can shelter some of the earnings of the company you buy with your company's tax loss carryforward.

The Birth of FoxMeyer

Tauscher and Bard realized that outside of Chapter 11, $85-million (revenues) Lag Drug Company was hopelessly insolvent. In

Chapter 11, the company would be solvent; it would have time to reorganize its debts. In Chapter 11, the unsecured creditors become partners of the debtor.

The pharmaceutical, health- and beauty-aids industry has witnessed so many bankruptcies that it owns a small auditorium on Lexington Avenue in New York City where debtors can address its credit managers. When Tauscher and Bard put Lag Drug Company into Chapter 11, they were urged to come to New York and take the stage. This was a first for all three of us. Our average age was 32, and we faced an audience of approximately 30 credit managers whose average age was 55 and whose average account receivable with Lag was about $400,000. Pfizer's credit manager was there, as was Clairol's, Richardson-Merrill's, Merck's, Upjohn's, R. J. Reynolds', American Tobacco's and others. We feared the worst.

Tauscher sat in the center with Bard and me on either side; we were his numbers men. The 29-year-old, six-foot-four-inch Tauscher told the angry creditors the truth. He was hired by Lag's president to set up the IBM System 36 computer that he had sold the company a few months earlier. He put all the customer records—inventory, payroll records and accounts payable — on the computer. When the president died suddenly, Tauscher was the only one who understood the company, and Bard was its secured lender. The owners of Lag Drug asked Tauscher to become its president, and he asked Bard to join him as chief financial officer. I had been asked to raise venture capital to turn the company around, and I had found several interested investors. The creditors squirmed in their seats with obvious disbelief. They had heard lots of stories from this stage over the years, but three young men, still wet behind the ears, had just told them something they normally laugh about at the nineteenth hole.

Tauscher continued. "Our plan to get you repaid is to acquire FoxVliet Drug Company in Wichita, Kansas. We can raise the purchase price by borrowing on FoxVliet's assets and by using the venture capital that we have raised, and we will repay the indebtedness out of FoxVliet's cash flow."

The creditors exploded. "You're going to trash one of our healthy customers? You're going to put two of our customers in bankruptcy?" they screamed. "What kind of story is this?"

But we held to our story. "If you gentlemen want to get your $12 million back, you're going to have to help us buy FoxVliet," Tauscher said.

"You're going to hock FoxVliet to the gills, stretch us out on $24 million in debt and ask us to keep shipping to you and to wish you well?" the Pfizer credit manager asked.

"That is what we're asking you to do. That is our plan of reorganization. We want you to go along with us," Tauscher said.

The meeting ended, but not the drama. The seller had to be held in place, and he had set a deadline of December 29. The secured lender in the leveraged buyout had to be convinced that the financing would happen, but Bard was experienced at speaking with asset-based lenders. The venture capitalists were the toughest group to hold in line because they were backing two young men with no track record who were financing out of Chapter 11. The owners of Lag Drug Company had to agree to suffer 80-percent dilution to permit a rescue of their company. Finally, the secured creditors had to approve the plan of reorganization.

The Lag Drug/FoxVliet deal was one of the first leveraged buyouts and easily the first bankruptcy LBO. It happened because Tauscher realized he could leverage the suppliers. He did this by communicating with them, by gaining their confidence and by making them believers.

Two years after the closing, the venture capitalists squeezed Tauscher's equity down to such a small amount that he walked out of the company. When FoxMeyer began to cough blood like a harpooned whale on the beach, the venture capitalists begged Tauscher to rejoin the company. He did so on his terms and nurtured FoxMeyer to sales of $3 billion, the second largest drug, health- and beauty-aid distributor in the country. In 1987, the venture capitalists backed Tauscher and Bard in their acquisition of Computerland Corporation.

Divisional Buyout

If you hear of a large corporation that is having problems, you might consider using LBO financing techniques to buy out one of its divisions. You can buy the division from the corporation by borrowing on the division's assets and repaying the loans from its cash flow. To enhance cash flow, you must take immediate cost-saving steps. Your ace in the hole is that the parent corporation's administrative service charge is eliminated. Unrelated activities and assets are spun off to raise additional cash. The parent corporation frequently will bend a little to help its managers finance the buyout if you spread some ownership among the division's managers.

The feasibility of accomplishing a management buyout takes some quick math. You first apply conventional lending ratios used by asset-based lenders to the division's principal assets to determine how much money you can raise. This usually results in an *equity gap* — a shortfall between the amount you can leverage and the probable asking price. That gap can be filled in a number of ways as we shall see. A second calculation will determine the *adjusted EBIT* — earnings before interest and taxes (remember this acronym!) — that are adjusted for the division's cost savings, once it is free from its parent and the corporate overhead charges. By cutting salaries and tightening the belt in other ways, you can increase the adjusted EBIT accordingly. For the third calculation, divide annual debt service on the acquisition debt into the adjusted EBIT to ascertain if there is sufficient cash flow (adjusted EBIT plus depreciation) to pay debt service while retaining something for you and your stockholders.

Let's put some numbers to this. Assume you spot a division whose balance sheet appears as shown in Figure 9.1.

Conventional loan ratios used by asset-based lenders are 80 to 85 percent of the value of accounts receivable less than 90 days outstanding, 50 percent of the value of raw materials and finished goods inventories and 75 percent of the liquidation (auction or quick sale) value of plant, machinery and equipment. There may be other assets off the balance sheet that can be used as collateral. The principal ones are customer lists, technological know-how and leaseholds, as discussed in chapter seven of this book.

Assuming that all of the accounts receivable are less than 90 days old and are acceptable to the lender, that two-thirds of the inventories are either raw materials or finished goods and that the net book value of the plant and equipment is equal to the liquidation value, then the division manager can raise the following cash from the division's balance sheet (see Figure 9.2).

FIGURE 9.1 Balance Sheet of Divisional Buyout Candidate

Assets		Liabilities and Net Worth	
Current assets:		Current liabilities:	
Cash	$ 350,000	Accounts payable	$ 900,000
Accounts		Accrued expenses	250,000
receivable	2,450,000		
Inventories	1,800,000	Note payable —	
		parent	1,200,000
Total current assets	4,600,000	Total current	
		liabilities	2,350,000
Plant, equipment		Stockholders' equity	3,250,000
(net)	850,000		
Other assets	150,000	Total liabilities and	
		and net worth	$5,600,000
Total assets	$5,600,000		

From the $3,320,000 cash advance, we must deduct the $1,200,000 note payable, which will have to be repaid by the new lender (unless it is owed to the corporation and is taken back by the corporation as part of the purchase price). The net cash available to pay the corporation is $2,120,000 or, to be safe, $2,050,000 after appraisal, legal and accounting fees and the lender's commitment fee.

Let's assume that the division's operating statement for the most recent 12-month period appears as in Figure 9.3.

To calculate the adjusted EBIT, add the division's profits, $1,982,750, to the corporate surcharge, $810,000; then add back the interest expense, $200,000, and the noncash charges and savings caused by belt tightening, perhaps $500,000. The elimination of perks would be substantial. In any event, let's assume that the adjusted EBIT is $2,502,550 per annum.

Is the adjusted EBIT large enough to cover the debt service? Assume the seller will hold the $1,200,000 note at 16.7 percent interest and will accept the $2,000,000 in cash that you offer as the down payment plus another $1,000,000 that you must raise outside plus a $4,000,000 five-year note secured by all of the assets in a second position to the asset-based lender at 18 percent annual

FIGURE 9.2   Raisable Cash

	Book Value	× Loan Ratio	= Cash Advance
Accounts receivable	$2,450,000	0.85	$2,082,500
Inventories	1,200,000	0.50	600,000
Plant, equipment (net)	850,000	0.75	637,500
Total	$4,500,000		$3,320,000

interest. Furthermore, assume that the note amortizes at the rate of $500,000 per annum with a fifth-year balloon of $2,500,000. The total purchase price is $9,520,000. Let's see the whether the adjusted EBIT will support this massive amount of leverage (see Figure 9.4).

The annual debt service of $2,216,000 is barely covered by the adjusted EBIT of $2,502,550. It is a "no hiccup" LBO: Just one hiccup, such as a two-point increase in interest rates or a small reduction in earnings, would jeopardize the division's ability to service its debt.

There is some leeway in the deal. An asset-based lender could ask the selling corporation to guarantee the collectibility of the accounts receivable. If the seller does so, the lender has the ability to loan 100 percent of the face amount of the accounts receivable. Second, the lender probably will ask you and your teammates, who will become stockholders, to guarantee the loan in proportion to your ownership. We will discuss the personal exposure of personal guarantees shortly. The fundamentals of personal guarantees are covered in chapter three.

The $1,000,000 that you must raise from outside sources can be obtained from LBO funds. These funds became extremely popular during the late 1980s and raised more than $25 billion from institutional investors to provide equity-gap or mezzanine financing.

Another way to improve the deal is to ask the corporation to take back the accounts receivable as part of the purchase price. The asset-based lender typically will not loan against the inventories if it does not tie up the accounts receivable. But in this instance, the face value of the accounts receivable is $2,450,000 and the initial takedown on the accounts receivable and inventory line is

FIGURE 9.3   12-Month Operating Statement of Divisional
                 LBO Candidate

	Percentage	
Sales	100.0	$13,500,000
Cost of goods sold	67.0	9,045,000
Gross profit	33.0	4,455,000
Selling expense	10.0	1,350,000
General and administration expenses	8.3	112,250
Corporate surcharge	6.0	810,000
Interest expense	1.5	200,000
Total operating expenses	25.8	2,472,250
Net profit contribution	7.2	$ 1,982,750

$2,682,500. Thus, by having the seller keep the accounts receivable, you must raise $232,000 more for the equity gap, but you save $593,000 in annual interest charges. Your current assets can be used as backup collateral if you need capital in the future.

Relatively high interest rates were used in this example on the assumption that the economy will be in a serious decline at the time you purchase your division. Indeed, interest rates could be five points higher and the buyout price could be $3 million higher, yet you still could make the purchase. That is the most exciting aspect of leveraged buyouts: They are highly doable with only a small amount of creative exertion.

There are asset-based lenders, mezzanine investors and LBO-experienced lawyers and accountants who are specialists in buyouts from boneyard to corporation divisions. They have fixed many deal brokers and have returned many remorseful sellers to the table to make the deal happen. When you buy a division or another company, contact one of these specialists whose names can be found in directories sold in large bookstores or made available in libraries. If your search proves fruitless, write me in care of Dearborn Financial Publishing.

FIGURE 9.4   Annual Debt Service of Divisional LBO Candidate

Loans	Face Amount of Loans	× Interest Rate	+ Annual Principal Payment	= Annual Debt Service
Asset-based:				
Revolving line	$2,682,500	.18	$ 478,000	—
PP&E loan	637,500	.18	115,000	$123,000
Existing note	1,200,000	.167	200,000	200,000
Seller's note	4,000,000	.18	720,000	400,000
Total	$8,520,000		$1,513,000	$723,000

Total annual debt service = $2,216,000

Tough Times Are Good Times for Buyouts

Whether you're planning an LBO or a facilities management buyout, if times are tough, remember that you are negotiating from strength and offer to put up very little of your own money.

Look at Ronald Jackson, president and chief executive officer of Kenner Parker Toys, Inc., of Beverly, Massachusetts, the fifth largest toy manufacturer in the United States. The company lost money as a subsidiary of General Mills Corporation and broke into the black one year after Jackson and his management team bought it for $350 million in an LBO (see Figure 9.5).

General Mills was happy to unload Kenner Parker because its mainstay products, Care Bears and Star Wars items, were being discontinued with no blockbuster toys or games in development. After gaining its independence, Jackson slashed costs, including advertising, from $49 million in 1985 to $36 million in 1986, while licensing Ghostbusters and SilverHawks to shore up revenues. Not long after going public, Kenner Parker was threatened by a takeover bid from New World Production, which owns the Marvel line of comic books and superheroes. Jackson protected his independence by selling Kenner Parker to Tonka Corporation for an acquisition price of $628 million. Jackson, who doubled his money in two

FIGURE 9.5   Kenner Parker Toys

($000s)	1985	1986	Percentage Change
Sales	$340	$503	48.0
Net profit	(58)	25	142.8

years, remains chief executive officer of Kenner Parker, which is nearly twice the size of Tonka.

WHEN LENDERS ASK FOR YOUR PERSONAL GUARANTEE

You may not be able to effect an LBO or finance a divisional buyout without giving the lender (which could be the seller, if it takes your promissory note) your personal guarantee. There are, however, negotiating tactics that you can employ to lessen your exposure.

The first step in negotiating a less punitive personal guarantee is to make a strong case against a *joint and several* guarantee. In a joint and several, each partner is liable personally for the full amount of the loan. If the loan is for $4 million and you and your three partners are each jointly and severally liable, then each of you is liable for the full $4 million. As that is clearly overkill, a good case can be made for several only — that is, your aggregate guarantees the total $4 million.

Bruce Engel, CEO of WTD, Inc., is unnerving to Weyerhauser and other lumber mills in the Pacific Northwest since he personally guaranteed $500,000 of creditor obligations to acquire a bankrupt sawmill in 1983. A bankruptcy lawyer and iconoclast, Engel had a personal net worth of $300,000 at the time. If the sawmill failed, there was no way he could repay the IOU. But Engel took his bluff a step further by persuading several backers to reschedule mortgage payments and convincing one creditor to forgo interest payments in exchange for a small percentage of the mill's monthly sales.

Engel was thrilled by the chance to prove himself. "Bruce came in as an outsider," says Chad Brown, a forest-products analyst at Kidder Peabody & Company, which took WTD public in 1988, creating $80 million in personal wealth for Engel. "Then he out-performed all the timber barons. He just loves that." Reviewing the mill's past, Engel decided to knock aside the most common prac-tices of the business. "I saw an overmature industry with costs too high and productivity too low, a business that was still dominated by an incredibly damaging macho ethic," Engel observed.[1]

Engel had reason to blink soon after he turned the mill around. Just when he sank WTD's new capital into two additional mills, the lumber market suffered another chilling downdraft. Engel did some calculations and realized that if he worked off the logs he had on hand at a manageable production rate, the company would lose hundreds of thousands of dollars in no time. So he faced down his suppliers and told them he was shutting down two of his three mills and wouldn't be able to pay them for three months. He also squeezed more favorable terms from his creditors because they saw his ship sail through rough water once before.

If you have several nonactive partners, for instance, those who fill the equity gap and own 25 percent of the new company, you might be able to eliminate 25 percent of the loan guarantee. Your argument to the lender would be that because your potential gain is only 75 percent of the enterprise, you should not be at risk on more than 75 percent of the loan. The deeper the recession and the more difficult the lender's ability to find good loan customers, the easier your negotiations will be to soften the personal guarantee.

BEGIN A DEVELOPMENT PROJECT

"Nothing propinks like propinquity," wrote Ian Fleming. And propinquity, or nearness, to cash is what the manager wants in tough times. Raising cash from buyouts and the sale of assets and off-balance-sheet assets is fine. But "selling smoke" often is a faster means to raise cash. By "selling smoke," I mean raising money by selling an idea, a conception of what the future might be, a project, a research-and-development (R&D) proposal, a job-development proposal, a joint venture, a spin-off right to something that does not yet exist. Hollywood, a $9-billion industry (U.S. box office receipts plus home video) has been doing it for 60 years. You can promote a package, package a pilot or pilot a promotional package just like the Beverly Hills bandits do for television specials. The premise is the same. Find the "sizzle" in your company and write a business plan for it. Here are some ways to raise cash from the sizzle.

R&D Grants

There are numerous sources of R&D grants, the most plentiful of which are 11 states that provide grant programs ranging from $35,000 to $500,000. In certain cases, you do not have to relocate your company to the states that offer grants to receive them. ScanTech Corporation in Santa Fe, New Mexico, has raised $350,000 in Ohio and $150,000 in Pennsylvania to develop the company's digital X-ray imaging products out of a circa 1610 adobe building in downtown Santa Fe. Here is how it works.

ScanTech's product is a system that combines X-ray and computer technologies to allow on-the-spot digital imaging that, unlike X-ray film, can be highlighted and manipulated to suit the viewer's needs. ScanTech is considering a variety of applications for its system. A Pittsburgh hospital is checking out the system for chest X-rays. General Electric is examining its use in aircraft turbine blades. Through a joint program with Ohio State University, ScanTech continues to explore welding applications on different metals. Using a grant from the Department of Energy, the company's president is working at a Los Alamos, New Mexico, laboratory to see whether linear accelerator technology can be used in ScanTech's system to accelerate electrons for X-ray generation. The systems's use in airport security systems is under study.

The company's founder, Everett Ellin, who learned fund raising several years ago as assistant director of the Guggenheim Museum, has raised nearly as much in state grant funds — $500,000 — as he has in venture capital from private investors.

You might think that grants take too long to get and are uncertain sources of capital. Not at all. The 11 states that provide R&D grants cite 10 1/2 to 15 weeks to process and fund a grant applica-

FIGURE 9.6   States Offering Grants

State	Grant Amount
Connecticut	$300,000
Illinois	100,000
Indiana	100,000
Michigan	250,000
Mississippi	100,000
New Jersey	150,000
New Mexico	500,000
North Carolina	50,000
Ohio	350,000
Pennsylvania	35,000
Rhode Island	100,000

tion. For information on how to raise grant money, contact the economic development directors of each state. The repayments are not odious. New Mexico charges 2 percent of the sales of the product developed with its funds for a period of eight years from the date of the grant. That is the equivalent of a noninterest-bearing eight-year participating unsecured loan. Most of the states that offer grants permit the company to add some portion of the financing for management services, consultants and travel. The 11 states that offer R&D grants and the amounts are listed in Figure 9.6.

Many of the states that offer grants also offer long-term, low-interest loans.[2] Ohio offers the 166 Program, which provides working capital to companies that locate manufacturing facilities in Ohio in amounts up to $1.6 million over 15 years at an interest rate of 6 percent per annum. To that you can add appropriate federal grant money. The Urban Development Action Grant (UDAG) provides up to 33 percent of the total project cost via a grant to the community, which, in turn, loans it to the company at interest rates as low as 4 percent per annum. A Community Development Block Grant (CBDG) provides up to $350,000 of the total project cost along the same lines. The local director of the economic development agency can help your company apply for a UDAG or a CBDG. Although these grants take a few months to generate funds, they are available in every state to applicants who develop or expand a business in a qualified Department of Housing and Urban Development (HUD) area. Such an area is defined by the age of its buildings and the absence of new development for many years. Two areas that are HUD-qualified, for example, are the South Bronx in New York and Beverly Hills, California.

If your company is at least 51 percent owned by Vietnam-era veterans, you can move to the head of the line for a Small Business Administration (SBA) 504 loan or an SBA loan guarantee to purchase equipment or component parts and for additional working capital. The SBA, which typically guarantees 90 percent of bank loans up to $550,000 and repayable over 84 months, will stretch to $1 million if your company produces goods for exports. Most small business owners can receive SBA assistance, but if you served in Vietnam, you will receive priority treatment. The SBA generally requires hard collateral and personal guarantees.

Let's look at several ways to use these direct-loan and loan-guarantee programs. If your company sells franchises or dealerships, you can help your clients obtain financing to build out, equip and purchase inventory for their location. Are you in the business of selling and installing equipment to small and medium-sized customers? To accelerate sales, take your customers to their local economic development agency and work on a loan- or lease-guarantee program. If you are in real estate development or construction, the UDAG and CBDG programs are hog heaven. You can renovate downtown America with these programs representing equity and conventional mortgage financing layered on top of them, then rent the renovated buildings out to quality tenants. For the street-level shops, purchase franchises of some of the best retail concepts; then finance your start-up costs with SBA loan guarantees. You can find able people to run the shops, and the franchising companies offer training in pizza throwing, ice cream serving and store layout. There are some beautiful old buildings with street-level shops in downtown New Orleans and Cleveland that you can buy and renovate with various grants, loans and loan guarantees. In this manner, the waterfront area in Portland, Maine, bounced back ten years ago.

The state of Oregon offers grants up to $250,000 for businesses that will operate on its waterfront. The state of Illinois will grant

$100,000 to early-stage companies with innovative new products. There are 27 states with innovative financing programs. Other states have offices that promote federal programs. Snatch your company from the jaws of disaster by packaging your development program, walking over to the nearest economic development office and finding out how to spin gold out of straw.

Foundation Grants

There are thousands of grants available from foundations established through entrepreneurial wealth from a previous generation — Kellogg, Carnegie, Ford and others. Several LBO millionaires support the National Foundation to Teach Entrepreneurship to Handicapped and Disabled Youth (NIFTY), a foundation of which I am a director. Recently, U.S. West announced that $20 million will be set aside for grants in its regional market. Entrepreneurs in service industries can obtain grants up to $500,000 to study problems that affect various aspects of society. The Kellogg Foundation provides grants for studies involving senior citizens. Park Communications provides grants in small towns in which it publishes newspapers. The Sam Walton Foundation provides grants in small towns in which it operates stores.

A list of foundations can be found in any major library or via CompuServe. Assign one of your less-overworked secretaries to contact them to determine their areas of interest. Then approach them with your development project.

R&D Limited Partnerships

If movies can be marketed via box office as well as home video, your development package can be marketed in two arenas as well. For example, with the same business plan that you use to pursue a grant from a state funding source, you can go after funding from an R&D limited partnership (RDLP) as well. There are three major RDLPs in the country, two of which are managed by R&D Funding Corporation, a division of Prudential-Bache Securities, Inc., in Sunnyvale, California, and one of which is managed by Merrill

Lynch Research & Development Fund, L.P., in New York City. These three funds have more than $300 million in aggregate capitalization. Their minimum investment is $1 million, with an emphasis on larger amounts.

R&D Funding Corporation and Merrill Lynch perform extensive due diligence prior to investing. They spend considerable time in investigating the patents, the market need, the competition, the capabilities of the scientists and the management team that will commercialize the product whose development they are funding. A senior officer of one of the RDLPs, with whom I worked closely on an $8.3-million funding, said, "We have to go beyond the normal due diligence that a venture capital fund would do because we take one more risk than they do: the development risk." As a result, to receive a commitment from R&D Funding Corporation or Merrill Lynch, you must have a very solid story to tell — that is, a qualified management team, a large market need, weak competition, a less expensive but more efficient product, an enlightened marketing strategy and an alert, helpful board of advisors. In addition, you will have to expect a four- to six-month due-diligence process.

Investment banking firms that do not have their own RDLPs also are capable of privately placing $1 million or more of RDLPs for your company. Their methods are more rigid, however, and they will perform lengthy due diligence. In addition, they will take time to prepare a private-placement memorandum. Furthermore, your company may have to commit to pay the investment bank's out-of-pocket expenses and legal fees if the financing aborts. Even if the investment bank gives your company a commitment letter, it is no better than a commitment to make its best effort. There are, however, success stories. Centocor, Inc., successfully raised $4 million via an RDLP through F. Eberstadt & Company in 1985 and investors received, in addition to some tax-shelter features, low-priced warrants to buy Centocor's common stock, which has tripled since the RDLP financing closed. The funds were used for research into oncogene therapy for certain kinds of cancer, and investors are considerably ahead on their 1985 investment.

If you have contacts with many wealthy people, your company can self-underwrite an RDLP as well and thereby save the investment banking costs. You will have to pay substantial legal fees, but you probably did most of the hard work when you wrote the grant application, so that the lawyer's task is to make it acceptable as an offering circular. Tell your lawyer to protect you from securities fraud but not to rewrite the business section of the RDLP offering. Borrow a handful of prospectuses from a local stock brokerage office to learn the layout and information requirements of an offering circular. This will hold down legal fees as well.

RDLPs provide that the technology and know-how that the limited partners pay for is to become their property. They take title to it. Your company may enter into a license agreement with the RDLP to "make, use and sell" the product for the RDLP at such time as a product is indeed developed. But the limited partners are informed in the prospectus that "there can be no assurance that it will." This lack of assurance places the limited partners at risk. And, being at risk, they can write off the losses incurred on research and development against their passive income (interest, rents and other license fees). Certain states provide a deduction against state income taxes as well for investors in RDLPs.

The prospectus states the amount of license fees the limited partners will receive at varying sales levels of the product. For example, 10 percent of sales up to $50 million, 5 percent from $50 million to $100 million and 2 percent thereafter for a total of 12 years. Note that RDLPs have finite time limits. They also have general partners that manage the development and receive a modest annual management fee — 3 to 5 percent of the amount raised per annum. This fee adds to your company's working capital.

The Roll-Up

If the product that the RDLP develops becomes a blockbuster success, the 10 percent fee on product sales that is owed to the limited-partner investors may become too large in terms of your company's ability to raise additional financing. Assume, for example, that the size of the RDLP is $5 million and your company has earnings of $1 million after taxes and 2 million shares of common stock outstanding. Then, if the blockbuster product has estimated sales of $10 million per annum, your company will be turning over to the RDLP $1 million per annum. If your company requires additional financing, the new investors are likely to protest shipping

$1 million per annum to the RDLP group when it could double the earnings and double the value of the stock. At this point, your investment bankers will doubtless advise you to do a *roll-up* — that is, thank the limited partners for their financial assistance, then get rid of the RDLP by exchanging shares of your company's common stock for limited-partnership interests.

Roll-ups are a novelty in the financial community because RDLPs are a five-year-old phenomenon and some positive successes are only recently being harvested. Genentech, Inc., rolled up two of its limited partnerships of $150 million in 1987 by giving away nearly 40 percent of Genentech's common stock! It seemed like a fair exchange, and the Genentech limited partners did not complain. On the other hand, *Forbes* recently reported that two real estate limited partnerships that were rolled up have given the partners 10 percent of the amount of their investment with little or no prospect for future upside potential. Remarkably, the partners took the roll-up lying down.

THE LITIGATION GAME

While assisting TIE/communications in Stamford, Connecticut, to raise capital in 1976, I learned enough survival strategies from founder Thomas J. Kelly, Jr. to last a lifetime. Kelly was battling AT&T at the time for the right to interconnect TIE's brand of telephones on AT&T's lines. It was hard enough just convincing customers to purchase TIE's telephones, rather than rent AT&T's, because of the service and reliability problem. Could a customer count on TIE to service the telephones if they broke?

Not only did Kelly and his chief operating officer, Leonard Fassler, push through a $350,000 R&D grant with the state of Connecticut—no mean feat when you are an importer/assembler without a product-development division—but Kelly treated TIE's adversarial situations as development projects. He was one of the first managers to "sell" litigation to investors. Kelly would treat his lawsuits from AT&T and against AT&T as assets that he could pledge. In the figurative sense, he would convince investors and lenders of TIE's eventual wins and huge settlements. Attorneys would agree to work on a contingency basis. Investors would buy off on the business plan and regard possible litigation wins as additional capital gains or downside protection. The financially astute venture capital partners of Allen & Company invested $300,000 in TIE after the company nailed down its R&D grant.

Others have carried litigation to a higher level by selling interests to pay legal fees. Dr. Glenn Gould for 30 years fought his claim to the invention of the laser with capital provided in part by Eugene Lang's Refac Technology Corporation. Gould was awarded the victory in 1987, which was expected to result in more than $30 million in royalties to him and his investors by 1992, of which Refac, an American Stock Exchange company, should receive close to $5 million.

Certain litigation wins, such as antitrust, provide treble damages to the winner. If two or three large suppliers stop shipments to you at the same time and effectively shut your company down, it is conceivable that they colluded. If not, why did each supplier stop shipping the same week? You may have an antitrust cause of action against them. A litigation attorney might be willing to take your company's case on a contingent-fee basis—that is, payment of his or her expenses plus one-third of the win. A distraught owner of a large computer retailer sold interests in his litigation to pay the legal bills.

As one who has litigated against large corporations, I know that small companies can beat the giants at the litigation game. The reason is simple. The big guys do not work as hard at it. One must move quickly in litigation, and big corporations are afraid that their image will suffer from having wronged a little guy.

I am not making a case for harassment lawsuits. Rather, if your company has been damaged and if it can point to the damages, add them up and show the flow of events that caused them, then by all means enter the litigation game as if it were a development project. A vigorous prosecution by an eager lawyer can get you a win and enable your company to raise money by leveraging the litigation.

THE ANNOUNCEMENT EFFECT

Public relations is a curious art. "If your actions speak loudly, you do not have to talk about them" is a familiar adage. But in a cash crunch, the folks in the trenches who are getting bashed by the creditors need to hand out material. They need a new story to tell the collection agencies and the in-house collectors — something to get their hopes up.

Therefore, when you are awarded a grant, telephone the local newspaper and get a story written about the event. Then you can photocopy the article and give copies to the accounts payable team to send to certain creditors (not the ones you are suing). Be sure your banker gets a copy to show the examiners and the loan committee.

Public relations can cut both ways. While you are entrenched in your workout plan, invisibility is your friend. The trade press can crucify you. Your creditors are the ones who buy advertising space in the trade press, so any sign of financial trouble at your shop will be gleefully reported there. If you are suing a big corporation, however, sending a photostat of the litigation article to the newspapers in the city where the corporation is headquartered is perceived as a good strategic move by some workout managers. Let the corporation get a call from its nervous banker about the $16-million lawsuit. This could send a dark cloud of concern over an otherwise bright day.

In litigation battles, the one who does the most homework wins. Lawsuits are won or lost before you set foot in court. In fact, 90 percent of commercial lawsuits are settled out of court. Go through all your files involving the litigants very carefully. Ask staff members for their correspondence. Investigate the tiniest detail. Follow the slimmest lead. You may find that the supplier that cut you off was supposed to give 30 days' notice. You may find incidences of defective merchandise. There may be inconsistencies in performance. You might find a possible conspiratorial trail.

In the pit of economic doom and gloom, pull your best innovative idea out of mothballs, bring it up to date and run it over to your state's economic development office. Find out if your package is doable in your state. If it is not one of the forward-thinking 27, check federal funding programs. You may be able to pull together five or six layers of funding without reaching for your own billfold. The states are competing for jobs. Take advantage of it.

Don't stop with state and federal funding programs. Use the package to attract research-and-development funds via RDLPs. You can approach the master limited-partnership investment banking firm or sell your own RDLP with the aid of an experienced attorney. If your innovation hits pay dirt by developing an important new product, you may have to roll up the RDLP later on.

Talk about your good news when you receive funding, then clip articles and let your accounts payable clerks tell your worried creditors about the news. Let them know that your company is valid and innovative and doing important things. The development projects may not be paying the bills, but they are showing strong forward momentum. Public relations can be a powerful weapon because people remember the stories they read about you but cannot remember where they read them. An article in your hometown newspaper when clipped, photostated and mailed to the company's key vendors should be used strategically as part of the company's overall redirect and grow plan.

Funding a litigation and funding a development project have much in common. You can leverage or sell interests in both. Both require preparing a written plan, doing lots homework and strategic thinking and carefully using public relations. Both require selling your vision of a future event to others, then reselling it in other markets to maximize your cash flow from a single event. When things look the grimmest, the time is best to go out and develop something.

When producing a biblical movie, the colorful director Samuel Goldwyn was heard to yell at his staff: "Why only twelve disciples? Go out and get thousands." Think big and involve lots of people. Bring in people who will have a stake in your success or failure, who will catch cold if you sneeze, who will go down with you if you go down.

LAY OFF THE RISK

During hard times, most people develop a bunker mentality. But you won't. You will reach out to the community to involve others in the success or failure of your company. Make them responsible for a portion of your success, with the knowledge that they will profit handsomely from a happy ending. If you'll share the credit with key people in the community, they'll move heaven and earth to help you succeed. If you operate in several communities, form regional boards of advisors. Implement this aspect of your survival plan meticulously, and be clear in delegating responsibility and establishing the rewards for success.

Movie producers seem to leverage people better than others. Their objective is to get many diverse people to assume a portion of the risk for the completion of the movie and to hold onto as much of the profit as they can. Take careful note of how the independent movie producer involves people. He juices them with points. He cajoles them with the idea of being involved. He twists their arms with pieces of the action. He uses, schmoozes and bemuses people until they commit. You can do it, too. Here's how it's done.

The independent movie producer obtains a 60-day commitment from the star and the director to block out 16 weeks at some date in the future. Now he has two key players at risk. They are leveraged. Then he asks the television network to advance a portion of the movie's budget for the rights to air the movie at a certain date in the future. The network will put up a letter of credit subject to a performance bond. The performance bond requires that the director create a budget. He agrees to do so if paid $60,000 for his time. The network is leveraged subject to the producer raising $60,000. That is made easier by the producer having the commitments of three players—the star, the director and the network. And so it goes. If the movie were to unravel, these three players would have to redo their plans, budgets and cash flow projections. The producer scampers around getting dozens of people committed for "dates certain" and fees or payments, and this creates a great deal of forward momentum.

In the field of movies, every player—except distribution companies, lenders and networks — is an agent, an entrepreneur if you will, living from deal to deal. When they commit their services to a block of time in the future, it becomes expensive and painful to adjust those plans. The players have a vested interest in the movie being made. Thus, they begin to assist the producer by widening his circle of contacts to assure that the movie is made.

You can transfer this people-leveraging strategy to your company and use it as a means of generating cash for a project, expansion, buyout or real estate development. The key players to contact are all those in the community who stand to benefit if your company pulls off its plan. Include all of those people, government agencies and entities who stand to benefit.

Begin with the region's economic development director. This person's job is to fill area plants with workers. She may have political ambitions that will be more attainable if she puts people to work. The economic development director will tell you what is available in state funding, job-training aid, federal funding, tax incentives and other economic-assistance programs. Ask for names of helpful people, venture capital clubs, wealthy investors and regional corporate pension funds.

A second important player is the president of the electric utility company in the region. Because people will use more electricity, the utility benefits if more jobs are created in the region. As a result, most electric utility companies set aside a portion of their capital—usually through employee pension funds—to invest in innovative businesses in the region. Innovation means new solutions to problems that affect large numbers of people. Innovation builds strong companies and creates jobs, and that translates into more electricity usage. Make the utility company feel part of your new product or project. Agree to locate it where they can showcase it. In consideration for gaining some credit for the project, they must assist you with financing or introductions to sources of financing.

Managers of pension funds in the region should be contacted to see if they invest a portion of their capital in venture capital projects. Investment departments of commercial banks also are candidates, as they frequently manage pension-fund assets. Many physician groups have sizeable pension funds, and if your project is medical in nature, you might consider offering a position on your medical board of advisors and additional stock options to the medical advisors in exchange for an investment.

Insurance companies are keenly interested in innovative investments. Practically all of them with assets in excess of $150 million have invested in venture capital funds or have made direct venture capital investments. Approximately 5 percent of an insurance company's assets may be invested in noninterest-bearing securities, under the rules of the state insurance commission. This 5 percent is known as the "basket." It grows every year as the insurance company's assets grow. The trade-off to the insurance company, in addition to potential capital gain on its investment, is to insure the company's officers, plant, equipment or other parts of the project. This is not a huge incentive to the insurance company, but if you involve the leading agent in the region who carries the ball for you to the investment committee, the premiums on your company's business will be very important to him or her.

Contact the various suppliers of equipment or inventory to the project. Fred Smith kicked off the $96 million financing for Federal Express Corporation by first going to his principal supplier, General Dynamics, from which Federal Express would purchase hundreds of Falcon jets. General Dynamics committed to a portion of the start-up financing. That level of commitment shows a great deal of faith in the project to other players because the supplier is risking capital and providing either extended shipping terms or credit.

If your project is science-based, the local university might agree to a joint venture with you and provide scientific assistance or laboratory space. It might manage a focus-group test of a new product for you at no charge. If your company has several alumni among its employees, a visit to the university endowment fund could prove beneficial. Many universities invest in venture capital funds or make direct venture capital investments. Grinnell College invested in Intel Corporation at an early stage, and Rochester University invested in Xerox Corporation when it was a strapling. Both universities now have multimillion-dollar endowments as a result. In consideration for the university's investment, you could agree to provide a gift of future personal capital gains to the endowment fund. You also might agree to hire accountants from the business school.

Do not overlook the local junior college president, whose goal it is to place graduates in jobs. If your project will require semiskilled workers, you can agree to hire graduates in consideration for the president's assistance in endorsing your project, introducing you to sources of capital and opening doors that have been closed to you. Perhaps he or she is on the board of the local insurance company or electric utility. A call from him or her to the presidents of those corporations beats a cold call from you.

Who else stands to benefit? When William C. Norris founded Control Data Corporation in 1967, he did so with a self-underwritten public offering. He and Control Data's chief financial officer, Willis K. Drake, drank countless cups of coffee with potential investors at Mrs. Strandy's Coffee House in St. Paul, Minnesota. One day when stock sales went too slowly, Norris called on the chairman of 3M Corporation and painted a glowing picture. But to no avail. While the coffee-shop investors became millionaires, the chairman of 3M Corporation, who turned Norris down, had to settle for sour grapes.

Commercial bankers are risk averse and unlikely to provide any up-front help. You can ask them what they might do and when, however, once the project has begun. For instance, perhaps the bank will commit to financing your accounts receivable from the beginning, before your company has positive net worth. Perhaps it will make an equipment loan, open credit-card accounts, provide a floor-plan inventory loan, provide you with a second mortgage, assist key employees in buying stock via loans on their cars, houses or boats. Be persuasive with several bankers and try to leverage one into helping you lift off to become the company's depository.

Consultants generally have excellent contacts, people who can get things done. "New York is a town where people are used to finding money," the saying goes. A New York streetwise consultant may be able to find the missing piece of the puzzle: the insurance firm that guarantees an equipment loan; the equity-gap lender; the publicity wizard who can place your story in the *New York Times*; the barter company and so forth. The small company manager should ask other companies to recommend consultants who have been helpful to them. Check their references. Establish explicit compensation packages with the cash portion tied to performance. Be clear and obtain the consultants' commitment to your company.

OTHERS TO INVOLVE

Even after you have involved ten or so outside people, there still are not enough key people working on your cash problem. More people must be leveraged. The troubled company must put itself in a position where others will suffer if it fails. A manager I once worked with whose background was in public relations knew how to do this very well. She brought eight organizations and people together in a room and made them her kitchen cabinet, making each one responsible for a part of the company's financing or acquisition, or whatever was to be accomplished. She would bring in the accountants to prepare the financial statement projections, their payment tied to a successful deal. The lawyers were leveraged in the same way. The local industrial-development agency that wanted to see jobs created in the region was pushed to dig deeper into its pockets. The insurance agent who might gain the key-man and liability business if he found money was pressured to find a loan or a creative form of financing. The stockbroker who might get the right to underwrite the company's new issue was asked to search through his Rolodex for names of investors. An agency of the federal government that might guarantee loans was leaned on. The commercial banker who might finance part of the transaction and earn the deposits was asked to reach. So was the commercial finance company officer who might take another piece of the loan. She also invited a venture capitalist and local venturesome individuals for the equity component. She then would squeeze them into her kitchen together, serve wine and a tasty meal and catalyze discussion to try to get a deal to happen. She schmoozed them, cajoled them, laughed with them and kept serving the wine and food. Nobody could leave without knowing *what* his or her role was and *when* he or she was expected to return with a done deal.

All the professionals were working on a speculative basis, so if a deal did not happen, they would not get paid. To leverage the local government agencies, she used the press effectively to announce several hundred jobs to be created or saved. Then, if the deal fell apart, their agencies would suffer the slings and arrows of public outcry, not she. When others are involved whose payment or reward depends on something happening, something usually happens. This woman knew how to get the most out of people.

FORM OR STRENGTHEN YOUR BOARD OF DIRECTORS

The obvious place to find assistance is the company's board of directors. It is critical to put together a strong board of directors. These people should be experienced businesspeople, not lawyers, accountants or bankers. You want board members who have lived through the downside, worked through crises and survived in markets that had been given up for dead. Your candidates also should know how to scale up production; how to design and implement a marketing plan; how to locate, interview, hire, compensate and manage middle managers; how to enter new markets; and how to terminate people without being sued. You can attract responsive, intelligent directors by getting them excited about your carefulness and competitiveness along with the company's growth prospects and by selling them a small amount of the company's common stock at a cheap price.

DO YOU COMMUNICATE WELL?

Raising money requires good communications skills. Many times in business, communications from the top down are extremely poor. The president has the corporate identity, product designs, marketing plan, production plans and advertising plans in his or her head. The president means to sit down one day and tell the key people the roles they are expected to play, but things keep cropping up that must be attended to. The company runs off like a loose flywheel, with predictable results. Sales of certain products fall; sales of others rise; personnel come; personnel go; some customers are satisfied; others bring litigation against the company. The results are uneven and productivity is less than it could be.

These kinds of difficulties normally are part of a larger problem or series of problems. It is not unusual in instances such as this for the president to be replaced by a more seasoned manager in the role of chief executive officer. If the commercial banker is being uncooperative, if the investors will not put in more capital and if the customers are complaining about service, a communications consultant may be able to locate the problems.

You might consider the services of a communications consultant to interview the key people in the company and make certain they understand clearly what is expected of them.

SUMMARY

The development of a redirect and grow plan is a forward-thinking process. Although you might want to shy away from bold moves when your company is in trouble, a crisis of survival calls for vision and courage to look beyond the here and now.

Remember, it is smart to buy something when you're broke. That's why $25 billion of mezzanine capital has been pulled together to help you effect a buyout, and ten times that amount, or $250 billion in leverage, is in the hands of skilled asset-based lenders to provide the bulk of the financing. Smart money moves to where the biggest profits are, and a quarter of a trillion dollars thinks there are big profits in buyouts. Join the smart sets and use the current hard times to buy out a competitor, a division, a healthy company or a boneyard company. Prices are not going to get much better.

By the same token, if your company has a development project that has not been worked on since the cookie jar became empty, now is the time to haul it out and dust it off. Thousands of grants are available from federal, state and private sources to innovative companies that are pursuing growth and redirection.

People are your greatest asset in launching your company on a new footing. If you know how to leverage key players — everyone from suppliers to pension-fund managers — you can open up new avenues by laying off risk with third parties.

Finally, don't let the turndowns get you down. Raising money is a numbers game. You might have to see five potential sources to get one investor, but when you get a turndown, try to get the reasons for it. Some company presidents believe that a resounding refusal is their best propellant.

Endnotes

1. *Success!*, December 1987, pp. 54-56.
2. For details, see another of my books, *Upfront Financing* (New York: John Wiley & Sons, Inc., 1988).

■ CHAPTER TEN ■

Implementing the Redirect and Grow Plan

We now enter the synthesis or rebuilding stage. The company has hit the bottom of the roller coaster. The enemies are known. The bullets that can put the company in the boneyard have been identified. Cash has been raised and husbanded. Teammates have been chosen. Time has been bought and used. Back-to-the-wall streetfight tactics have been resorted to when needed. The company is ready to spring back like a slingshot and soar to new heights of achievement and profitability. Now follows the rebuilding plan.

The president and the chief financial officer should meet on a Sunday and thoroughly analyze the company's cash position. The amount of available or raisable cash and the size of the bullets that could strike the company (which determines the size of the reserve) will determine which strategies to use in the redirect and grow plan. If the company has only 90 days' cash on hand, a grant proposal may not be practical. Perhaps the technology should be licensed or sold outright. The proceeds could be plowed into finding and buying an LBO target. If the company has only 60 days' cash on hand, a bankruptcy lawyer probably should be retained to put the company in Chapter 11 quickly if needed. An LBO can be achieved out of Chapter 11; and don't forget the option to go public via the Chapter 11 route. In any event, all strategies emanate from the weekly cash flow statement.

WHEN ECONOMIC VIABILITY IS NEGATIVE

The workout has been accomplished. The creditors have agreed to a standstill. Free cash flow has been generated to pay the bullets. The criticals are reasonably satisfied to wait 90 days for the first payment on an installment note that they have agreed to. The occasionals are in the same boat: waiting to be paid 20 cents on the dollar in 90 days or to accept a stretchout. Some creditors have opted to become stockholders. There still are problems for the Lion to address, as one or two lawyers try to play hero on behalf of a national creditor to obtain more of its legal business. The Ferret has to wrap up one or two asset sales. The Bulldog is seeking replacements for some key production components and must keep the sales team inspired. But in the main, the company made it through the workout and it is the hour of the Beaver: the rebuilder of the company's business.

But what business should he or she rebuild? The company's present business is not viable. Competitors stole its customers by announcing its death in the trade press and discounting prices for months to win new customers. The successfully worked-out company fails the DEJ factor test explained in chapter three of this book. It is a nonstarter. The Beaver's job is to find a new business to get into and to buy it within 90 days. As the jobs of the Ferret, the Bulldog and the Lion become less time-consuming, the Beaver can enlist some of their time to help with the redirect and grow plan.

My favorite redirect and grow plan, and one used over and over again by vulture capitalists and boneyard buyers, is the "when you're broke buy something" plan. That is, use the carcass of the wound-down company to buy a cash flow-positive company using LBO financing techniques, and apply the excess cash flow of the acquired company to service the stretched-out debt negotiated during the informal reorganization. This strategy can be used for the plan of reorganization in Chapter 11 as well, as was demonstrated with Lag Drug Company, Itel Corporation, Wickes Lumber Company, Penn Central Corporation and others.

Not wanting all my eggs in one basket, I prefer to supplement the LBO strategy with a development project using community support, as described in the previous chapter, based on job saving and job creation. If both redirect and grow plans come through, all the better. But if only one can happen in the 90-day period allowed by the creditors, then put the major emphasis behind LBO financing. It is more time-tested and believable to creditors; and if some of them have agreed to take company stock in lieu of cash payments, it gives them an upside they can look to and salute.

To accomplish an LBO and an RDLP in 90 days takes a coordinated effort using the skills of the crisis management team, quick decision making, clear communications and accuracy. Once again, I recommend the weekly meeting — perhaps on Sundays to leave five full days for activity. The chief crisis officer should lead the discussions by first reviewing the cash position, then asking for comments from the Lion and Bulldog on trouble areas, then leaving the bulk of the meeting to the Beaver's report on getting the company into a new line of business. The Ferret reports first, as follows:

> We have a war chest of $250,000 in CDs with a brokerage firm back East. It is earning interest at 9 percent per annum in safe securities. I have a few more asset sales pending, and I expect to see cash from them of about $70,000 this month. I have begun helping the Beaver analyze acquisition candidates.

The Ferret knows how to squeeze cash out of operating expenses and balance sheets, and he or she is used for due-diligence purposes by the Beaver. (We will discuss three critical areas for due diligence later in this chapter.) The Ferret is sent in to analyze target acquisitions to see if their overheads can be slashed to produce a larger-than-reported bottom line, thus freeing up more cash flow to service the turnaround company's installment payment plan.

The Lion reports next:

> We have signed standstill agreements with all creditors. They expire in 87 days, and I doubt if we can obtain renewals without making a cash payment to some of the larger ones. We have had to take a couple of lawyers to the disciplinary commission for overreaching, and we have motions for sanctions working in two instances. If we win, which I doubt because we're acting *pro se*, and judges

dislike *pro se* because they feel they have to explain everything to us, we might pick up some serious money.

In the meantime, I am helping the Beaver with due diligence on some of the acquisition candidates. My task is analyzing the upside potential of the acquisition targets. I'm doing some serious research on their markets, whether or not there is room to grow, can growth be achieved without additional expenditures and how will growth come — from taking market share from others or from opening new distribution channels. My results will be in shortly and I will be able to estimate if the cash flow from the most attractive acquisition targets will be sufficient to pay the installment debt *and* finance some new acquisitions. But I check the critical list every morning to be sure nothing is slipping through the cracks. I'm a skeptic, and I have dealt with our enemies the longest. One of them could slap a very serious RICO suit on us just before the closing of our LBO and scare the sellers away.

The Lion's report reminds all the teammates that workouts never really are over, and they always take longer than planned. They usually get to the end of the standstill period short some dollars and not having the LBO closed and the RDLP wrapped up.
The Bulldog reports as follows:

I have wound down operations to one shift and a skeleton crew at night to wrap, ship and sweep up. Income from sales is covering all of the company's expenses and I have not concluded whether or not we should continue operating at this level — as a small, niche supplier — or if we should sell the operation to another company or to a competitor. My best guess is that if we complete the LBO or RDLP and no longer need the current operation, we might be able to sell it to the workers for a long-term payout or probably to a competitor who will buy it and shut it down.

I am assisting the Beaver with business due diligence. My job is to go into the target companies and see if their businesses are sound. I also examine their liabilities. But my biggest task is to make sure we don't buy a pig in a poke.

When not on the road, I assist the CCO and the Beaver in filing papers with the community and meeting with community helpers to see if they want to pump in some money to enable us to develop a new product that our present workers and sales team can produce and sell and thereby return some jobs to the community. I'm pretty busy, but I still talk to the sales team when I'm traveling and find time to buy raw materials at the best prices to keep the shop running smoothly.

The chief crisis officer gives a summary report on how the RDLP is doing with the community leaders and with possible limited-partner investors from the area. He then provides an overview:

We are going to need a little more than the $250,000 in cash and the $75,000 expected from the sale of assets to buy the target company that looks the most attractive, and to fund the activities of our small group of warriors plus the two word-processing operators on staff. I suggest that we make plans to sell the operation for at least $350,000 and bring our redirect and grow war chest up to $700,000. We can live with $550,000 for the next 90 days, but I would be happier with $700,000. If the LBO aborts, we will need an additional $100,000 to find a second LBO target.

PREPARE YOUR CASH FLOW STATEMENTS ON SUNDAY

The team members must continually gauge themselves against the available funds in the war chest. Each Sunday, a new cash flow statement should be prepared with great attention to detail. The object of the weekly update is to keep generating cash to meet emergencies.

FIGURE 10.1   Cash Flow Statement Projection

Seven team members for six months	$ 72,000
FICA, insurance	18,000
Utilities	5,000
Telephone	10,000
Rent	9,000
Postage, couriers	5,000
Travel	10,000
Legal fees	15,000
LBO up-front fees, expenses	75,000
Consumables, supplies	5,000
Subtotal	224,000
Reserve to fund second LBO target	100,000
Total	$324,000

For example, assume that you begin with $250,000 cash in hand (actually, it is in your out-of-county banks, partially on deposit and partially in a money market account). In your first cash flow statement projection, you allocated it as in Figure 10.1.

The cash flow statement indicates that enough funds are on hand to finance an LBO, but nothing is available to finance the equity gap: the difference between the debt one can raise for an LBO and the purchase price. That might have to be finessed with public stock, sellers' notes or, if you have the courage to ask for it, convincing several creditors in the informal reorganization to put up the capital. Why not ask for it? What have you got to lose?

Let's take a closer look at LBOs.

TARGETING THE LBO

Let's assume that in your informal reorganization, the Lion has located all of the debt, knocked some of it down, added back unpaid interest to some of it and come up with the total amount owing of

$3.8 million. Assuming equal monthly payments over 60 months of $63,333, potential LBO candidates should be cash flowing at least $2 million per annum, or about $166,667 per month. My rule of thumb is that after servicing the debt raised to buy the LBO target, there should be two times the debt service to pay the informal reorganization debt, or in this case $40,000:

$$
\begin{array}{r}
\$\ 166,667 \\
-\ 126,667 \\
\hline
\$\ \ \ 40,000
\end{array}
$$

Clearly, $40,000 per month will not service LBO-incurred debt, thus the need to find an LBO candidate where significant expenses can be slashed to increase the $40,000 monthly figure by at least three times, with more upside potential from increased sales. You can see why doing an LBO requires a team effort.

You cannot announce the repayment plan until you identify the LBO target and enter into a letter of intent. Let's step back and see what kind of a stretchout plan the crisis management team might be planning, given a $3.8 million debt facing it.

THE STRETCHOUT PLAN

When either the "buy something" or the "develop something" plans appear to be happening, it is time to announce to the creditors how you plan to pay them and when. As a first step, the 400 creditors should be organized according to the following categories of criticality:

A — priority claims, taxes
B — secured creditors
C — unsecured, over $25,000
D — unsecured, $10,000 to $24,999
E — unsecured, $ 1,000 to $ 9,999
F — unsecured, under $999
G — special exceptions

You may have another arrangement in mind, particularly if there is a bulge in the $1,000 to $10,000 group and you need to break it up into two categories. The object of grouping the creditors into categories is to offer them different repayment plans.

Assume that the LBO target will be able to provide a cash flow of $200,000 per month to the company postacquisition. To be conservative, plan on having only half or $100,000 per month. Then use half of that number, or $50,000, to pay the salaries and benefits of the survival team, and $25,000 for utilities, legal fees and general and administrative expenses. If the "develop something" strategy has been successful, then the survival team has an additional 3 to 5 percent (of the grant) available in the form of a project management fee. Save this money because it will serve as telemarketing and direct-mail marketing dollars when the product upgrade is ready to be marketed.

If all creditors are paid equally, it will take 38 months to repay $3.8 million, at $100,000 per month. That is too large. However, the smaller creditors may not go along with a 60-month plan because the individual payments to them will be very small and their need for cash usually is very great. You may have to offer them cents on the dollar up front or in a 12-month stretch. Creditors owed $5,000 to $10,000 usually are difficult to deal with. They will need some careful negotiating. The larger creditors can take a longer stretch, plus an interest rate and perhaps an upside opportunity, such as warrants to buy stock, as consideration for their forbearance. Therefore, an effective stretchout plan recognizes the needs of all of the creditors as well as the degree to which they can be leveraged.

Common Stock

Do not rule out the possibility of offering common stock to your creditors for all or part of the amount owing. If your crisis management team has been clear, intelligent, open and forthcoming, if the LBO target has an interesting story — solid, dependable cash flow without a requirement for capital expenditures — and if the product-upgrade story has an excitement, there is no reason not to try to sell your stock to the creditors. Tell your creditors that fortunes are made in adversity. The creditors who will be needed to sell you components for the product upgrade are more likely to accept common stock rather than a promissory note paid out over 48 months.

Promissory Note

Another plan might include five series of promissory notes— with or without conversion features into common stock—with interest at a very low rate of 5 to 7 percent payable in the 60th month. The larger the creditor, the longer the term. However, there may be special exceptions, such as the creditor you need badly as a supplier but who will go out of business unless he or she is paid more quickly. This creditor is category G. The upside or sweetener could be to accelerate the note if the company's earnings turn around dramatically. An alternate upside is to have the balance of the note convertible into common stock; then, if earnings head north, the loyal creditors who convert a large portion of their note into stock could make a pile of money on your adversity.

What follows then is the promissory note that you would like them to sign and return to you and the cover letter that accompanies it. A sample cover letter and promissory note that fit the example that we have been using appear in Appendixes I and II at the end of this book. Now, let's buy a company to service 60 months of installment notes.

WHEN YOU'RE BROKE, BUY SOMETHING

You have called on merger and acquisition brokers to submit sellers to you and completed due diligence on the ones that have EBIT of $2 million or more. Your hypothetical target company has a balance sheet as shown in Figure 10.2.

Assume that the target company's plant and equipment have been substantially depreciated but that their combined liquidation value as determined by a competent appraiser is $6 million. This frequently occurs when property values in a neighborhood appreciate.

FIGURE 10.2   Balance Sheet of Hypothetical Target Company

($000s) Assets		Liabilities and net worth	
Cash	$ 50	Accrued expenses	$ 450
Accts. receivable	5,000	Accts. payable	2,500
Inventory	3,000		
Total current assets	$8,050	Total liabilities	2,950
Net plant and		Stockholders' equity	5,500
equipment	400		
Total assets	$8,450	Total liabilities and stockholders' equity	$8,450

How Much Can You Borrow?

There is a quick test to determine how much senior secured debt you can borrow on the assets of a takeover target. If the quick test indicates 80 percent or more of the seller's asking price can be raised from asset-based lenders, you can be reasonably safe in assuming that you can buy the company and maintain a majority ownership position in its common stock.

The quick test has two components:

1. How much debt service will the target company's cash flow support?
2. How much of the purchase price can be borrowed on the seller's assets?

Using the hypothetical target company, if you divide 18 percent into the target's reconstructed cash flow of $2 million, the resulting number is $11.1 million. The 18-percent ratio includes interest of approximately 12 percent per annum and 6 percent per annum to retire the term debt. Following more thorough due diligence, you may learn that $2 million of cash flow is too low or too high a number, but for the quick test it appears that the target company would be able to service debt of more than the $10-million asking price.

The target company's accounts receivable are $5 million, and its inventory is $3 million. You can assume that an asset-based lender will provide a loan equal to 80 percent of the target company's qualified accounts receivable (those under 90 days old) and that it will advance about 50 percent of the target company's inventory, although this number can vary widely. Thus, approximately $5.5 million can be raised by borrowing on the target company's current assets.

$5,000,000 × .80 = $4,000,000

3,000,000 × .50 =   1,500,000

Total revolving line of credit $5,500,000

This loan will revolve rather than be repaid. As the company's accounts receivable and inventory grow, the loan will grow; should they decline, the loan will decline.

Many sellers can be persuaded to guarantee the collectibility of the target company's accounts receivable. They also can be persuaded to pledge a portion of the purchase price—say, 5 percent—to put some teeth in their guarantee. If you can achieve this with your seller, then the advance rate against the target company's accounts receivable would increase to 100 percent. The total revolving line of credit in this example would increase thereby to $6 million.

The advance ratio to be applied against the seller's equipment is approximately 75 percent of its *liquidation value*. This is neither market value—the replacement cost—nor book value—the $400,000 at which it is carried on the company's financial statements. Liquidation value is the dollar amount that the plant and equipment would bring in an auction to be held within a few weeks after the lender forecloses on the assets. To a quick test, it is necessary to obtain an equipment list and a recent appraisal of the plant. The seller should have a copy of the latter for insurance purposes, and the equipment list should be in the controller's file.

Assume that the plant is insured for $6 million and the equipment cost $8 million to buy. As a rule of thumb, liquidation value probably will be approximately 50 percent of the market value. In this case, the quick-test liquidation value would be $3 million, and 75 percent of that is $2.25 million.

The equipment loan would necessarily be repaid over not more than seven years, or roughly $320,000 per annum (which, by the way, is approximately 3 percent of $10 million, not the 6 percent that was previously estimated). There is room in this transaction for an overadvance by the asset-based lender because cash flow is relatively high in relation to the target company's asset size.

The two hypothetical loans aggregate $8.75 million plus perhaps $750,000 in the form of an overadvance added to the term loan. Accordingly, you are within $500,000 of buying the target company at the seller's asking price of $10 million without an air ball or an equity gap to fill. The seller may be persuaded to take $9.5 million in cash and $500,000 in the form of a consulting fee to provide advice and assistance for two years. Or the seller might take back a subordinated note in the amount of $500,000.

The quick test is just that. It means that this particular target company probably can be purchased by a boneyard buyer using 100-percent leverage. Naturally, the asset-based lender will want the company that has just barely survived Chapter 11 to invest at least 15 percent of the amount of its loan, but this can be arranged in several ways, as we have seen.

Where To Find the Money

Once you have analyzed the leveraged buyout in detail, it is time to prepare a secured financing memorandum and call on the asset-based lenders listed in Appendix III at the back of this book. Study their size and industry criteria before calling on them. You don't have time to waste on turndowns.

If you have a large equity gap, one too large to fill with sellers' notes, or if the asset-based lender wants to see $1 million in equity capital provided under its loans and your creditors have responded to your requests with a Bronx cheer, then turn to the investors in troubled companies listed in Appendix IV at the back of this book. These investors don't come cheap. They are used to getting control, but you may be able to hold them under 51 percent by showing how thoroughly you have done your homework and how well you have backed off and stretched out the debt. They should be impressed with the crisis management team having been battle-scarred and ready to take on a solid LBO target and grow it threefold.

Again, read their investment and size criteria before calling on them because turndowns are very time-consuming.

CADENCE OF THE TAKEOVER

Once you have established via the quick test that the target company is at least 80 percent acquirable with senior secured loans and that it is in a line of business that interests you, that you know something about and to which you can bring some marketing improvements, then there are certain steps you must take to determine whether or not you want to buy the target company. I refer to this as the *cadence* of the takeover process because it has a *form* and *rhythm*—a beginning, middle and end. The tune lasts about 60 days, sometimes less, but rarely more. You will know when the music stops because you will encounter a deal breaker. But if the rhythm continues within the form established by thousands of LBOs that have occurred before yours, you will literally feel the cadence moving you along to a closing.

DEAL BREAKERS

Downside planning is the rule rather than the exception when doing a leveraged buyout because of the multiple players and their interrelationships. Anyone of them can abort the deal: the seller, the buyer, the lender, the mezzanine lender, counsel for each of these, accountants for the seller and buyer, or an outside variable such as legislation or a creditor of the seller who insists on an unreasonable requirement. It is strongly recommended that you act clearly in all of your negotiations so that the potential deal breakers surface as early as possible. That way you won't have to deal with them at the eleventh hour.

There are an infinite number of factors that can break a deal. These are stone walls typically created by the seller's or buyer's counsel or financial advisor around which the buyer cannot maneuver. Deals break down over price, terms, tax consequences and legal issues. If the issues cannot be resolved, the buyout will not occur. Seller's counsel may break the deal for the simple reason of not wanting to lose a client.

It is my experience that deal breakers arise much more in the buyout of privately held and family-owned companies than in divisions of publicly held companies. The reasons for this are several. Privately held companies frequently have family members as owners, some of whom have unreasonable expectations of value. They occasionally have interpersonal rivalries that express themselves a week before the closing.

Accounting and tax matters present more problems in the buyout of privately held companies than in divisions of publicly held companies. In the first place, many privately held companies never have been audited prior to the buyer's audit. Surprises can occur that cause the buyer to adjust the price downward. For example, inventory stored in the warehouse and carried on the target company's books at cost may, in fact, be worthless or worth perhaps 10 cents on the dollar.

DON'T FALL IN LOVE WITH A TARGET

No matter how well suited you are to manage a particular company, no matter how much money you have gathered to purchase the company and irrespective of the fact that a particular company has "gone platinum" and everyone seemingly wants to buy it, do not fall in love with a target company. There will be another one just around the corner.

W.T. Grimm & Company, a division of Merrill Lynch, which has been the principal scorekeeper in the mergers and acquisition business for about 25 years, reported that there were 1,365 acquisitions in the first half of 1989. The average acquisition was valued at $203.7 million; however, that figure is overstated because of the $16.1 billion acquisition of SmithKline Beckman by Beecham Group plc and the $11.7 billion acquisition of Warner Communications, Inc., by Time, Inc. When the megadeals are eliminated, the average price comes down to a level that the first-time buyer can identify with.

Corporate divestitures accounted for 45 percent of the acquisitions according to the Grimm report. Accordingly, your acquisition opportunities can be selected relatively equally from each camp: column A, division of large corporations; column B, privately owned companies. With more than 2,700 companies being acquired each year in the United States, there is no reason for you to fall in love with only one target company. It can only lead to buying mistakes, such as agreeing to solve a deal breaker by accepting the seller's possible future liability for underpayment of taxes.

YOUR TEAM

You cannot buy a company without the services of a lawyer, an accountant and, in most cases, an equipment appraiser. The purpose of the team is to conduct due diligence.

The costs of this team are paid for out of the cash flow of the target company if you make the acquisition. If the takeover aborts, you must make payments. The three teammates are selling their services on an hourly basis; thus, their fees are negotiable. For example, the accountant you hire to conduct financial due diligence may quote a low hourly rate if he or she expects to be awarded the auditing contract after the acquisition. The lawyer may offer a flat fee payable partially up front and the balance at closing, or a small fee up front plus a "success bonus" if the deal closes. The appraiser, who generally is the least expensive player, will charge an hourly fee payable at least one-half before the appraisal and one-half on submission of the appraisal. If the acquisition involves a plant and real estate, an appropriate appraiser will be required for those assets.

Try to locate and hire teammates who have acquisition experience, particularly LBO experience. The more experience they have, the more quickly and efficiently they will do their jobs. They have solved numerous deal breakers in the past and can help persuade the seller and his or her teammates to be more accommodating.

FIGURE 10.3   Range of Up-front Fees and Expenses

Service	Retainer	Maximum
Accounting due diligence	$ 5,000	$ 18,000
Legal due diligence	5,000	35,000(a)
Equipment appraisal	10,000	10,000
Plant, real estate appraisal	7,500	7,500
Commitment fee to lender	10,000	20,000
Cost of search for money	10,000	10,000
Total	$47,500	$100,500

(a) Includes a "success fee" of $15,000 that when agreed to, reduces the retainer.

THE UP-FRONT COSTS OF DOING AN LBO

Before you can get on with the exciting part of the closing and takeover of the target company, you must pay for due diligence in time and money. It is best not to shortcut the due diligence process because you may pay for inexpensive due diligence the rest of your life.

Figure 10.3 shows the range of up-front fees and expenses, assuming a $2 million to $20 million acquisition price.

The crisis management budget, you will recall, allowed for $75,000 to consummate an LBO.

The retainer column totals $50,000, which is the amount of money *you will spend on an aborted acquisition.* The maximum column totals more than $100,000, which is the amount of money *the target company will spend on a consummated acquisition.* If the acquisition is consummated with inadequate due diligence, the payor may pay ten times that amount or more for the rest of his or her or the company's life, whichever is longer.

It is extremely important, therefore, to abide religiously by the two first laws of leveraged buyouts:

1. Know when to fold 'em.
2. Be relentless in your due diligence.

If your due diligence indicates that the target company is not economically viable, you might have difficulty in repaying the indebtedness you incurred to buy the company.

DUE DILIGENCE

The expression *due diligence* comes out of a famous lawsuit of the early 1960s in which Johns Hopkins University purchased an investment called Barcrist Corporation from the brokerage firm of Eastman Dillon Union Securities, Inc., the forerunner of Dillon Read & Company. The investment went south almost immediately, and Johns Hopkins sued Eastman Dillon for failing to be duly diligent in its investigation of Barcrist prior to offering it to the university. The court agreed, and from that time onward, investment bankers and buyers of companies have conducted due diligence to avoid remorse. To do otherwise is to buy in haste, repent at leisure.

There are three elements of due diligence: audit, legal and business. They relate to the three critical areas in the target company where problems are most likely to surface:

- Its financial statements and records, some of which may be missing;
- Its contractual agreements, or their absence, and its liabilities, both disclosed and undisclosed; and
- Its business, including its management, products, markets, research and development, competition, capital equipment, regulation and employee relations.

Audit Due Diligence

It is especially important to have an outside certified public accountant (CPA) audit the financial statements of a privately held target company, especially one that never has been audited. Although a financially experienced crisis manager can analyze the financial statements of any target company, you should show appropriate caution by engaging the services of an experienced CPA who can play a defensive role—someone who can spot things that might go wrong plus comment on accounting regulations, tax matters and technical issues such as the value of off-balance-sheet assets. Experienced auditors have audited more companies than have most crisis managers. They have seen dozens of deceptive bookkeeping tactics—false billings to overstate sales, inventory purchases overstated to minimize income taxes and numerous personal expenses billed to the company.

Jacob or Esau.   When a company is for sale, it probably has been spruced up before it is presented to prospective buyers. You will frequently see target companies that have been profitable only since its owners decided to sell. Sprucing up is to be expected, and there are means of determining if the profits will evaporate when ownership changes. One of the most common ways to show profits is to refrain from paying bills for raw materials. Another is to record inventories at less than their full value. A third is to book sales that have not occurred. The role of the auditor is that of Isaac in the Old Testament: to distinguish the voice of Jacob and the hands of Esau.

Why Are You Selling?   One of the first questions to ask a seller is "Why are you selling this business?" Your task then is to obtain evidence for the reason given. Be suspicious if the reason for selling is a sudden turn in events such as a divorce or a need to move to a drier climate for health reasons, particularly if profits have just turned up. It is most unusual to show a sudden increase in profits in these situations unless bills are not paid.

If you inherit a company with 90 days of unpaid bills on top of the LBO debt that you must service, plus the informal reorganization debt, you probably won't be able to turn the company around. One of the auditor's most important due-diligence steps is to ask suppliers how responsibly the target company pays its bills. Another is to compare the company's accounts receivable with amounts that customers believe they owe. Your auditor will do this as a routine step. The audited accounts receivable are more reliable in the eyes of your asset-based lender as well.

The Income Tax Comparison.   Before buying any company, ask to see its income tax returns for the previous three years and compare those with the financial statements the company has submitted to you. Look for differences between the financial statements and the income tax returns, primarily in the inventory and accounts payable area.

If the seller has been overstating the cost of the company's inventory for 20 years—a fact you can determine easily by comparing the two statements—but says that the reason for selling is quite sudden, such as a divorce or the spouse's bad health, there are red flags all over the place. The real reason for selling may be that the company has been bled dry and a new competitor has been spotted in the bushes. The seller is trying to sell a company that appears to be turning profitable, whose bills have not been paid in 90 days and whose market is about to be carved in half by a tough competitor. You spot the deception by comparing tax records with financial statements. If the seller will not provide income tax returns, do not even consider the deal.

Legal Due Diligence

Investigating the target company's records is a critical step in the preacquisition process. The company may not have adequately protected its trademarks or its patented products. It may be in violation of environmental or labor regulations. Its insurance may be inadequate or nonexistent. It may be operating under incorrect assumptions concerning distribution agreements or licenses.

All of the target company's contracts require a legal review. If you have experience in reading contracts, and if there are relatively few of them, you may avoid a legal review. In this case, have your counsel review the contracts when drafting the closing papers.

Undisclosed Suits and Liabilities.   We have discussed one of the major deal breakers—undisclosed future income tax liability from inventory understatements—in buying privately held companies. But there are more, such as the failure to clean up environmental spills, undisclosed personnel liabilities or underfunded pension-fund liabilities. Certain of these occur more frequently in buying divisions and others in buying privately owned companies. They are all potential deal breakers, and they need to be brought up onto the negotiating table.

Employee Relations. Unfunded pension-fund contributions are an off-balance-sheet liability that can present a massive cash drain to a buyer. The U.S. Department of Labor will not permit a seller to walk away from this liability. Nor will it permit an entrepreneurial buyer using massive amounts of leverage to complete the purchase with a promise to fully fund the employee pension fund after the acquisition. The Labor Department will block the acquisition until the deficiency is made up.

Cash-poor corporate sellers may want to walk away from their responsibility to fill the employee pension fund, and aggressive raiders may have the best of intentions to put the toothpaste back into the tube, but intentions are not adequate. This liability is a real one, and your lawyer can help you to either eliminate it as a liability to be assumed by you or lower the price by that amount and contribute the cash savings to the unfunded pension fund.

Business Due Diligence

Certain areas in the investigative process are the purview of the Beaver's team and are not assignable to your accountant or lawyer:

1. *The target company's market.* Is the market growing? If so, at what rate? Where is the growth coming from? Are competitors entering or leaving the market? What is the effect of foreign competition?

2. *The target company's product or service.* Have sales in- creased over the past three years? Has the gross profit margin changed? If so, is this due to changes in price or cost? Have sales per employee increased over the past three years? Net profits per employee? Have sales per advertising expenses increased over the past three years?

3. *The target company's management team and personnel.* Can this company operate efficiently without the seller's presence on a full-time basis? Is the management team competent,

FIGURE 10.4   The Mathematics of Business Due Diligence

The Market Factor

- Growth in excess of 10 percent per annum over the past three years.   ✕
- No major competitor has more than a 25 percent market share.   ✕
- No institutional or legislative barriers to entering new markets.   ✕
- Advertising expense/sales ratio is less than 5 percent per annum and not increasing.   ✕
- Interviews with customers are positive, indicating an intent to reorder.   ✕
- Customers do not require customizing of the product.   ✕
- The market is particularly well known in certain regions and niches and there is an opportunity to expand nationally.   ✕
- Prices have not been raised for two years.   ✕
- The company has used traditional advertising to obtain customers and has not conducted market research in years.   ✕
- There are no material foreign or "knock-off" competitors.   ✕

---

hardworking, intelligent and loyal to their owner, past or future?

The Mathematics of Business Due Diligence.   These three factors—market, product and management team—must have positive values for you to proceed with an acquisition. They are not additive factors. Rather, they are multiples. If one of these has a zero value, it will wipe out the value of the company.

In doing your business due diligence, assign a maximum value of ten to each of the three categories. Then see if each has ten positive factors. A rating of five or less for any of the three categories would indicate a decision to fold. Figure 10.4 represents an example of the mathematics of business due diligence prior to a takeover.

This example describes a market that is growing despite the target company's lack of market testing or attempts to expand

FIGURE 10.5 The Mathematics of Business Due Diligence

The Product Factor

1. Has the product's (or service's) name been protected legally?
2. How many channels is the product sold through, and can additional products be sold through its presents channels?
3. Can the product or products be sold through additional channels?
4. Is there a users group, customers' club or membership organization among the products' (or services') customers; or if not, could they be formed to generate additional revenues?
5. Is the company aggressively marketing to its "noncustomers" — that is, to those who have an interest in the generic product or service but buy a competitor's offerings?
6. Has any market research been done to determine why noncustomers buy competitive products or services?
7. What is, the product's life cycle? How frequently must innovations be introduced, and what is the company's capability for innovation?
8. Does the company rent its customer list (or former customer list) to other companies and organizations to generate additional income?
9. Does the product or service have an expandable market, or must the company introduce innovations every three to five years? If the latter situation exists, at what cost?

beyond its niches. It would get a ranking of ten in the market category, the highest possible. It sparkles with growth opportunities.

But assume that the target company has been spending more for advertising in recent years and experiencing level sales or a modest growth in sales that is a function of price increases only. Furthermore, assume that the target company has experimented with certain nontraditional forms of advertising and marketing, such as target marketing rather than magazine advertising and credit-card inserts rather than sales reps, but still is unable to increase sales. The combination of these factors casts a pall on the market that the company is addressing. Four of the ten market factors flash red warning lights. The Beaver is put on notice to proceed with caution.

The second factor — product — can be measured quantitatively by seeking answers to the nine important questions listed in Figure 10.5.

These are not the only questions a buyer should ask about the target company's product or service, but they are the critical ones in determining the ability to generate cash rapidly and on an annuity basis. This ability is critical to service debt after the acquisition, particularly if there is an industry downturn or recession. It is extraordinarily difficult to survive a recession or industry downturn if you buy a capital-equipment or high-technology products manufacturer via a leveraged buyout. These companies produce equipment against future payment, and they require working capital to meet the cash flow deficits between ordering the parts, paying the workers and overhead, delivering the finished product to the customer and receiving payment. Imagine trying to borrow working capital money on a fully leveraged balance sheet. It can't happen. You must sell something to cover the deficit—an asset, a division or equity securities—and that is an expensive proposition in hard times.

Thus, you need additional sources of cash flow. A number of capital-equipment manufacturers generate ancillary cash flow by selling parts, providing maintenance and repair services, creating user groups, providing seminars for customers and publishing newsletters for customers that contain paid advertisements. User groups can generate as much as $5,000 per customer per year, paid up front, with the proceeds used for research and development of new products. Customer seminars can generate an additional $1,000 per customer per year. List rentals of the names of customers and noncustomers can generate a much smaller number, but require no effort on the part of the company.

Retired Navy Admiral Bobby R. Inman led a takeover of Tracor Corporation, a $600-million (revenues) Austin, Texas, defense contractor, financing the purchase in August 1988 with $400 million in junk bonds privately placed by Merrill Lynch Capital Markets Group and a $330 million bridge loan provided by Shearson Lehman Hutton. The price/earnings ratio of the acquisition was 23x, which is roughly 15x cash flow. That is an exorbitant price for any company, but censurable naivete for a defense contractor.

Twelve months after the buyout, and shortly after Shearson sold its bridge loan to Merrill Lynch, Tracor fell on hard times. Defense spending slowed with Glasnost, and the Pentagon had grown more tightfisted about cost overruns. The buyers knew before the purchase that the Pentagon was investigating Tracor for price rigging. A bloodied Inman told *The Wall Street Journal,* "The conclusion I have come to is that you shouldn't leverage in the defense business."[1] Inman resigned in January of 1990, and soon thereafter Tracor filed for protection under Chapter 11.

Consumer-products companies, distribution companies and channel companies (i.e., wholesalers and retailers) are easier acquisitions to manage postacquisition because they are more propinquitous to cash. Their customers pay up front or concomitant with the sale. Nonetheless, intensive due diligence is essential in the more cash-flow-intensive companies as well as in the capital-equipment companies.

Preparation for Management Due Diligence

Even when the market and the product factors produce high positive values, a zero value for the target company's management and personnel can turn an attractive takeover into a difficult workout. Of course, you can change management and personnel and replace them with more experienced people, but that can be costly and time-consuming as well.

To provide you with the tools to conduct a meaningful investigation of the managers, division heads and key personnel prior to an acquisition, learn the key operating and efficiency ratios of the industry in which the target company operates; then compare those figures with the ratios of the target company. *Operating ratios* include the following:

- Gross profit margin (three-year trend)
- Net cash flow/sales (three-year trend)
- Selling expenses/sales (three-year trend)

- Accounts receivable turnover (three-year trend)
  (sales/accounts receivable)
- Inventory turnover (three-year trend)
  (cost of goods sold/inventory)
- Accounts payable turnover (three-year trend)
  (cost of goods sold/accounts payable)
- Sales increases past three to five years

These ratios measure the company's ability to generate cash flow and the trend in which its operations are heading. An attenuation of gross profit margins over time probably means that the target company's product line needs upgrading. This will cost you money after the acquisition, when you won't have it. An up-and-down gross profit margin trend usually signals a cyclical industry and a company that is whiplashed by its customers. This circumstance occurs frequently among component suppliers to the automobile, aerospace, appliance and electronics industries. It occurs less often in industries that distribute, store, haul, collect and reprocess the used materials of companies in a diversified array of industries. *Your most desirable target is a company whose cash-flow-generating capability is rising year to year.*

A rise in the selling expenses/sales ratio is a red flag. This means that it takes a greater expenditure of advertising dollars and salespersons' commissions to generate the same dollar amount of sales. The product line probably is growing stale. This could be the reason the company or division is for sale. If you have experience in marketing, a rising selling expenses/sales ratio could represent an opportunity to catch a falling star and hurl it back up into the brightest constellation.

A slowdown in accounts receivable, inventory and accounts payable turnover ratios, which you can determine by dividing the ratios into 365 days, can mean several things. A stretchout in accounts receivable days on hand could mean that the company is offering extended terms to achieve sales. It is also a signal of management inefficiency. An expansion of accounts receivable could mean that the accounts receivable clerks are less aggressive in collecting receivables than they could be.

A buildup of inventory days on hand could mean some deadwood in inventory. If it is nonsaleable, you might be able to negotiate a reserve and hold back some of the purchase price against the eventual sale of the inventory. This opportunity presents itself more frequently in the purchase of privately held companies. For due-diligence purposes, you certainly will want to ask the seller or the plant manager why inventory is turning over more slowly.

An increase in accounts payable days on hand could mean a number of things as well. If it trends up sharply, this ratio could suggest that invoices are not being paid on time to window dress the company for a sale. If it trends down, it could mean that suppliers are demanding payment more rapidly. In either event, knowing what this important ratio has been over the past three years is critical prior to interviewing management.

Efficiency ratios are a measure of how well or poorly management and personnel are doing their jobs. Remember, these ratios are more important when measured over time and when juxtaposed against industry variables. The two most important measures of efficiency are sales/employee and net profits/employee. If these ratios are lower than those for comparable companies in the industry, then the company is relatively less efficient than its competitors. Perhaps you will be able to eliminate some personnel following the takeover. Family-owned businesses frequently regard their positions in their communities as a sacred bond. Terminating an elderly employee who no longer is useful is simply not done because it is considered irresponsible behavior on the part of a community employer. A target company that is more efficient than its competitors does not present the same cost-saving postacquisition opportunities. However, it suggests that some people in the company, maybe dozens of them, are putting in lots of overtime without busting the budget. You will want to find out who these people are and perhaps promote them after you own the company.

Other measures of efficiency include:

- Sales/book value of equipment
- Overhead expenses/sales
- Sales/net worth
- Sales/working capital

The sales/book value of equipment ratio, if relatively large and trending up, indicates that the company probably takes very good care of its equipment or that it has excellent maintenance engineers in the plant and that the equipment is sufficiently well maintained to warrant a higher advance rate than usual from your asset-based lender. A relatively low ratio could indicate that the company owns excess equipment or that the equipment breaks down frequently. In effect, a low ratio suggests that the company's production department is not efficiently managed. Once you understand this ratio and its significance, then you know what questions to ask and of whom.

The ratio of overhead expenses/sales can point you to waste and fat, primarily in the general and administrative expense category. Overhead is comprised of many factors, but the largest are legal fees, health care and other employee benefits, insurance, rent, travel and entertainment expenses, and utilities. If this ratio has increased over the past three years, it could mean that the company has grown fat and complacent or that its costs of doing business have increased. Product-liability insurance, employee health insurance and other employee benefits have been increasing in many industries. But they may be out of line in the takeover company. Be certain to look at the raw numbers in addition to the ratios, and then ask the company's administrative officers for the reasons behind the increases in overhead expenses. Ask about each line item in a persistent manner; you may find ways to cut costs and generate cash after the acquisition.

In a company that I visited recently to perform due diligence on behalf of a proposed buyer, I found product-liability insurance to be $150,000 per annum. The amount was 20 times larger than the industry norm. When I asked why, I was told that a relative of the owner was in the insurance business, and the payment was essentially nepotistic. The posttakeover saving of $142,500 was apparent.

The ratios of sales/net worth and sales/working capital are relatively broad measures of efficiency. The number explains how hard the company works its assets. A low number could indicate a relatively lazy group of workers. These two ratios are tip-off numbers.

Obtaining Permission To Perform Due Diligence

You would no more grant a stranger access to your records and your key personnel than tell a belligerent creditor to "be fruitful and multiply, but not in those words," as Woody Allen once said to a guy who ran into his car. What makes you think the seller of a company would do something you wouldn't do? The answer is the *letter of intent*.

The letter of intent (LOI) is your ticket of admission to perform due diligence. It expresses your intent to purchase the target company at a specified price and by a certain date, and it is signed by you and the seller. You normally have 45 to 60 days to perform, after which the seller can negotiate with other buyers if you fail to close. The seller takes the company off the market for that period of time and agrees to be helpful to you in your due diligence.

A sample LOI that you can use with appropriate modifications is provided in Figure 10.6. I have used it in dozens of LBOs and it works time and again.

THE NONBINDING AGREEMENT

The LOI does not bind either party to perform. Like the deal sheet of a Hollywood movie, the term sheet of a private placement or the outline of a manuscript submitted to a publisher, the LOI sets forth the proposed deal, but either party can choose later on, in the words of Samuel Goldwyn, to "include me out."

Yet the LOI is critical to obtaining the financing. No asset-based lender worth his or her salt will begin analyzing the assets, cash flow and buyer's integrity without an LOI. All too many buyouts abort because the seller is not serious about selling, or the buyer is inexperienced in buying; unless there is a signed LOI, the asset-based lender has better things to do with his or her time and energy.

You can be sued by the seller for failing to close on an LBO. Anyone can sue anyone else for failure to carry out a specified intent. However, if your due diligence indicates that the company is Esau rather than Jacob, or if you cannot raise the financing, you have a rationale for not closing on the deal, at least on the agreed

FIGURE 10.6 Sample Letter of Intent

Date
Chief Executive Officer
Target Corporation
Any Street
Middletown, AK 07000

Dear Mr. Seller:

This will confirm certain acquisition terms proposed by us on behalf of Target Holdings, Inc. ("Holdings"), a corporation to be formed and majority-owned by the undersigned and key employees of Target Corporation upon your acceptance of the terms herein. It is Holdings' intention to offer to purchase certain of the assets and to assume certain of the assets and liabilities of Target Corporation ("Target") pursuant to a formal purchase offer as described below, which Holdings will make to you. The offer would be subject to the following principal terms and conditions:

1. Holdings agrees to pay the sum of ten million dollars ($10,000,000) as the Purchase Price.
2. The Purchase Price will consist of $9,500,000 in cash at the closing and $500,000 in the form of a consulting agreement payable to you at the rate of $8,333 per month over 60 months. Your duties under the contract are subject to further discussion.
3. The assets that Holdings intends to purchase include every asset of Target on its financial statements as of the closing date, plus non-balance-sheet assets including its trade name, customer lists, contracts, blueprints, technical know-how and any and all other off-balance-sheet assets.
4. The liabilities that Holdings intends to assume include every liability of Target on its financial statements as of the closing date, with the exception of notes payable to the bank, the management contract, the sales commission agreement with you and its airplane lease.
5. Holdings will obtain a portion of the capital for the purchase price at the closing from outside sources and from encumbering and borrowing against the assets of Target.

FIGURE 10.6   Sample Letter of Intent   (Continued)

6. This offer is contingent upon further due diligence by Holdings, including an appraisal of tangible assets, a review of all Target contracts and agreements, and raising capital to consummate the purchase, which activities are expected to consume 60 days.

7. You agree that you will not withdraw cash from Target during the 60-day period, except to meet normal and recurring obligations of the business, and that you will not reduce, or cause others to reduce, the net worth of Target during the 60-day period below its level on the August 31, 1991, balance sheet of $5,500,000.

8. This letter is not intended to create a binding legal agreement or obligation, but to outline our intent to proceed in good faith on the general terms stated above. You will continue to provide full access to Target's financial records by Holdings' outside auditors, appraisers, personnel and attorneys, and you agree to keep Holdings informed with respect to any matters material to the business of Target that would affect its willingness to go forward with this transaction.

9. We will both use our reasonable best efforts to consummate this transaction within sixty (60) days from today. We will proceed to instruct our counsel to draft a definitive purchase agreement for your review upon your signing this letter. If this transaction is not closed within sixty (60) days from this date, by written notice to the other party, either party hereto may suspend negotiations after that date and any further obligation to cooperate shall thereupon cease.

   In the event of cancellation of this agreement after expiration of the above time period, each party shall bear its own expenses incurred in connection with this transaction.

10. You agree that you will not negotiate for the sale of Target, its assets or its stock until the period described in paragraph 9 has expired.

Sincerely yours,

_____
President
Target Holdings, Inc.   Dated:_____

AGREED TO AND ACCEPTED BY:

_____
Chief Executive Officer
Target Corporation

terms. Thus, the lawsuit probably will evaporate in a dismissal via summary judgment.

Some sellers will insist that you place some money in escrow — the so-called "binder" or "commitment fee" — but this can (and should) be negotiated away. Explain that if the seller had better buyers than you, he or she wouldn't be talking to you at all.

WILL THE REDIRECT AND GROW PLAN WORK?

The EBIT of the target company is $2 million per year. The Lion and the Bulldog have completed their due diligence and believe it can be upped to $3 million per year immediately by slashing health insurance, management perks, owners' salaries and advertising expenses. In the subsequent years of the stretchout, some new marketing channels will mature and add an additional $300,000 per annum.

The crisis management team gets out its sharpest pencil and multiplies $10,000,000, the amount of debt being raised, by .18, and sees that the annual debt service will be $1,800,000, or $150,000 per month. It needs $63,333 to pay the $3.8 million of informal reorganization debt, so the difference exists and on paper the target company is the one to buy.

The asset-based lender that is putting up the $9.5 million will surely want the buyer to put up $1 million in equity to show its seriousness. It's time to go to the creditors and ask them to fund the equity gap by taking second-lien positions on the assets. They can be persuaded by showing them what little choice they have and by offering them equity in the company. The war chest still has some money left in it. You can offer $100,000 from the war chest as well. Bear in mind the discussion of personal guarantees in chapter three of this book. If you need to provide them, you have the know-how to do it right.

SUMMARY

Happy endings are achievable, even for companies faced with the prospect of bankruptcy.

You have come a long way with me and I appreciate your patience. The workout and turnaround process is not easy. You have to manage both the crisis and the workout. Business schools and executive seminar programs do not teach workouts and turnarounds, and this book hopefully fills the void.

Remember these few things.

1. Your company probably is a terrible candidate for Chapter 11 and an excellent candidate for an informal reorganization.

2. Gather a crack team to effect the workout and turnaround; then run the company with a weekly cash flow statement and frequent crisis team meetings.

3. Take control of the crisis early. Call it what it is: a troubled company that needs immediate attention. Put out all fires and bullets immediately to preserve the workout plan.

4. Find or raise free cash flow. You cannot save and turn around a company without cash, whether in a Chapter 11 or outside of one.

5. The workout and turnaround stage of a troubled company is an intellectual process. It requires your being quick and alert 14 hours a day. Warn your family in advance that you will need their patience for about six very interesting months.

Endnote

1. Roger Lowenstein, "Tracor, Struggling in Wake of LBO, Finds Defense Sector Transformed into Mine Field," *The Wall Street Journal*, August 3, 1989, p. C2.

Cover Letter to Creditors To Seek Their Agreement to an Informal Reorganization

December 15, 19__

_____
_____
_____
_____

Dear _____:

Following the recent telephone conversation, Phoenix Management Corp. ("PMC") and its subsidiary, Phoenix Product Upgrade Corp., have been unable to meet their obligations. Furthermore, the situation has deteriorated and PMC owes in excess of $3.8 million while having assets of less than $300,000, all of which are claimed by a secured creditor. The situation does not lend itself to a Chapter 11 reorganization or a Chapter 7 windup and liquidation as there would be virtually no payout to unsecured creditors.

As a result, PMC intends to effect an informal reorganization with repayment to its creditors over time. The company has two assets that make an informal reorganization and repayment program possible: a seasoned management team that refuses to give up and a customer base of more than 1,500 users who we believe will purchase our product upgrades.

December 15, 19__
Page 2

PMC has located a company in an unrelated business that PMC intends to purchase via a leveraged buyout using debt secured by the target company's assets. After allowing for repayment on the leveraged buyout financing, the new combined company will generate positive cash flow. It is from this cash flow that PMC will repay you and its other creditors.

As a condition of the buyout, however, we must receive approval of the creditors of PMC to a restructuring of PMC's debt. We propose, therefore, to convert the indebtedness to a five- (5) year note bearing interest at 7.5 percent per annum as set forth in the attached Promissory Note.* The attached Promissory Note includes a limited release ("Note and Release") from you to enable the acquisition to occur.

In this informal reorganization, it is essential that we receive your approval for the plan. If we cannot effect the buyout, we will be forced to liquidate the Company for the benefit of the secured creditor, leaving you and other creditors with almost nothing.

Please consider our offer as a sincere attempt to repay you in full with interest and vote in favor of this plan. To vote in favor and agree to the terms outlined in the Note and Release, please sign the attached blank Note and Release where indicated and return it to us at the following address by January 14, 19__. We then will send you the executed Note and Release. (The extra copy is for your records until the fully executed Note and Release is returned to you.)

Send Note and Release to my attention at:
Your Name
Phoenix Management Corp.
Your Address
City, State, Zip Code

---

* This language varies at this point for each category of creditor.

December 15, 19__
Page 3

If we have creditor consent to this plan, payments will begin in 120 days. Without consent, we will be forced to file for protection under Chapter 7 of the Bankruptcy Act and liquidate the Company, in which event you will not receive payment on the indebtedness.

Sincerely yours,

Your Name
Chairman

Enclosure: Note and Release (2)

Accompanying the letter in Appendix I is the Promissory Note and Release. The value of the "buy something" and "develop something" strategies have that extra little suggestion of leverage: Lenders in the LBO will want 100 percent of the creditors to sign on to the stretchout plan; or the state wants 100 percent acceptance of the plan before it funds the product-development plan. (Do not forget to add this very important statement.)

Sample Nonnegotiable Note and Release: Five-Year Term

December 15, 19__

Payee: _____

Address: _____

_____

Principal Amount: $_____

Due: _____

FOR VALUE RECEIVED, Phoenix Management Corp., a Delaware corporation, (hereinafter the "Company" or "PMC") its successors and assigns, whose address is Your Address, City, State Zip Code, hereby promises to pay, subject to the conditions set forth below to payee above, (the "Payee"or "Holder") at the address set forth above, or such other place(s) as Payee shall direct, the principal sum set forth above plus interest of seven and one-half percent (7.5%) per annum for five (5) years payable as follows: sixty (60) equal monthly installments of $_____ each, the first installment to be paid December 31, 19__, subsequent installments to be paid monthly thereafter;

plus

(i) if the Company's pre-tax annual earnings for any of the next ten years exceed $3.0 million, a payment of $_____ representing the balance of the principal and interest due and unpaid for the five (5) year period beginning December 31, 19__ ("Balance"), to be paid ninety (90) days after the thirty-sixth (36th) monthly payment is made hereunder.

Note and Release
Page 2
December 15, 19__

In an event of default by the Company in performance of this Note and Release ("Note") and payment of any amount or installment of principal and interest to the Holder of this Note, the Holder of this Note shall be entitled to acceleration of the balance of principal and interest of this Note. Upon declaration of acceleration by the Holder hereof, the entire balance of principal and interest shall become due and payable in full subject to the conditions set forth below. Other rights, powers, privileges and remedies of the Holder of this Note are cumulative and not exclusive of any rights, powers, remedies and privileges which the Holder might have.

Notwithstanding anything herein to the contrary, the Company covenants and agrees with the Holder, and Holder by acceptance hereof, covenants, expressly for the benefit of the present and future holders of "Senior Indebtedness," defined as any debt due and owing in connection with the acquisition of entities to be acquired by PMC, that the payment of the principal and interest of this Note is expressly subordinated in right of payment to the payment in full of up to $3.0 million principal and interest of Senior Indebtedness of the Company. Upon any terminating liquidation of assets of the Company, upon the occurrence of any dissolution, winding up, liquidation, whether or not in bankruptcy, insolvency or receivership proceedings, the Company shall not pay thereafter, and the Holder of this Note shall not be entitled to receive thereafter, any amount in respect of the principal and interest of this Note unless and until the above specified amount of Senior Indebtedness shall have been paid or otherwise discharged.

The Holder hereof, by its acceptance of this Note, covenants and agrees for itself, its successors and assigns, that in the event of Company's default hereunder and the Holder obtains judgment thereon in a court of competent jurisdiction, the Holder shall not execute such judgment upon the assets of the Company, its successors and assigns, unless and until, and only to the extent that, the then book value of such assets exceeds the total amount of Senior Indebtedness, not to exceed $3.0 million.

This Note may be prepaid at any time without penalty.

Note and Release
Page 3
December 15, 19__

The Company hereby waives presentment for payment, protest, notice of protest, notice of nonpayment and diligence in bringing suit. The Company agrees to pay all costs of collection, including reasonable attorney's fees, if a default shall occur under this Note.

The Holder, upon acceptance hereof, shall have no further claims against the Company or any surviving or successor entity should the Company be sold or acquired, or the Company's subsidiaries or their employees, for payment and specifically no claims against the subsidiaries (or their assets) of the Company presently owned, or hereafter acquired, except as set forth herein. The Holder specifically releases the Company and any surviving entity and its subsidiaries from any further claim except the amount specified by this Note.

IN WITNESS WHEREOF, the undersigned has executed and delivered this Note the day and year above written.

ACCEPTED AND AGREED TO:

By:_____   Date:_____
    Your Name, Chairman
    Phoenix Management Corp.

By:_____   Date:_____
    Name of Creditor Officer

Title:_____
    Office Held

Directory of Lenders to Troubled Companies

Codes:

Sm: Small, begins at $100,000
Med: Medium, begins at $1,000,000
Lg: Large, begins at $5,000,000
Ch 11: Borrower must be in Chapter 11
WO: Borrower need not be in Chapter 11

Name	Principal Location	Size	Ch 11/ WO
Access Capital, Inc.	New York City	Sm.	Both
Alcor Business Capital	Los Angeles, CA	Sm.	Both
Allstate Financial Corporation	Arlington, VA	Sm.	Ch 11
Ambassador Factors	New York City	Med.	Both
Bankers Capital	Northbrook, IL	Med.	Both
Barclays Business Credit	Chicago, IL	Lg.	Both
BFC Financial Corporation	Encino, CA	Sm.	Both
Boatmen's Bank	St. Louis, MO	Lg.	Ch 11
CAMCO	Baltimore, MD	Med.	Both
Chase Leasing Company	Overland Park, KS	Sm.	Both
Chase Manhattan Bank, N.A.	New York City	Lg.	Both
Chrysler Capital Corporation	Stamford, CT	Lg.	Both

Name	Principal Location	Size	Ch 11/ WO
CIT Group/Business Credit	New York City	Lg.	Both
Citibank	New York City	Lg.	Both
Congress Financial Corporation	Dallas, TX	Lg.	Both
DAIWA Bank	Dallas, TX	Lg.	Both
Enterprise Financial Corporation	Atlanta, GA	Sm.	Both
Financial Guild of America	Los Angeles, CA	Med.	Ch 11
Fleet/Norstar	Providence, RI	Lg.	Ch 11
GE Capital Corporate Finance Group	Los Angeles, CA	Lg.	Both
Goodman Factors, Inc.	Dallas, TX	Sm.	Ch 11
Hampshire Capital Corporation	New Castle, NH	Sm.	Both
Hibernia National Bank	Dallas, TX	Med.	Ch 11
Hinden/Owen/Engelke, Inc.	Los Angeles, CA	Lg.	Both
IBJ Schroder Bank & Trust Company	New York City	Lg.	Ch 11
J&D Financial Corporation	North Miami, FL	Sm.	Ch 11
KBK Financial, Inc.	Houston, TX	Sm.	Both
Lighthouse Financial Corporation	Greensboro, NC	Med.	Ch 11
Marine Midland Business Credit	Wilmington, DE	Lg.	Ch 11
Mellon Bank, N.A.	Philadelphia, PA	Lg.	Both
Metro Factors, Inc.	Dallas, TX	Med.	Both
National City Bank	Cleveland, OH	Lg.	Ch 11
NCNB Texas	Dallas, TX	Lg.	Ch 11
Nederlandsche Middenstandsbank	New York City	Lg.	Both
Pace Financial Associates, Inc.	New York City	Med.	Both
Philadelphia National Bank	Philadelphia, PA	Lg.	Both

Name	Principal Location	Size	Ch 11/ WO
Premium Commercial Services	Huntington Beach, CA	Sm.	Both
Prestige Capital Corporation	Fort Lee, NJ	Med.	Both
Rosenthal & Rosenthal, Inc.	New York City	Lg.	Both
Star Bank, N.A.	Cincinnati, OH	Med.	Ch 11
Transwestern Funding, Inc.	Midland, TX	Sm.	Ch 11
Triad Financial	Bloomfield Hills, MI	Sm.	Ch 11
Trust Company of New Jersey	Jersey City, NJ	Lg.	Ch 11
United Credit Corporation	New York City	Lg.	Both
U.S. Bancorp Financial, Inc.	Los Angeles, CA	Sm.	Both

Access Capital, Inc.
232 Madison Avenue
New York, NY 10016
800-421-0034 or
   212-689-8500
Fax: 212-689-8622

Collateral for loans: Accounts
   receivable
Profit participations or ownership:
   None
Loans to DIPS, workouts or both: Both
Additional covenants if any: Standard
   covenants
Number of loans last 12 months: 15
*Aggregate dollar amount of these
   loans:* $5 million
Contact persons: Miles M. Stuchin
Branch offices and contact persons:
   None

Alcor Business Capital
5655 Wilshire Boulevard
Los Angeles, CA 90036
800-222-4595 or
   213-937-0535
Fax: 213-857-0319

Collateral for loans: Accounts
   receivable, inventory
Profit participations or ownership:
   None
Loans to DIPS, workouts or both: Both
Additional covenants if any: None
Number of loans last 12 months:
   Undisclosed
*Aggregate dollar amount of these
   loans:* Undisclosed
Contact persons: Ed Stein
Branch offices and contact persons:
   None

Allstate Financial Corporation
2700 South Quincy Street
Suite 540
Arlington, VA 22206
703-931-2274
Fax: 703-998-5470

Collateral for loans: Accounts receivable, inventory
Profit participations or ownership: Yes
Loans to DIPS, workouts or both: DIPS
Additional covenants if any: None
Number of loans last 12 months: 4
Aggregate dollar amount of these loans: Undisclosed
Contact persons: John Gallo, Mike Clark
Branch offices and contact persons: None

Ambassador Factors
1450 Broadway
New York, NY 10018
212-221-3000
Fax: 212-221-3981

Collateral for loans: Accounts receivable, inventory
Profit participations or ownership: None
Loans to DIPS, workouts or both: Both
Additional covenants if any: None
Number of loans last 12 months: Undisclosed
Aggregate dollar amount of these loans: Undisclosed
Contact persons: William Paolillo, Executive Vice President
Branch offices and contact persons: None

Bankers Capital
Lake Cook Corporate Center
4201 Lake Cook Road
Northbrook, IL 60062
800-323-4380 or
709-564-5353
Fax: 708-564-5412

Collateral for loans: Machinery and
equipment
Profit participations or ownership:
None
Loans to DIPS, workouts or both: Both
Additional covenants if any: None
Number of loans last 12 months:
Undisclosed
*Aggregate dollar amount of these
loans:* Undisclosed
Contact persons: Howard H. Migdal,
Vice President, Marketing
Branch offices and contact persons:
None

Barclays Business Credit
Madison Plaza
200 West Madison Street
Chicago, IL 60606
312-346-8370
Fax: 312-346-7038

Collateral for loans: Accounts
receivable, inventory, machinery
and equipment, real estate
Profit participations or ownership: Yes
Loans to DIPS, workouts or both: Both
Additional covenants if any: As
warranted by the situation
Number of loans last 12 months:
Undisclosed
*Aggregate dollar amount of these
loans:* Undisclosed
Contact persons: Jeffrey C. Gentsch,
Regional Vice President
Branch offices and contact persons:
Irwin Teich, Division President
1000 Parkwood Circle
Suite 420
Atlanta, GA 30339
404-988-9492

BFC Financial Corporation
15760 Ventura Boulevard
Suite 532
Encino, CA 91436-3095
818-905-7775
Fax: 818-501-4635

Collateral for loans: Accounts receivable, inventory
Profit participations or ownership: None
Loans to DIPS, workouts or both: Both
Additional covenants if any: None
Number of loans last 12 months: Undisclosed
Aggregate dollar amount of these loans: Undisclosed
Contact persons: Kenneth L. Bernstein, President
Branch offices and contact persons: None

Boatmen's Bank
One Boatmen's Plaza
St. Louis, MO 63101
314-466-6264
Fax: 314-466-6340

Collateral for loans: Accounts receivable, inventory, machinery and equipment
Profit participations or ownership: None
Loans to DIPS, workouts or both: DIPS
Additional covenants if any: None
Number of loans last 12 months: Undisclosed
Aggregate dollar amount of these loans: Undisclosed
Contact persons: John Rouse
Branch offices and contact persons: None

CAMCO
7400 York Road
Baltimore, MD 21204
301-828-1171
Fax: 301-296-2114

Collateral for loans: Accounts
   receivable, inventory, machinery
   and equipment
Profit participations or ownership: Yes
Loans to DIPS, workouts or both: Both
Additional covenants if any: None
Number of loans last 12 months: 2
*Aggregate dollar amount of these
   loans:* $7 million
Contact persons: Michael D. Quinn,
   President
Branch offices and contact persons:
   None

Chase Leasing Company
5750 West 95th Street
Suite 120
Overland Park, KS 66207
913-381-8800
Fax: 913-381-1819

Collateral for loans: Machinery and
   equipment
Profit participations or ownership:
   None
Loans to DIPS, workouts or both: Both
Additional covenants if any: None
Number of loans last 12 months: 3
*Aggregate dollar amount of these
   loans:* $80,000
Contact persons: John Chase
Branch offices and contact persons:
   None

Chase Manhattan Bank, N.A.
1 Chase Plaza
New York, NY 10081
212-552-7138
Fax: 212-552-5529

Collateral for loans: Accounts receivable, inventory, machinery and equipment
Profit participations or ownership: None
Loans to DIPS, workouts or both: Both
Additional covenants if any: None
Number of loans last 12 months: Undisclosed
Aggregate dollar amount of these loans: Undisclosed
Contact persons: Robin Weiss
Branch offices and contact persons: In many states

Chrysler Capital Corporation
225 High Ridge Road
Stamford, CT 06905
203-975-3396
Fax: 203-975-3906

Collateral for loans: Accounts receivable, inventory, real estate and equipment
Profit participations or ownership: Yes
Loans to DIPS, workouts or both: Both
Additional covenants if any: Performance measures
Number of loans last 12 months: 3
Aggregate dollar amount of these loans: $45 million
Contact persons: Phil Sweetland, L. Frank Melazzo
Branch offices and contact persons:
Orange, CA, 714-565-5200
Dallas, TX, 214-392-2400
Lincolnshire, IL, 708-634-1101

CIT Group/Business Credit
270 Park Avenue
28th Floor
New York, NY 10017
212-270-2720
Fax: 212-286-1607

Collateral for loans: Accounts receivable, inventory, equipment
Profit participations or ownership: None
Loans to DIPS, workouts or both: Both
Additional covenants if any: Normal financial covenants plus super-priority status
Number of loans last 12 months: 3
Aggregate dollar amount of these loans: $150 million
Contact persons: David M. Weinstein, Vice President; Victor Russo, Vice President
Branch offices and contact persons:
Raul E. Herrera
300 South Grand Avenue
3rd Floor
Los Angeles, CA 90071
213-621-8301
Fax: 213-621-8309

Citibank
399 Park Avenue
New York, NY 10043
212-559-5307
Fax: 212-793-0875

Collateral for loans: Accounts receivable, inventory, machinery and equipment
Profit participations or ownership: Not typically
Loans to DIPS, workouts or both: Both
Additional covenants if any: Court-related reporting requirements, but each situation is tailor-made.
Number of loans last 12 months: 3
Aggregate dollar amount of these loans: $420 million
Contact persons: Ann Lane, John Podkowsky, 212-559-3540
Fax: 212-421-0321
Branch offices and contact persons:
Many offices throughout the U.S. and abroad

Congress Financial Corporation
1201 Main Street
Suite 1625
Dallas, TX 75250
214-761-9044
Fax: 214-748-9118

Collateral for loans: Accounts receivable, inventory, machinery and equipment
Profit participations or ownership: None
Loans to DIPS, workouts or both: Both
Additional covenants if any: None
Number of loans last 12 months: Many
Aggregate dollar amount of these loans: $100 million+
Contact persons: Peter J. Levy
Branch offices and contact persons:
100 South Wacker Drive
Chicago, IL 60606
312-332-0420

DAIWA Bank
1601 Elm Street
Dallas, TX 75201
214-979-0925
Fax: 214-979-0571

Collateral for loans: Accounts receivable, inventory
Profit participations or ownership: None
Loans to DIPS, workouts or both: Both
Additional covenants if any: None
Number of loans last 12 months: Undisclosed
Aggregate dollar amount of these loans: Undisclosed
Contact persons: Paul Patrick, Vice President
Branch offices and contact persons: Many throughout the U.S.

Enterprise Financial Corporation
6100 Lake Forest Avenue
Suite 530
Atlanta, GA 30328
404-255-4400
Fax: 404-847-9301

Collateral for loans: Accounts receivable, inventory, equipment
Profit participations or ownership: None
Loans to DIPS, workouts or both: Both
Additional covenants if any: As warranted by the situation
Number of loans last 12 months: 3
Aggregate dollar amount of these loans: $700,000
Contact persons: Connie Warne, President
Branch offices and contact persons: None

Financial Guild of America
4154 Whiteside Street
Los Angeles, CA 90063-1691
213-268-9213
Fax: 213-260-7431

Collateral for loans: Accounts receivable, inventory, machinery and equipment
Profit participations or ownership: None
Loans to DIPS, workouts or both: DIPS
Additional covenants if any: Lender's attorney's costs to be paid by borrower
Number of loans last 12 months: 3
Aggregate dollar amount of these loans: $1,000,000
Contact persons: Darlene Diedrich
Branch offices and contact persons: None

Fleet/Norstar
111 Westminster Street
Providence, RI 02903
401-278-5598
Fax: 401-278-3133

Collateral for loans: Accounts
   receivable, inventory, equipment
Profit participations or ownership:
   None
Loans to DIPS, workouts or both: DIPS
Additional covenants if any: None
Number of loans last 12 months: 4
Aggregate dollar amount of these
   loans: Undisclosed
Contact persons: Keven McGrath
Branch offices and contact persons:
   None

GE Capital Corporate
   Finance Group
1999 Avenue of the Stars
Suite 3000
Los Angeles, CA 90067
213-203-0335
Fax: 213-785-0644

Collateral for loans: Accounts
   receivable, inventory, machinery
   and equipment
Profit participations or ownership: Yes
Loans to DIPS, workouts or both: Both
Additional covenants if any: Priority
   administration claims status, plus
   standard asset-based loan covenants
Number of loans last 12 months: 7
Aggregate dollar amount of these
   loans: $1.5 billion
Contact persons: Jeffrey H. Coats,
   Senior Vice President and Manager
Branch offices and contact persons:
   Richard S. Allen
   535 Madison Avenue, Suite 2700
   New York, NY 10022
   212-826-5959
   Kenneth T. Millar
   100 Galleria Parkway, Suite 900
   Atlanta, GA 30339
   404-955-9299
   Jerry E. Roberts
   15301 Dallas Parkway, Suite 1100
   Dallas, TX 75248
   214-458-3232

Goodman Factors, Inc.
3001 LBJ Freeway
Suite 230
Dallas, TX 75234
214-241-3297
Fax: 214-243-6285

Collateral for loans: Accounts
   receivable
Profit participations or ownership:
   None
Loans to DIPS, workouts or both: DIPS
Additional covenants if any: None
Number of loans last 12 months: 4
*Aggregate dollar amount of these
   loans:* Undisclosed
Contact persons: Keith Reid,
   Jack Correro
Branch offices and contact persons:
   None

**Hampshire Capital
   Corporation**
P. O. Box 178
New Castle, NH 03854
603-431-1415
Fax: 603-431-7755

Collateral for loans: Accounts
   receivable, inventory, machinery
   and equipment, real estate
Profit participations or ownership: Yes
Loans to DIPS, workouts or both: DIPS
Additional covenants if any: None
Number of loans last 12 months: 1
*Aggregate dollar amount of these
   loans:* Undisclosed
Contact persons: Philip G. Baker
Branch offices and contact persons:
   None

Hibernia National Bank
1601 Elm Street
2nd Floor
Dallas, TX 75201
214-969-6133
Fax: 214-969-6096

Collateral for loans: Accounts receivable, inventory, machinery and equipment
Profit participations or ownership: None
Loans to DIPS, workouts or both: DIPS
Additional covenants if any: None
Number of loans last 12 months: Undisclosed
Aggregate dollar amount of these loans: Undisclosed
Contact persons: E. L. "Chip" Scoggins
Branch offices and contact persons: None

Hinden/Owen/Engelke, Inc.
10920 Wilshire Boulevard
Suite 1400
Los Angeles, CA 90024
213-208-8184
Fax: 213-824-4092

Collateral for loans: Accounts receivable, inventory, machinery and equipment, real estate
Profit participations or ownership: None
Loans to DIPS, workouts or both: Both
Additional covenants if any: None
Number of loans last 12 months: 1
Aggregate dollar amount of these loans: $5 million
Contact persons: Russell Hindin
Branch offices and contact persons:
Jack Engelke
116 South Michigan Avenue
Suite 1400
Chicago, IL 60603
312-606-0551
Fax: 312-372-8681

IBJ Schroder Bank & Trust Company
1 State Street
New York, NY 10004
212-858-2117
Fax: 212-858-2768

Collateral for loans: Accounts receivable, inventory
Profit participations or ownership: None
Loans to DIPS, workouts or both: DIPS
Additional covenants if any: None
Number of loans last 12 months: 5
Aggregate dollar amount of these loans: $50 million
Contact persons: Peter A. Handy, Ron Winter
Branch offices and contact persons: None

J&D Financial Corporation
12747 Biscayne Boulevard
North Miami, FL 33181
305-893-0300
Fax: 305-891-2338

Collateral for loans: Accounts receivable, inventory, machinery and equipment
Profit participations or ownership: None
Loans to DIPS, workouts or both: DIPS
Additional covenants if any: As warranted by the situation
Number of loans last 12 months: Undisclosed
Aggregate dollar amount of these loans: Undisclosed
Contact persons: Jack Carmel
Branch offices and contact persons: None

KBK Financial, Inc.
1320 Neils Esperson
  Building
Houston, TX 77002
713-224-4791
Fax: 713-237-8616

Collateral for loans: Accounts
  receivable
Profit participations or ownership:
  None
Loans to DIPS, workouts or both: Both
Additional covenants if any: None
Number of loans last 12 months: 2
*Aggregate dollar amount of these
  loans:* $250,000
Contact persons: Doyle Kelley,
  President
Branch offices and contact persons:
  Jimmy Cazalot
  Odessa, TX
  915-337-6361

Lighthouse Financial
  Corporation
P. O. Box 3545
Greensboro, NC 27402
919-272-9766
Fax: 919-230-2262

Collateral for loans: Accounts
  receivable, inventory
Profit participations or ownership:
  None
Loans to DIPS, workouts or both: DIPS
Additional covenants if any: None
Number of loans last 12 months: 1
*Aggregate dollar amount of these
  loans:* $1,500,000
Contact persons: Barry D. Yelton
Branch offices and contact persons:
  None

**Marine Midland Business
  Credit**
One Christiana Center
301 North Walnut Street
Wilmington, DE 19801
302-573-6712
Fax: 302-573-3513

Collateral for loans: Accounts
  receivable, inventory, machinery
  and equipment
Profit participations or ownership:
  None
Loans to DIPS, workouts or both: DIPS
Additional covenants if any: None
Number of loans last 12 months:
*Aggregate dollar amount of these
  loans:*
Contact persons: Ted Prushinski
Branch offices and contact persons:
  Atlanta, GA, 404-452-0029
  Boston, MA, 617-273-4455
  Buffalo, NY, 716-841-7407
  Charlotte, NC, 704-535-1234
  Chicago, IL, 312-876-3320
  Cincinnati, OH, 513-721-2221
  Dallas, TX, 214-385-3500
  Kansas City, MO, 816-474-0202
  Los Angeles, CA, 213-437-4545
  New York, NY, 212-503-6558

Mellon Bank, N.A.
1735 Market Street
Philadelphia, PA 19101
215-553-3483
Fax: 215-553-0201

Collateral for loans: Accounts
  receivable, inventory, machinery
  and equipment
Profit participations or ownership:
  None
Loans to DIPS, workouts or both: Both
Additional covenants if any: None
Number of loans last 12 months:
  Undisclosed
*Aggregate dollar amount of these
  loans:* Undisclosed
Contact persons: Frank Sannella, Jr.
Branch offices and contact persons:
  Douglas A. Hoffman, Vice President
  OMBC 4942
  Pittsburgh, PA 15250, 412-234-3097
  Jack Hoekstra
  Oakbrook Terrace, IL, 312-341-6670

Metro Factors, Inc.
P. O. Box 38604
Dallas, TX 75238
214-363-4557
Fax: 214-369-1944

Collateral for loans: Accounts
  receivable
Profit participations or ownership:
  None
Loans to DIPS, workouts or both: Both
Additional covenants if any:
  Super-priority lien status
Number of loans last 12 months: 6
*Aggregate dollar amount of these
  loans:* $2,500,000
Contact persons: Richard Worthy,
  President
Branch offices and contact persons:
  None

National City Bank
1900 East Ninth Street
Cleveland, OH 44114
216-575-3198
Fax: 216-575-3160

Collateral for loans: Accounts
  receivable, inventory
Profit participations or ownership:
  None
Loans to DIPS, workouts or both: DIPS
Additional covenants if any: None
Number of loans last 12 months:
*Aggregate dollar amount of these
  loans:* $10 million
Contact persons: Alan M. Zang
Branch offices and contact persons:
  600 Vine Street
  Suite 304
  Cincinnati, OH 45202-4122
  513-381-7474
  Fax: 513-381-4951

NCNB Texas
901 Main Street
Dalls, TX 75283
214-508-0403
Fax: 214-508-0425

Collateral for loans: Accounts
receivable, inventory, machinery
and equipment
Profit participations or ownership: Yes
Loans to DIPS, workouts or both: DIPS
Additional covenants if any: None
Number of loans last 12 months:
Undisclosed
*Aggregate dollar amount of these
loans:* Undisclosed
Contact persons: Bob Cochran
Branch offices and contact persons:
David Bowers
700 Louisiana Street
Houston, TX 77002
713-802-7717
Fax: 713-247-7175

**Nederlandsche
Middenstandsbank**
135 East 57th Street
New York, NY 10022-3101
212-446-1706
Fax: 212-750-8935

Collateral for loans: Accounts
receivable, inventory, machinery
and equipment
Profit participations or ownership: As
warranted by the situation
Loans to DIPS, workouts or both: Both
Additional covenants if any: As
warranted by the situation
Number of loans last 12 months: 4
*Aggregate dollar amount of these
loans:* $100 million
Contact persons: Barry Iseley,
Tracey Rudd
Branch offices and contact persons:
None

Pace Financial Associates, Inc.
43 West 89th Street
New York, NY 10024
212-874-4890
Fax: 212-873-9611

Collateral for loans: Accounts receivable, inventory, machinery and equipment
Profit participations or ownership: Yes
Loans to DIPS, workouts or both: Both
Additional covenants if any: None
Number of loans last 12 months: 3
Aggregate dollar amount of these loans: $2.5 million
Contact persons: Austin Bleich
Branch offices and contact persons:
AAA
Bill Gatehouse Road
Falls Church, VA 22047

Philadelphia National Bank
P. O. Box 7618
Philadelphia, PA 19101
215-973-3575
Fax: 215-973-6054

Collateral for loans: Accounts receivable, inventory
Profit participations or ownership: Undisclosed
Loans to DIPS, workouts or both: Both
Additional covenants if any: Standard asset-based loans policies
Number of loans last 12 months: Undisclosed
Aggregate dollar amount of these loans: Undisclosed
Contact persons: Ronald K. Wallace, Senior Vice President
Branch offices and contact persons: Affiliated with Congress Financial Corporation (see separate listing). Both companies are subsidiaries of CoreState Financial Corporation.

Premium Commercial Services
P. O. Box 2480
Huntington Beach, CA
92647
714-893-4250
Fax: 714-893-6184

Collateral for loans: Accounts
receivable, inventory
Profit participations or ownership:
None
Loans to DIPS, workouts or both: Both
Additional covenants if any: None
Number of loans last 12 months:
Undisclosed
*Aggregate dollar amount of these
loans:* Undisclosed
Contact persons: Cole Allen
Branch offices and contact persons:
7100 Hayvenhurst
Penthouse F
P. O. Box 8255
Van Nuys, CA 91409
818-785-5500
Fax: 818-785-5841

Prestige Capital Corporation
2 Executive Drive
Fort Lee, NJ 07024
201-944-4455
Fax: 201-944-9477

Collateral for loans: Accounts
receivable
Profit participations or ownership:
None
Loans to DIPS, workouts or both: Both
Additional covenants if any: None
Number of loans last 12 months: 3
*Aggregate dollar amount of these
loans:* $3.2 million
Contact persons: Harvey L. Kaminski,
President
Branch offices and contact persons:
None

Rosenthal & Rosenthal, Inc.
1451 Broadway
New York, NY 10036
212-790-1405
Fax: 212-790-0900

Collateral for loans: Accounts receivable, inventory, machinery and equipment, real estate
Profit participations or ownership: Yes
Loans to DIPS, workouts or both: Both
Additional covenants if any: None
Number of loans last 12 months: Many
Aggregate dollar amount of these loans: $20 million
Contact persons: Michael J. Rosenberg
Branch offices and contact persons: None

Star Bank, N.A.
425 Walnut Street
Cincinnati, OH 45202
513-632-4205
Fax: 513-632-2040

Collateral for loans: Accounts receivable
Profit participations or ownership: None
Loans to DIPS, workouts or both: DIPS
Additional covenants if any: Borrower-specific
Number of loans last 12 months: 1
Aggregate dollar amount of these loans: $2 million
Contact persons: Steven L. Fields
Branch offices and contact persons: Barry Sullivan
6500 Rockside Road
Cleveland, OH
216-524-0009

Transswestern Funding, Inc.
310 West Illinois
Suite 140
Midland, TX 79701
915-685-0181
Fax: 915-687-0861

Collateral for loans: Machinery and equipment
Profit participations or ownership: None
Loans to DIPS, workouts or both: DIPS
Additional covenants if any: None
Number of loans last 12 months: 1
Aggregate dollar amount of these loans: $267,000
Contact persons: Stephanie Leonard
Branch offices and contact persons: None

Triad Financial
1750 Telegraph
Suite 103
Bloomfield Hills, MI 48302
313-253-0100
Fax: 313-253-0059

Collateral for loans: Accounts receivable, inventory
Profit participations or ownership: None
Loans to DIPS, workouts or both: DIPS
Additional covenants if any: None
Number of loans last 12 months: Undisclosed
Aggregate dollar amount of these loans: Undisclosed
Contact persons: Doreen Zajac
Branch offices and contact persons: None

Trust Company of New Jersey
35 Journal Square
Jersey City, NJ 07306-9998
201-420-4910
Fax: 201-420-2543

Collateral for loans: Accounts receivable, inventory, machinery and equipment
Profit participations or ownership: None
Loans to DIPS, workouts or both: DIPS
Additional covenants if any: Borrower must achieve predetermined earnings goals, plus standard asset-based covenants
Number of loans last 12 months: 3
Aggregate dollar amount of these loans: $5.5 million
Contact persons: Robert J. Figurski, Senior Vice President
Branch offices and contact persons: 30 in New Jersey

United Credit Corporation
10 East 40th Street
New York, NY 10016
212-725-9480
Fax: 212-725-0903

Collateral for loans: Accounts receivable, inventory, machinery and equipment
Profit participations or ownership: None
Loans to DIPS, workouts or both: Both
Additional covenants if any: None
Number of loans last 12 months: 12
Aggregate dollar amount of these loans: $5 million
Contact persons: Leonard R. Landis
Branch offices and contact persons: None

U.S. Bancorp Financial, Inc.
201 North Figueroa
Suite 900
Los Angeles, CA 90012
213-580-5620
Fax: 213-580-5678

Collateral for loans: Accounts receivable, inventory, equipment
Profit participations or ownership: None
Loans to DIPS, workouts or both: Both
Additional covenants if any: Borrower-specific
Number of loans last 12 months: Undisclosed
Aggregate dollar amount of these loans: Undisclosed
Contact persons: Louis Hajjar
Branch offices and contact persons: None

Directory of Investors in Troubled Companies

Codes:

Sm: Small, begins at $100,000
Med: Medium, begins at $1,000,000
Lg: Large, begins at $5,000,000
Ch 11: Investee must be in Chapter 11
WO: Investee need not be in Chapter 11

Name	Principal Location	Size	Ch 11/ WO
Alliance Recovery Group, Inc.	Baltimore, MD		Both
Allsop Venture Partners	Cedar Rapids, IA	Lg.	Both
American Acquistion Partners	Morristown, NJ	Lg.	Both
Applied Technology	Lexington, MA	Med.	Ch 11
Ardshiel, Inc.	New York City	Lg.	Both
Baytree Investors, Inc.	Rosemont (Chicago)	Lg.	Both
Benefit Capital, Inc.	Inglewood, CA	Med.	Both
BT Securities Corporation	New York City	Lg.	Both
Capital for Business, Inc.	St. Louis, MO	Med.	Ch 11
Capital Partners	Greenwich, CT	Lg.	Both
Carl Street Partners	Chicago, IL	Med.	Both
Castle Harlan, Inc.	New York City	Lg.	Both
Chase Manhattan Capital Corporation	New York City	Lg.	Ch 11

Name	Principal Location	Size	Ch 11/ WO
Code, Hennessy & Simmons	Chicago, IL	Lg.	Both
Cohen, Arnold S., Financial Consultants	New York City	Med.	Ch 11
Comann, Howard & Flamen	Menlo Park, CA	Lg.	Both
Continental Equity Capital Corporation	Chicago, IL	Med.	Ch 11
Controlled Investments	Beverly Hills, CA	Med.	Both
DeMuth, Folger & Terhune	New York City	Lg.	Both
Diehl & Company	Newport Beach, CA	Lg.	Both
Edison Venture Fund	Lawrenceville, NJ	Med.	Both
Equity Opportunity Associates	Greenwich, CT	Lg.	Both
FHL Capital Corporation	Birmingham, AL	Lg.	Both
First Century Partners	New York City	Lg.	Both
Galef (J. M.) & Company, Inc.	New York City	Lg.	Both
Gibb, Parker & Company, Inc.	New York City	Med.	Both
Golder, Thoma & Cressy	Chicago, IL	Lg.	Both
Grubb & Williams, Ltd.	Atlanta, GA	Sm.	Both
Heller Equity Capital Corporation	Chicago, IL	Lg.	Both
Investors Equity Corporation	Princeton, NJ	Lg.	Both
Johnsen Securities	New York City	Med.	Both
Lepercq Capital Management	New York City	Lg.	Both
Lubar & Company, Inc.	Milwaukee, WI	Med.	Ch. 11
McCown De Leeuw & Company	New York City	Lg.	Ch. 11
Merrill Lynch Capital Partners, Inc.	New York City	Lg.	Both
National City Venture Corporation	Cleveland, OH	Sm.	Both
Poly Ventures	Great Neck, NY	Med.	Ch. 11

Name	Principal Location	Size	Ch 11/ WO
Premier Venture Capital Corporation	Baton Rouge, LA	Med.	Both
Scandinavian Corporate Development Group	Westport, CT	Lg.	Ch 11
Schroder Venture	New York City	Lg.	Both
Sprout Group	New York City	Lg.	Both
TDH II Limited	Radnor, PA	Lg.	Both
Venture Investors of Wisconsin, Inc.	Madison, WI	Sm.	Both
Walnut Capital Corporation	Chicago, IL	Sm.	Both
Weinstein Associates Limited	Milwaukee, WI	Lg.	Both
Weiss, Peck & Greer Investments	New York City	Lg.	Both
Welsh, Carson, Anderson & Stowe	New York City	Lg.	Both
Westfield Capital Corportion	Stamford, CT	Lg.	Both

Alliance Recovery Group, Inc.
7400 York Road
Suite 300
Baltimore, MD 21204
301-828-1171
Fax: 301-296-2114

Invest in DIPS, workouts or both: Both
Obtain control position: No
Assume active management role: Yes
Investment is generally secured by assets: Yes
Number of investments last 12 months: Confidential
Aggregate dollar amount of these investments: Confidential
Contact persons: Michael D. Quinn, Chairman, CEO
Branch offices and contact persons: None

Allsop Venture Partners
Corporate Center East
Suite 210
2750 First Avenue, Northeast
Cedar Rapids, IA 52402
319-363-8971
Fax: 319-363-9519

Invest in DIPS, workouts or both: Both
Obtain control position: Yes
Assume active management role: Yes
Investment is generally secured by assets: As warranted by the situation
Number of investments last 12 months: 2
Aggregate dollar amount of these investments: $5.5 million
Contact persons: Robert W. Allsop, General Partner
Paul D. Rhines, General Partner
Branch offices and contact persons: Robert L. Kuk, General Partner
Bart A. McLean, Principal
111 West Port Plaza
Suite 600
St. Louis, MO 63146
314-434-1688

**American Acquisition
Partners**
175 South Street
Morristown, NJ 07960
201-267-7800
Fax: 201-267-7695

Invest in DIPS, workouts or both: Both
Obtain control position: Yes
Assume active management role: No
*Investment is generally secured by
  assets:* No
Number of investments last 12 months:
  Undisclosed
*Aggregate dollar amount of these
  investments:* Undisclosed
Contact persons: Ted Bustany,
  Managing Partner
Branch offices and contact persons:
  None

Applied Technology
One Cranberry Hill
Lexington, MA 02173
617-862-8622
Fax: 617-862-8367

Invest in DIPS, workouts or both: DIPS
Obtain control position: Yes
Assume active management role: Yes
*Investment is generally secured by
  assets:* Yes
Number of investments last 12 months:
  Undisclosed
*Aggregate dollar amount of these
  investments:* Undisclosed
Contact persons: Frederick B. Bamber
Branch offices and contact persons:
  None

Ardshiel, Inc.
230 Park Avenue
Suite 2527
New York, NY 10169
212-697-8570
Fax: 212-972-1809

Invest in DIPS, workouts or both: Both
Obtain control position: Yes
Assume active management role: Yes
*Investment is generally secured by
    assets:* No
Number of investments last 12 months:
    3
*Aggregate dollar amount of these
    investments:* Undisclosed
Contact persons: Dennis McCormick
Branch offices and contact persons:
    Frank Bryant
    300 South Corand Avenue
    Los Angeles, CA 90071
    213-629-4824

Baytree Investors, Inc.
6300 North River Road
Suite 701
(Rosemont) Chicago, IL
    60018
708-318-6161
Fax: 708-318-6163

Invest in DIPS, workouts or both: Both
Obtain control position: No
Assume active management role: No
*Investment is generally secured by
    assets:* Yes
Number of investments last 12 months:
    11
*Aggregate dollar amount of these
    investments:* $100 million
Contact persons: Christopher A.
    Jansen, President
Branch offices and contact persons:
    Chicago, IL, 708-381-6161
    Cleveland, OH, 216-292-8283
    Pensacola, FL, 904-435-8877
    Fargo, ND, 701-232-0182
    Salt Lake City, UT, 801-355-8600
    Fort Lee, NJ, 201-592-5832
    Providence, RI, 401-521-0639
    Dallas, TX, 214-233-6161
    Hartford, CT, 203-520-4560
    Silver Springs, MD, 301-587-1814

Benefit Capital, Inc.
9920 South La Cienega
   Boulevard
9th Floor
Inglewood, CA 90301
213-641-3767
Fax: 213-417-5478

Invest in DIPS, workouts or both: Both
Obtain control position: No
Assume active management role:
   Typically
Investment is generally secured by
   assets: Yes
Number of investments last 12 months:
   2
Aggregate dollar amount of these
   investments: $1,123,000
Contact persons: Robert W. Smiley, Jr.,
   Chairman, CEO
Branch offices and contact persons:
   3701 Birch Street, #47
   Newport Beach, CA 92660
   714-756-3212
   Fax: 714-756-0607

BT Securities Corporation
280 Park Avenue
New York, NY 10017
212-454-3758
Fax: 212-454-1047

Invest in DIPS, workouts or both: Both
Obtain control position: Not typically
Assume active management role: No
Investment is generally secured by
   assets: As warranted by the situation
Number of investments last 12 months:
   5
Aggregate dollar amount of these
   investments: $50 million
Contact persons: Arthur B. Schoen, Jr.,
   Managing Director
Branch offices and contact persons:
   Tom Ventling
   300 South Grand Avenue
   40th Floor
   Los Angeles, CA 90071
   213-620-8375
   Fax: 213-620-8394
   Lou Kovonda
   233 South Wacker Drive
   Chicago, IL 60606
   312-993-8100
   Fax: 312-993-8096

BT Securities Corporation
(Continued)

Charlie Donner
2323 Bryan Street, Suite 1510
Dallas, TX 72701
214-954-1212
Fax: 214-969-5474

Capital for Business, Inc.
11 South Meramec
Suite 800
St. Louis, MO 63105
314-854-7427
Fax: 314-726-8739

Invest in DIPS, workouts or both: DIPS
Obtain control position: No
Assume active management role: No
*Investment is generally secured by
    assets:* No
Number of investments last 12 months:
    Undisclosed
*Aggregate dollar amount of these
    investments:* Undisclosed
Contact persons: Nathaniel E. Sher
Branch offices and contact persons:
    Bart Bergman, Executive Vice
        President
    1000 Walnut Street, 18th Floor
    Kansas City, MO 64106
    816-234-2357
    Fax: 816-234-2333

Capital Partners
One Pickwick Plaza
Suite 300
Greenwich, CT 06830
203-625-0773
Fax: 201-625-0423

Invest in DIPS, workouts or both:
    Both, but the company must be
    economically valid and its problems
    due to excessive leverage
Obtain control position: Yes
Assume active management role: No
*Investment is generally secured by
    assets:* No
Number of investments last 12 months:
    1
*Aggregate dollar amount of these
    investments:* $8 million
Contact persons: A. George Gebauer,
    Partner
Branch offices and contact persons:
    None

Carl Street Partners
414 North Orleans Street
Suite 308
Chicago, IL 60610
312-527-4700
Fax: 312-527-1896

Invest in DIPS, workouts or both: Both
Obtain control position: Yes
Assume active management role: No
Investment is generally secured by assets: Yes
Number of investments last 12 months: 1
Aggregate dollar amount of these investments: $3 million
Contact persons: Anthony R. Pesavento
Branch offices and contact persons: None

Castle Harlan, Inc.
150 East 58th Street
New York, NY 10155
212-644-8600
Fax: 212-207-8042

Invest in DIPS, workouts or both: Both
Obtain control position: Yes
Assume active management role: No
Investment is generally secured by assets: No
Number of investments last 12 months: 1
Aggregate dollar amount of these investments: $20 million
Contact persons: John K. Castle, General Partner
Leonard M. Harlan, General Partner
Branch offices and contact persons: None

Chase Manhattan Capital Corporation
One Chase Manhattan Plaza
13th Floor
New York, NY 10081
212-552-6275
Fax: 212-552-5529

Invest in DIPS, workouts or both: DIPS
Obtain control position: No
Assume active management role: No
Investment is generally secured by assets: Yes
Number of investments last 12 months: Undisclosed
Aggregate dollar amount of these investments: Undisclosed
Contact persons: Robin Weiss, 212-552-7138
Branch offices and contact persons: Affiliated with Chase Manhattan Bank (see Asset-Based Lenders Directory)

Code, Hennessy & Simmons
10 South Wacker Drive
Suite 3175
Chicago, IL 60606
312-876-1840
Fax: 312-876-3854

Invest in DIPS, workouts or both: Both
Obtain control position: Yes
Assume active management role: Yes
Investment is generally secured by assets: No
Number of investments last 12 months: Undisclosed
Aggregate dollar amount of these investments: Undisclosed
Contact persons: Andrew Code, Daniel Hennessy, Brian Simmons, Jon S. Vesely
Branch offices and contact persons: None

**Cohen, Arnold S.,
Financial Consultants**
110 East 57th Street
16th Floor
New York, NY 10022
212-753-1490
Fax: 212-753-2983

Invest in DIPS, workouts or both: DIPS
Obtain control position: Yes
Assume active management role: Yes
*Investment is generally secured by
assets:* Yes
Number of investments last 12 months:
1
*Aggregate dollar amount of these
investments:* Undisclosed
Contact persons: Arnold S. Cohen
Branch offices and contact persons:
None

**Comann, Howard &
Flamen**
2884 Sand Hill Road
Menlo Park, CA 94025
415-854-1800
Fax: 415-854-3848

Invest in DIPS, workouts or both: Both
Obtain control position: Yes
Assume active management role: Yes
*Investment is generally secured by
assets:* Not applicable
Number of investments last 12 months:
1
*Aggregate dollar amount of these
investments:* $45 million
Contact persons: Tyler K. Comann,
Partner
Timothy E. Howard, Partner,
Daniel P. Flamen
Branch offices and contact persons:
None

Continental Equity Capital Corporation
231 South LaSalle Street
Chicago, IL 60697
312-828-8021
Fax: 312-987-0887

Invest in DIPS, workouts or both: DIPS
Obtain control position: Yes
Assume active management role: Yes
Investment is generally secured by assets: No
Number of investments last 12 months: 1
Aggregate dollar amount of these investments: $5 million
Contact persons: Burton E. McGillivray, Managing Director
Branch offices and contact persons: None, but affiliated with Continental Bank

Controlled Investments
425 South Beverly Drive
Beverly Hills, CA 90212
213-556-2155
Fax: 213-556-4664

Invest in DIPS, workouts or both: Both
Obtain control position: Yes
Assume active management role: Yes
Investment is generally secured by assets: Yes
Number of investments last 12 months: Undisclosed
Aggregate dollar amount of these investments: Undisclosed
Contact persons: William Shaw
Branch offices and contact persons: None

**DeMuth, Folger &
    Terhune**
One Exchange Plaza
New York, NY 10006
212-509-5628
Fax: 212-363-7965

Invest in DIPS, workouts or both: Both
Obtain control position: Yes
Assume active management role: Yes
*Investment is generally secured by
    assets:* No
Number of investments last 12 months:
    Undisclosed
*Aggregate dollar amount of these
    investments:* Undisclosed
Contact persons: Donald F. DeMuth,
    Partner
    Thomas W. Folger, Partner
    J. Michael Terhune, Partner
Branch offices and contact persons:
    None

Diehl & Company
1500 Quail Street
Suite 200
Newport Beach, CA 92660
714-955-2000
Fax: 714-955-1812

Invest in DIPS, workouts or both: Both
Obtain control position: Yes
Assume active management role: Yes
*Investment is generally secured by
    assets:* Yes
Number of investments last 12 months:
    2
*Aggregate dollar amount of these
    investments:* $7 million
Contact persons: Michael D. Henton,
    Partner
Branch offices and contact persons:
    None

Edison Venture Fund
997 Lenox Drive, #3
Lawrenceville, NJ 08648
609-896-1900
Fax: 609-896-0066

Invest in DIPS, workouts or both: Both
Obtain control position: No
Assume active management role: No
*Investment is generally secured by
    assets:* No
Number of investments last 12 months:
    Undisclosed
*Aggregate dollar amount of these
    investments:* Undisclosed
Contact persons: John H. Martinson,
    General Partner
Branch offices and contact persons:
    None

**Equity Opportunity
    Associates**
210 River Run at the Mill
Greenwich, CT 06831
203-531-4576
Fax: 203-629-2235

Invest in DIPS, workouts or both: Both
Obtain control position: Yes
Assume active management role: Yes
*Investment is generally secured by
    assets:* No
Number of investments last 12 months:
    Undisclosed
*Aggregate dollar amount of these
    investments:* Undisclosed
Contact persons: W. Brewster Kopp,
    General Partner
Branch offices and contact persons:
    None

FHL Capital Corporation
825 Financial Center
Birmingham, AL 35203
205-328-3098
Fax: 205-328-4010

Invest in DIPS, workouts or both: Both
Obtain control position: Yes
Assume active management role: As
  warranted by the situation
*Investment is generally secured by
  assets:* As warranted by the situation
Number of investments last 12 months:
  Undisclosed
*Aggregate dollar amount of these
  investments:* Undisclosed
Contact persons: H. Jack Callaway,
  Managing Director
Branch offices and contact persons:
  None

First Century Partners
1345 Avenue of the
  Americas
New York, NY 10105
212-698-6688
Fax: 212-698-5517/8

Invest in DIPS, workouts or both: Both
Obtain control position: Yes
Assume active management role: No
*Investment is generally secured by
  assets:* Yes
Number of investments last 12 months:
  1
*Aggregate dollar amount of these
  investments:* $5 million
Contact persons: David S. Lobel
Branch offices and contact persons:
  Sage Givens
  350 California Street
  San Francisco, CA 94104
  415-955-0021

Galef (J.M.) & Company, Inc.
1414 Avenue of the
  Americas
New York, NY 10019
212-223-2200
Fax: 212-223-0053

Invest in DIPS, workouts or both: Both
Obtain control position: Yes
Assume active management role: No
*Investment is generally secured by
  assets:* No
Number of investments last 12 months:
  2
*Aggregate dollar amount of these
  investments:* $5 million
Contact persons: James M. Galef
Branch offices and contact persons:
  None

Gibb, Parker & Company, Inc.
230 Park Avenue
Suite 903
New York, NY 10169
212-682-3603
Fax: 212-682-4025

Invest in DIPS, workouts or both: Both
Obtain control position: Yes
Assume active management role: Yes
*Investment is generally secured by
  assets:* No
Number of investments last 12 months:
  Undisclosed
*Aggregate dollar amount of these
  investments:* Undisclosed
Contact persons: Jeffrey M. Parker
Branch offices and contact persons:
  None

Golder, Thoma & Cressy
120 South LaSalle Street
Chicago, IL 60603
312-853-3322
Fax: 312-853-3354

Invest in DIPS, workouts or both: Both
Obtain control position: Yes
Assume active management role: Yes
*Investment is generally secured by
   assets:* No
Number of investments last 12 months:
   Undisclosed
*Aggregate dollar amount of these
   investments:* Undisclosed
Contact persons: Carl D. Thoma
Branch offices and contact persons:
   None

Grubb & Williams, Ltd.
1790 The Lenox Building
3399 Peachtree Road
Atlanta, GA 30326
404-237-6222
Fax: 404-261-1578

Invest in DIPS, workouts or both: Both
Obtain control position: Yes
Assume active management role: Yes
*Investment is generally secured by
   assets:* Yes
Number of investments last 12 months:
   2
*Aggregate dollar amount of these
   investments:* $500,000
Contact persons: Stephen Grubb,
   Managing Director
Branch offices and contact persons:
   None

**Heller Equity Capital
 Corporation**
200 North LaSalle Street
Chicago, IL 60601
312-621-7200
Fax: 312-621-7208

Invest in DIPS, workouts or both: Both
Obtain control position: Usually
Assume active management role:
   Active on board and selection of
   management
*Investment is generally secured by
   assets:* Yes
Number of investments last 12 months:
   Undisclosed
*Aggregate dollar amount of these
   investments:* $20 million minimum
   per investment
Contact persons: Erwin A. Marks,
   Managing Director
Branch offices and contact persons:
   None

**Investors Equity
 Corporation**
The Stone House
Carnegie Center
Princeton, NJ 08540
609-243-0400
Fax: 609-243-0481

Invest in DIPS, workouts or both: Both
Obtain control position: Yes
Assume active management role: No
*Investment is generally secured by
   assets:* Yes
Number of investments last 12 months:
   3
*Aggregate dollar amount of these
   investments:* $15 million
Contact persons: Kirby Westheimer
Branch offices and contact persons:
   None

Johnsen Securities
767 Third Avenue
7th Floor
New York, NY 10017
212-838-7778
Fax: 212-593-0734

Invest in DIPS, workouts or both: Both
Obtain control position: Yes
Assume active management role: Yes
Investment is generally secured by assets: No
Number of investments last 12 months: 1
Aggregate dollar amount of these investments: $2 million
Contact persons: Walter Johnsen
Branch offices and contact persons: None

Lepercq Capital Management
1675 Broadway
New York, NY 10019
212-698-0795
Fax: 212-262-0144 or 212-262-0155

Invest in DIPS, workouts or both: DIPS
Obtain control position: Yes
Assume active management role: Yes
Investment is generally secured by assets: As warranted by the situation
Number of investments last 12 months: 1
Aggregate dollar amount of these investments: $5.3 million
Contact persons: Michael J. Connelly
Branch offices and contact persons: None

Lubar & Company, Inc.
3380 First Wisconsin Center
Milwaukee, WI 53202
414-291-9000
Fax: 414-291-9061

Invest in DIPS, workouts or both: DIPS
Obtain control position: Yes
Assume active management role: No
Investment is generally secured by assets: Not customarily
Number of investments last 12 months: Undisclosed
Aggregate dollar amount of these investments: Undisclosed
Contact persons: Joe Froehlich
Sheldon B. Lubar
David J. Lubar
Branch offices and contact persons: None

McCown De Leeuw & Company
900 Third Avenue
28th Floor
New York, NY 10022
212-418-6539
Fax: 212-418-6584

Invest in DIPS, workouts or both: DIPS
Obtain control position: Yes
Assume active management role: Via board control
Investment is generally secured by assets: Typically
Number of investments last 12 months: Undisclosed
Aggregate dollar amount of these investments: Undisclosed
Contact persons: David E. De Leeuw, Managing Partner
Branch offices and contact persons:
George E. McCown,
Managing Partner
3000 Sand Hill Road
Building 3, Suite 290
Menlo Park, CA 94025
415-854-6000
Fax: 415-854-0853
Steven A. Zuckerman
455 East Eisenhower Parkway
Suite 117
Ann Arbor, MI 48108
313-662-9732
Fax: 313-662-9824

Merrill Lynch Capital Partners, Inc.
767 Fifth Avenue
48th Floor
New York, NY 10153
212-339-8502
Fax: 212-339-8585 or
212-339-8586

Invest in DIPS, workouts or both: Both
Obtain control position: Yes
Assume active management role: No
Investment is generally secured by assets: No
Number of investments last 12 months: 1
Aggregate dollar amount of these investments: $200 million
Contact persons: James J. Burke, Jr.
Branch offices and contact persons: None

National City Venture Corporation
1965 East Sixth Street
Suite 400
Cleveland, OH 44114
216-575-2491
Fax: 216-575-3355

Invest in DIPS, workouts or both: Both
Obtain control position: As warranted by the situation
Assume active management role: No
Investment is generally secured by assets: As warranted by the situation
Number of investments last 12 months: 4
Aggregate dollar amount of these investments: $7 million
Contact persons: Philip L. Rice, Vice President
Daniel L. Kellogg, Vice President
Carl E. Baldassarre, Vice President
Branch offices and contact persons: None

Poly Ventures
199 Middle Neck Road
Great Neck, NY 11021
516-829-4625
Fax: 516-466-5561

Invest in DIPS, workouts or both: DIPS
Obtain control position: Yes
Assume active management role: As
   warranted by the situation
*Investment is generally secured by
   assets:* No
Number of investments last 12 months:
   1
*Aggregate dollar amount of these
   investments:* $2 million
Contact persons: Herman Fialkov,
   General Partner
Branch offices and contact persons:
   Robert Brill
   Poly Ventures II
   Polytechnic University Office
   Route 110
   Farmingdale, NY 11735
   516-249-4710
   516-249-4713

**Premier Venture Capital
   Corporation**
451 Florida Street
Baton Rouge, LA 70801
504-389-4421
Fax: 504-389-4299

Invest in DIPS, workouts or both: Both
Obtain control position: Yes
Assume active management role: No
*Investment is generally secured by
   assets:* Yes
Number of investments last 12 months:
   Undisclosed
*Aggregate dollar amount of these
   investments:* Undisclosed
Contact persons: Thomas J. Adamek
Branch offices and contact persons:
   None

Scandinavian Corporate Development Group
P. O. Box 52
Westport, CT 06881
203-227-1682
Fax: Call first

Invest in DIPS, workouts or both: DIPS
Obtain control position: Yes
Assume active management role: Yes
Investment is generally secured by assets: No
Number of investments last 12 months: Undisclosed
Aggregate dollar amount of these investments: Undisclosed
Contact persons: C. E. Jacobsson, Managing Partner
Branch offices and contact persons: Viktor Rydbergsgatan 15
S-41132 Gothenburg, Sweden
031-162195

Schroder Venture
787 Seventh Avenue
New York, NY 10019
212-841-3880, x886
Fax: 212-582-1405

Invest in DIPS, workouts or both: Both
Obtain control position: Yes
Assume active management role: As warranted by the situation
Investment is generally secured by assets: No
Number of investments last 12 months: Undisclosed
Aggregate dollar amount of these investments: Undisclosed
Contact persons: Timothy F. Howe
Branch offices and contact persons: None

Sprout Group
140 Broadway
New York, NY 10005
212-504-3600
Fax: 212-504-3444

Invest in DIPS, workouts or both: Both
Obtain control position: As warranted
by the situation
Assume active management role: As
warranted by the situation
*Investment is generally secured by
assets:* As warranted by the situation
Number of investments last 12 months:
3
*Aggregate dollar amount of these
investments:* $10 million
Contact persons: Richard Kroon,
Managing Partner
Branch offices and contact persons:
Keith Geeslin, Partner
Russell Pyne, Partner
Jon Stone, Partner
3000 Sand Hill Road, Building 1
Suite 285
Menlo Park, CA 94025
415-854-1550
Fax: 415-854-8779

TDH II Limited
259 Radnor-Chester Road
P. O. Box 6780
Radnor, PA 19087-5218
215-964-0112
Fax: 215-964-0830

Invest in DIPS, workouts or both: Both
Obtain control position: As warranted
by the situation
Assume active management role: No
*Investment is generally secured by
assets:* As warranted by the situation
Number of investments last 12 months:
Undisclosed
*Aggregate dollar amount of these
investments:* Undisclosed
Contact persons: Stephen Harris
Branch offices and contact persons:
None

Venture Investors of Wisconsin, Inc.
University Research Park
565 Science Drive
Suite A
Madison, WI 53711
608-233-3070
Fax: 608-238-5120

Invest in DIPS, workouts or both: Both
Obtain control position: Yes
Assume active management role:
Active on board and selection of management
Investment is generally secured by assets: Yes
Number of investments last 12 months: Undisclosed
Aggregate dollar amount of these investments: Undisclosed
Contact persons: Roger Ganser, President & CEO
Branch offices and contact persons: None

Walnut Capital Corporation
2 North LaSalle Street
Suite 2410
Chicago, IL 60602
312-346-2033
Fax: 312-346-2231

Invest in DIPS, workouts or both: Both
Obtain control position: No
Assume active management role: Yes
Investment is generally secured by assets: Yes
Number of investments last 12 months: 1
Aggregate dollar amount of these investments: $200,000
Contact persons: Burton W. Kanter
Branch offices and contact persons: None

Weinstein Associates Limited
324 East Wisconsin Avenue
Suite 1010
Milwaukee, WI 53202
414-289-0990
Fax: 414-289-0522

Invest in DIPS, workouts or both: Both
Obtain control position: Yes
Assume active management role: Via active executive committee
Investment is generally secured by assets: Yes
Number of investments last 12 months: Undisclosed
Aggregate dollar amount of these investments: Undisclosed
Contact persons: Stanley Weinstein, President
Branch offices and contact persons: None

Weiss, Peck & Greer Investments
One New York Plaza
New York, NY 10004
212-908-9555
Fax: 212-908-0112

Invest in DIPS, workouts or both: Both
Obtain control position: No
Assume active management role: No
Investment is generally secured by assets: No
Number of investments last 12 months: 2
Aggregate dollar amount of these investments: Undisclosed
Contact persons: Mary Bechmann
Branch offices and contact persons:
Dieter Heidrich, Partner
1113 Spruce
Boulder, CO 80302
303-938-8278

Welsh, Carson, Anderson & Stowe
One World Financial Center
Suite 3601
New York, NY 10281
212-945-2000
Fax: 212-945-2016

Invest in DIPS, workouts or both: Both
Obtain control position: Yes
Assume active management role: As warranted by the situation
Investment is generally secured by assets: No
Number of investments last 12 months: Undisclosed
Aggregate dollar amount of these investments: Undisclosed
Contact persons: Bruce K. Anderson, General Partner
Branch offices and contact persons: None

Westfield Capital Corporation
72 Cummings Point Road
Stamford, CT 06902
203-977-1139
Fax: 203-967-2886

Invest in DIPS, workouts or both: Both
Obtain control position: Yes
Assume active management role: Yes
Investment is generally secured by assets: No
Number of investments last 12 months: 3
Aggregate dollar amount of these investments: $14 million
Contact persons: J. Herbert Ogden, Jr.
Branch offices and contact persons: None

Index